Madame du Barry

Madame du Barry

THE WAGES OF
BEAUTY

JOAN HASLIP

GROVE WEIDENFELD
New York

Published by Grove Weidenfeld
A division of Grove Press, Inc.
841 Broadway
New York, NY 10003-4793

First published in Great Britain in 1991 by George Weidenfeld and Nicolson Limited, London

---

Library of Congress Cataloging-in-Publication Data

Haslip, Joan, 1912–
    Madame du Barry : the wages of beauty / Joan Haslip.
      p.   cm.
    Includes bibliographical references.
    ISBN 0-8021-1256-0 (acid-free paper)
    1. Du Barry, Jeanne Bécu, comtesse, 1743–1793. 2. Louis XV, King of France, 1710–1774—Relations with women. 3. Favorites, Royal—France—Biography. 4. France—Kings and rulers—Mistresses—Biography. I. Title.
DC135.D8H35   1992
944′.034′092—dc20
[B]   91-33808
                                                   CIP

Manufactured in the United States of America

Printed on acid-free paper

First American Edition 1992

1 3 5 7 9 10 8 6 4 2

Contents

Illustrations

For Margot

Why should I be afraid to admit it?
Margot's the one for me.
Yes, Margot. You think that's strange?
What does her name matter? It's what she is that counts.
I know her background isn't anything to boast about,
Nor make one feel particularly good,
But all that is vain anyway.
She was born so poor
That neither money nor style
Could conceal it for a moment.
And without education or wit
Her conversation's so dull
I never know what to say to her.
Still, Margot has such lovely eyes
That one look from her
Is worth more to me than fortune, wit or birth.

Oh, you've got me completely hooked.
Sweetness, I'm completely obsessed.
But all this time I spend writing to you
Is without a doubt just wasted.
You'll never read this, Margot,
Since you don't know how to read.
But forgive me for this old habit of mine,
I can't stop myself brooding.
And at least it's you
And you alone I'm thinking about.
Come back and be with me,
All your happiness is here.
Come, and at once I'll exchange
The chill wreaths of Parnassus
For the sweet garlands of love.

AFTER CHODERLOS DE LACLOS
Verses considered to have been
addressed to Madame du Barry

Acknowledgements

My thanks go to Madame Victor Moritz, the late owner of Louve-ciennes, who furnished me with many details of Madame du Barry's life at the *pavillon* and, in particular, of her little-known love affair with Henry Seymour, for which she supplied me with the portrait included among the illustrations.

I also wish to thank Monsieur Pierre Lemoine, until recently the curator of Versailles, who gave me so much information and allowed me to visit 'les Petits Appartements' before they were opened to the public; also the directors of the present Hôtel du Commerce which formerly belonged to Madame du Barry.

For the second time I wish to thank my friends the Baroness Elie de Rothschild and Bernard Minoret for the help and encouragement they have given me. My gratitude is also due to Hilary Laurie for the trouble she took in editing the book, and to Maria Ellis for the wonderful way she succeeds in unravelling my indecipherable hand-writing.

1

The little girl who, on 19 April 1743, was christened Jeanne in the church of Vaucouleurs on the borders of Lorraine had nothing to inherit other than her beauty. Only three people, one of whom acted as her godmother, signed the register and they had come at the bidding of the *curé* rather than out of friendship for the mother. None of Anne Bécu's six brothers and sisters had troubled to be present. Serving in aristocratic households, they preferred to ignore the relative who had not even confessed to the *curé* as to who might be the father of her child. It was rumoured in Vaucouleurs that Anne Bécu, who was a seamstress by trade, had been seduced by a handsome monk when she was sewing sheets in the monastery of the Picpus. The monk, who went by the unsuitable name of Brother Angel, was a certain Jean-Baptiste Gomard de Vaubernier, who was shortly afterwards dismissed from the order and sent to Paris where he was later attached to the church of St Eustache, becoming a popular preacher and a favourite confessor to rich old ladies.

The Bécus, who were originally a peasant family from Lorraine, were known for their extraordinary good looks. The father, Fabien, one of the handsomest men of his day, had kept an eating house in Paris, where he had attracted the notice of an aristocratic widow, a Comtesse Mondidier de Cantigny, who had been foolish enough to marry him, thereby forfeiting all her hereditary rights and privileges. After a few unhappy years of matrimony, during which her husband squandered the whole of her modest patrimony, the countess died, leaving Fabien Bécu with no other alternative than to go back to his old profession. Adopting the more elegant name of Cantigny, to which he had no right but against which no one protested, he returned to Vaucouleurs and became a cook in a neighbouring château, where he married the lady's maid and fathered no less than seven children, all of whom inherited his beauty and a certain refinement of manner he had acquired from his first wife. These assets gained them employment in the houses of the nobility either as maids or lackeys, one of them becoming personal valet to King Louis xv's father-in-law, the exiled King of Poland, who held his court at Nancy.

The only one of Fabien's children who refused to settle down was Anne, a pretty, flighty girl who preferred to eke out a modest living as a seamstress rather than submit to the discipline of a grand household. Vaucouleurs was a garrison town, and neither officers nor soldiers were immune to the blue eyes of the obliging little seamstress. Her favours always brought her in a few *écus* to spend on silk for a new dress or a yard of lace to trim the bonnet of the baby Jeanne, who from her earliest years promised to be ravishingly pretty. Tripping along the streets of Vaucouleurs holding her little girl by the hand, Anne Bécu attracted the notice of every passer-by. One summer, in 1746, an important visitor came to Vaucouleurs, a Monsieur Billard-Dumonceaux, paymaster of the city of Paris and inspector of the army commissariats. He only stayed a few days, but in that short time he managed to get Anne Bécu in the family way and nine months later she gave birth to a second child, this time a boy called Claude.

It is not known whether Anne left Vaucouleurs of her own accord or at the instigation of Monsieur Dumonceaux. But in 1747, when Jeanne was four years old, she was taken to Paris by her mother where they found lodgings with Anne's sister, housekeeper to the King's librarian. Hélène Bécu, the loveliest of all Fabien's children and known in the *quartier* as 'la belle Hélène', was rigidly respectable and would never have taken in her irresponsible young sister and her two bastards if there had not been a rich protector in the background who contributed to their maintenance. Anne's baby boy died only a few months after their arrival in Paris, after which Monsieur Dumonceaux took both her and Jeanne into his home, where he lived officially with a beautiful Italian mistress called Francesca, known in the Paris *demi-monde* as Madame Frédérique. Francesca appears to have been sufficiently broadminded to engage Anne Bécu, who had inherited her father's culinary talent, as a cook, on the condition that her lover did not pay too many visits to the kitchen. Being a warmhearted Italian, she was fond of children and the lovely little Jeanne was given free run of the house and spoilt and indulged in every whim.

The two years spent in the luxurious home of a celebrated courtesan formed the tastes and character of the future Madame du Barry. At five years old she was already made aware of her beauty. Francesca took pleasure in dressing her in pretty clothes, in teaching her to dance and entertain the guests, while Dumonceaux, who fancied himself as an artist, delighted in painting her in the role of a nymph or cupid in the manner of Boucher. Anne was relegated to the kitchen, but her daughter spent hours in Francesca's bedroom admiring herself in the gilded mirrors, stroking the soft velvet chair covers and playing with the gold utensils which littered the dressing table. The voluptuous Italian, reclining on a bed hung with taffeta and covered in scented cushions, was infinitely more appealing than the mother bending over her copper pots in the steaming kitchen. And Anne, who had been quite happy in Vaucouleurs, flirting in the local taverns, felt lonely and unwanted. Watched by a jealous mistress, Dumonceaux was no longer so assiduous in his visits to the kitchen, and Anne began to listen to the sensible elder sister who kept telling her it was time for her to settle down and that she knew of a respectable widower who was looking for a wife. The fact that Nicolas Rançon was plain and pockmarked in no way detracted from his advantages as a husband. A gentleman's gentleman of good standing whose master had died leaving him a small annuity, he was ten years younger than Anne and might never have considered her a suitable wife had not the amiable Monsieur Dumonceaux been prepared to supplement his income by appointing him as a storekeeper to the army commissariat for Corsica, where Paoli's patriot armies were keeping thousands of French troops immobilized.

Her mother's marriage brought a dramatic change in the life of the six-year-old Jeanne. Acting largely on the instigation of Francesca, Dumonceaux decided to have her educated in a convent. The choice they made was a wise one, for St Aure was not one of those fashionable establishments where dancing and deportment were included in the curriculum. Situated in the heart of Paris, it was run by an order of nuns known as 'the worshippers of the Sacred Heart' and was intended as a school for decent girls of limited means who might otherwise be led into corruption. Apart from religious instruction, the pupils were taught domestic trades enabling them to earn a modest living. That the education was by no means as narrow as might have been expected was shown by the fact that both drawing and music were taught at St Aure, and that the talent for drawing she displayed as a child later developed in Jeanne du Barry into a genuine appreciation of the arts which made of her the friend and patroness of the leading artists of the day. It was only later that she realized how much she owed to the good nuns of St Aure, and the day on which Francesca's carriage left her at the convent door was the unhappiest in her life. The portmanteau holding her pretty clothes was taken away and replaced by a uniform of coarse white serge, her golden curls were covered by a plain black veil, and her pretty feet encased in rough yellow boots. But even the hideous, ill-fitting uniform could not hide a beauty which even the austere Mother Superior found hard to resist.

Little is known of the nine years Jeanne spent at St Aure. Being easy and accommodating by nature, she soon adapted herself to her surroundings and the tears she shed in the first days quickly dried. Anxious to please, she was both regular in her prayers and obedient in her duties, but every now and then her normal high spirits would assert themselves and she would go dancing down the corridors to the horror of the nuns, or be found admiring her reflection in the shining copper pans in the refectory. There were no mirrors in the convent, but the open admiration of her companions assured her that she was the loveliest of them all.

An occasional visit from her mother was for nine years her only contact with the outside world. But she still kept the memory of the sunlit house by the Seine and the gardens where she played with Francesca's little spaniel. Not even the most optimistic of nuns was under any illusion that the lovely golden-haired girl would ever take religious vows. Outwardly she was good, sweet and submissive, but there was a roguish look in her blue, almond-shaped eyes and her small red mouth was all too ready for laughter. After nine years at St Aure, Jeanne was little different from the child who had sat on Francesca's knee.

Jeanne's first visit to her former benefactors was cruelly disappointing. Francesca was no longer the triumphant beauty whose drawing room was crowded with aspiring gallants. Nine years had brought the first onslaught of middle age, the first grey hairs and wrinkles, and she was now a woman desperate to preserve her fading youth and keep her hold on a lover to whom she had become a habit rather than a passion. The radiant loveliness of the fifteen-year-old Jeanne,

4

which not even the convent uniform could disguise, was too insolent to be borne. The child she had loved had become a dangerous rival to be dismissed with a small gratuity to buy herself a new dress. Billard-Dumonceaux was probably never told of Jeanne's return, and the girl who expected so much from life had to content herself with a corner of her mother's modest attic in a mean and crowded street, where her stepfather's absence in Corsica enabled her to have a bed.

What was to become of her? There were endless discussions between Anne and the various relatives who, now that she was a respectable married woman, were ready to give their advice. The peasant family from Lorraine, whether lackeys, priests or small tradesmen, had all grown into shrewd, hardened Parisians who were under no illusions as to the dangers which awaited a girl of Jeanne's sensational appearance. As usual it was her aunt, Hélène Bécu, who had the wisest suggestion to make. Her mistress had a young hairdresser who was doing well in his profession and was in need of an apprentice, and by the end of 1758, before Jeanne had celebrated her sixteenth birthday, she had not only found a job for which she was eminently suited, but her employer, a certain Lametz, had also fallen madly in love with her to the extent of sharing with her his small but elegant apartment, which seemed like paradise in comparison to the sordid, stuffy attic in the rue neuve St Étienne. For six months they lived in bliss with the infatuated hairdresser squandering his savings on the charming mistress who, for all her angelic face and convent education, was all too ready to accept whatever he had to offer.

Finally there came the day when Madame Lametz, the young man's mother, heard of her son's disastrous attachment to a lowborn girl who was robbing him of his savings. Bent on vengeance, she descended on Anne Rançon and stormed into her kitchen, accusing her in the foulest language of being nothing but a procuress who had prostituted her daughter when she was still a minor and threatening to denounce her to the local priest who would have them both sent to the dreaded *Hôpital*, a place of detention for women picked off the streets. But Anne was more than a match for Madame Lametz. Knowing that her innocent-looking daughter would melt the heart of the toughest police inspector, she went straight to the court of the Châtelet and lodged a complaint for defamation of character. The judgment was in her favour. Accused of corrupting a minor and at the same time

5

crippled with debts, the unfortunate Lametz had to sell up his business and flee the country. Jeanne's first romance, perhaps the only purely sentimental romance she ever had, ended in tears, and though Vatel and most of Madame du Barry's authoritative biographers deny she ever had a child, one suspects that Madame Rançon's complaint at the Châtelet, followed by Lametz's sudden flight to England, had to do with a little girl born in the same year and officially fathered by Jeanne's uncle, Nicolas Bécu, who was serving in the household of the Duchesse d'Antin.

Many years later, when Jeanne Bécu had become the Comtesse du Barry and the King's favourite, her mother, though still legally married to Nicolas Rançon, retired to a convent frequented by the nobility where she was known under the more aristocratic name of Madame de Montrabé and where she was accompanied by a niece, Marie Joséphine, daughter of Nicolas Bécu. Long after the King was dead and Madame du Barry had returned from exile to her château of Louveciennes, a constant visitor was this same Marie Joséphine, generally known as Betsi, whose enchanting little face, immortalized by Drouais as a young girl playing with a cat, hung on the drawing-room wall. The other relatives, all of whom profited by the bounty of Madame du Barry, were jealous of Betsi who in 1781, at the age of twenty, was married off with a large dowry to a Marquis de Boisse-son, considerably older than herself, and even after their marriage she continued to have rooms reserved for them at the château of Louveciennes. No documents survive to ensure the truth of Betsi's origins. But her extraordinary resemblance to Madame du Barry, the same almond-shaped eyes the colour of aquamarines, the same sweet smile and charming ways, give substance to the legend.

Little is known of the life of Jeanne Bécu from the end of 1759 to 1761, when at the age of eighteen she found employment with the rich old widow of a *fermier général*, a provincial finance minister, living at a short distance from Paris in the château of Courneuve. Though originally taken on as a lady's maid, it was not long before she was promoted to the position of companion by a lonely old woman who loved society and was enchanted to find that the beautiful young girl attracted people to her house who had rarely bothered to come before, and that her two sons had never been so assiduous in their visits.

The luxurious château, the constant come-and-go of people, the pretty clothes given her by a generous mistress soon made Jeanne forget the unfortunate Lametz. This was the world she had always longed for, the world of rich financiers such as Billard-Dumonceaux, where men were ready to pay for their pleasures and women like Francesca accepted their gifts as their right. Of Madame de la Garde's two sons, one was a *fermier général*, the other paymaster to the army. Both were married to unattractive wives and were all too ready to instruct their mother's enchanting companion in the various amatory arts. For Jeanne it was all a delightful game, and so long as they visited their mother at different times it was a game that was all too easy to play. But the situation took an unpleasant turn when one of their wives, a notorious lesbian with particularly vicious habits, came up from the provinces to visit her mother-in-law, and had no sooner arrived than she conceived a violent passion for Jeanne and molested her in such a way that the girl, who at heart was still a normal little peasant, took fright and complained to her mistress. But jealous servants, who resented one of their class being treated as an equal by the gentry, had been busily pouring venom into the old lady's ears, telling of nocturnal visits to Jeanne's room, of her improper relations with the two young masters and the money she extorted both from them and their friends. This combined with her daughter-in-law's hysterical scenes, decided Madame de la Garde to get rid of the all-too-pretty companion. And by the end of the year Jeanne found herself again without a job.

But the year at Courneuve had brought her into the world of high finance among men who, fascinated by her dazzling looks, continued to take an interest in her future career. And in the spring of 1762 she was taken on as apprentice at the most exclusive fashion house in Paris, run by a Monsieur Labille, whose clients included all who were rich and famous in society and the *demi-monde*.

2

'A la Toilette', situated in the rue neuve des Petits Champs, was a little shop of glittering glass which stood out in brilliant contrast to the dreariness of the surrounding houses. It was more of a showcase than a shop with its air of unbridled luxury, its banks of exotic flowers, which even in the depth of winter arrived from the south of France and whose delicious perfumes wafted into the street. Looking into the window, you could see the pretty little *grisettes* displaying their wares against a background of panelled walls and taffeta hangings, where the newest of feathered hats and ribboned bonnets were shown on gilded stands and every drawer and table overflowed with laces and muslins, sword-knots and painted fans. Everyone who was anyone came to Labille's, the great ladies and the courtesans looking for the latest novelty, the courtiers and the young officers in search of the most elegant of sword-knots, and the libertines who came for no other reason than to flirt with the shopgirls who were known to be the prettiest ones in town.

Monsieur Labille was a stern taskmaster, and the girls he employed had to sleep on the premises, where there were large airy dormitories, and everyone had to be in bed by nine o'clock. But in spite of his severity there was plenty of opportunity for secret assignations. When goods were being delivered to favoured clients, hopeful gallants would be waiting at street corners for the girls from Labille's to pass by carrying the large striped, ribboned boxes which were as elegant as everything else in the shop. On Sundays and other feast days the girls were free to enjoy themselves to their hearts' content, and many a romantic tryst was kept in the gardens of St Cloud or at the fair of St Germain.

Few of the girls at Labille's lived on their salaries, but none were as successful as Jeanne Bécu, who at eighteen had already learnt which of her suitors was ready to pay the highest price for her favours. Rich merchants, bankers and government officials provided grist for her mill. Whether young or middle-aged, they all found her irresistible with her spontaneous gaiety, her roguish smile and small red mouth so ready to burst into laughter. All the descriptions of the future Madame du Barry speak of her '*yeux fripons*', the blue slanting eyes with the veiled lids, tender and sensual, mocking and mischievous at will. No one enjoyed her favours for very long, no one could claim her as an official mistress. She longed for luxury, never so much as now that she worked at Labille's where thousands of *livres* were squandered on the merest trifles. But instinctively she felt that higher things were in store for her, and she went her way, charming and teasing, but never committing herself in full. Monsieur Labille might disapprove of her laziness and immorality, but he could hardly afford to dismiss a girl who attracted the richest and most spendthrift of clients, and with whom his partner, the wealthy silk merchant Monsieur Bruffault, was said to be so infatuated that he had offered to set her up in an establishment of her own. But for the time being Jeanne was happy at Labille's where she had made friends with her employer's daughter, a talented young artist who was later to achieve considerable fame as a portrait painter, and whose loyalty to her first patronesses, Mesdames de France, Louis xv's unmarried daughters, prevented her from later attaching herself to the court of the woman who had become their father's mistress.

Adelaide Labille-Guiard's fascinating portrait of Madame Henriette which today hangs in the Louvre makes us regret that she has left us no portrait of Madame du Barry, which would have been so much more interesting than the somewhat insipid versions of Helbes and of Floras with which the court painters immortalized the reigning favourite.

The modest talent for drawing Jeanne had acquired at the convent was encouraged by her friend, who brought her into the world of artists, introducing her both to the court painter Drouais and the sculptor Pajou, who has left us a bust of her in those early days when she still retained that look of intrinsic sweetness which Comte d'Espinchal, whose journals show us Madame du Barry in the various phases of her career, describes seeing her for the first time when she was known as Mademoiselle Lange and 'was so striking in appearance and in every way so pretty and agreeable that she was already known to all the connoisseurs in the capital and several painters were anxious to have her as a model'. The Prince de Ligne, who was a prince of the Holy Roman Empire but spent half his year in Paris and was a connoisseur of beautiful women, waxes enthusiastic on 'the charms of the little *grisette* who worked at Labille's, a girl who was tall, well made and ravishingly blonde with a wide forehead, lovely eyes with dark lashes, a small oval face with a delicate complexion marked by two little beauty spots, which only made her the more *piquante*, a mouth to which laughter came easily and a bosom so perfect as to defy comparison'.

The police reports were somewhat more prosaic, for by the end of 1762 Jeanne, who by now had taken on the name of Vaubernier, derived from her putative father, the monk Gomard de Vaubernier, was already appearing in the records at the Châtelet as 'a pretty little *grisette* ready to accept whatever came her way – in short, a kept woman living with various men to whom she was not married, but in no sense a prostitute or a *raccrocheuse* guilty of soliciting in the streets'. This proves the accusations brought against her by the Duc de Choiseul and his party to have been entirely fictitious. Jeanne was never one of the girls of the celebrated procuress Sarah Gourdan – a libel denied by Madame Gourdan herself – and the police were not seriously interested in Jeanne up to the time when she became attached to Jean du Barry, known as '*le roué*' ('the rake'), notorious for his dissolute morals but sufficiently clever always to remain on the right side of the law.

It was during the peace celebrations of 1763 that Jeanne met for the first time the man who was to have a decisive influence on her life. The court painter Drouais had invited her and Adelaide to view the unveiling of Bouchardon's equestrian statue of Louis XV, placed on a pedestal designed by Pigalle in the newly completed Place Louis Quinze. This great square, situated on what had formerly been an area of wasteland between the river, the Tuileries gardens and the Champs Elysées, was first planned in 1748, the year of the battle of Fontenoy, one of the most glorious in French history, when the English were defeated and the King was still 'Louis the well beloved'. At that time the unveiling of his statue would have been hailed with joyful demonstrations by his loyal subjects. Now, at the end of the disastrous Seven Years' War, it roused more mockery than praise. The four allegorical figures on Pigalle's splendid pedestal, representing

Force, Prudence, Justice and Peace, were given the names of the King's four most notorious mistresses, Mailly, Vintimille, Châteauroux and Pompadour, all of them hated in their day, but none so hated as the last, whose driving ambition had led the peace-loving King to war.

The loss of Canada to the British in the Seven Years' War and the failure of Dupleix in India to gain new territory meant less to the Parisians than the heavy taxes at home, the military drafts and conscription of young men sent to fight in Maria Theresa's wars. It was this unpopular Austrian alliance for which the people blamed the King and his favourite. But though the treasury was empty, the festivities were magnificent. There were fireworks and sham battles on the Seine, processions and dancing in the streets, fountains running with wine and distributions of meat in the poorer quarters of the town. And the Parisians, who loved a fête, forgot their grievances in the beauty of the scene.

Nineteen tents of red linen lined with damask, each lit by a chandelier, had been put up for King Louis and his entourage. Built on the river in front of the Palais Bourbon, these tents gave the people the opportunity of seeing the King who came so rarely to his capital. At fifty-three he was still one of the handsomest men of his day. But his was the sad, disillusioned face of a man who knew that he had lost the love of his subjects and was too lazy and egotistical to try to win it back, preferring to shut himself up in Versailles and go hunting in the forests of the Île de France, letting himself be dominated by a woman who had the magic gift of banishing his boredom which in middle age was turning to melancholia.

But the aura of Bourbon majesty was still sufficiently compelling to win him the plaudits of the crowds, and the people cheered their King, his dowdy little Queen, the heavy unattractive Dauphin and his Saxon wife. They even cheered Mesdames, the four spinster daughters who had been too proud to marry beneath their rank. But there was very little cheering for the Marquise de Pompadour, sitting beside her brother who, as minister of works, had superintended every detail of the evening's festivities. For all her elegance and grace, the cruel lights of the chandelier showed up the havoc wrought by illness, the pallor beneath the rouge, the puffy cheeks and dark circles under the eyes of a woman who was slowly dying at the age of forty-two. Everything in her life had been sacrificed to her ambition, to keep a footing on the slippery pinnacle of power. For nearly twenty years this little bourgeoise, born Jeanne Poisson, had reigned as uncrowned queen of France, enthralling by her talents the most difficult of men, fighting her natural frigidity with unhealthy diets which destroyed her beauty and her youth, till in the end she had to swallow her pride and accept the little girls who had to be supplied for the King's pleasure. She whom they called the King's favourite had for the past ten years been no more than a friend, but a friend more powerful than any mistress, who chose his ministers and dictated the policy of France. The people blamed her for the war, but she had wanted to make Louis into a great king, and the tragedy of her life was that she still loved him as much as when she had first met him twenty years before at a hunt in the forest of Senart.

From her seat on one of the wooden stands, Jeanne saw for the first time the glittering pageantry of royalty and cheered with such enthusiasm as to attract the attention of her neighbours, who smiled benevolently at the lovely girl, with her blue eyes shining, her cheeks flushed with excitement. One man in particular was watching her, a man who had already seen her at Labille's and knew that Mademoiselle Vaubernier, formerly Mademoiselle Lange, was no more than Jeanne Bécu, a peasant girl from Lorraine, whose mother had been a cook in the household of a paymaster-general. Jean du Barry made it his business to know the origins of the little actresses and *grisettes* he took under his protection. Coming from a noble and impoverished family of Toulouse, he had found life in his native town too restricted for his liking. The eldest of six children, the two thousand *livres* he had inherited from his father, a dedicated army officer and a chevalier de St Louis, a military order given by the King, more or less equivalent to the Légion d'honneur, had lasted him little over a year. The death of a godfather who left him a small turreted manor house and eighty acres of good farming land in Languedoc enabled him to make a suitable marriage with another army family and to add a title to his name. As 'the high and mighty Lord of Levignac and Count of Ceres' he cut a dash in Toulouse society, living so far above his income that by the end of a few years he had nothing left but debts.

Leaving his wife and baby son in the country, he set out for one of those fashionable watering places where high play at the faro table, and wealthy valetudinarian ladies with nothing to do, provided endless opportunities for ambitious and unscrupulous young men. After making some useful connections to pave his way on his arrival in the capital, Jean-Baptiste du Barry arrived in Paris in the spring of 1753 intending to make a fortune and a great name for himself. But an attempt to get into diplomacy through the then foreign minister, Rouillé, who was a distant connection of his wife's, ended in failure and he was forced to resort to more devious methods better suited to his talents for duplicity and intrigue. Neither rich nor handsome, he was nevertheless possessed of a certain fascination which convinced the most hardened businessmen that he was the very person to carry out a successful contract and the most sophisticated women that he was the most satisfying of lovers. To quote from Rostand's immortal *Cyrano*, du Barry was a real '*cadet de Gascogne, menteur et bretteur, sans vergogne*' ('liar and swashbuckler without shame'). But such was his charm that men who knew him to be a cardsharper were still willing to be fleeced, and women who recognized him as a heartless debauchee were still ready to share his bed.

In the ten years which elapsed between his arrival in Paris and his first meeting with Jeanne Vaubernier, du Barry had earned himself the reputation of being one of the most dissolute men in the capital. But it was his very immorality which won him entry into a group of hardened libertines comprising some of the greatest names in France, among whom were the Duc de Nivernais and the Maréchal de Richelieu, both of them in their seventies, still passionate amorists, ready to be on friendly terms with anyone who could pander to their lusts. If du Barry lived in a sumptuous style, collecting old masters and driving in the most elegant of carriages, it was not so much due to the profitable army contracts he succeeded in obtaining through his connections with the ministry of war as owing to his successful operations with women. He was no more than a common pimp, picking up girls of every class, from shopgirls to small-time actresses. They had only to be beautiful, easy in character and ready to accept his training which was arduous. Polished and groomed, yesterday's *grisette* might end in becoming the mistress of a duke.

By the summer of 1755 the police were already reporting on 'a certain Comte du Barry who supplied young ladies to his acquaintances and took for himself a large percentage of their earnings.' So successful were these transactions that the Duc de Richelieu was reported to have appointed him to 'furnish his pleasures.' But even the police were inclined to be tolerant, referring to him under the soubriquet of '*le roué*', and no serious effort was made to put a curb on his activities, though the whole of Paris knew that the greater part of his income came from cardsharping and women. The ambitions of a young man who had set out from his manor house in Languedoc hoping to become a great ambassador had sadly changed over the years. Now he had but one ambition left: to force his way into Versailles by supplying a mistress for the King. There was a moment he came near to succeeding, when one of his protégées, a water carrier's daughter from Strasbourg, attracted the notice of King Louis. But the watchful eyes of Madame de Pompadour soon put an end to the affair. Though the marquise might be forced to accept the little girls in the Parc aux Cerfs, she would never tolerate a rival coming from the tainted stable of a du Barry. With the help of his doctors, there had been no difficulty in persuading the King, always fearful for his health, that a relationship with the protégée of a notorious debauchee might have unpleasant consequences.

But by 1763 the Marquise de Pompadour was a dying woman. On the night of the peace celebrations, the smiling face in the illuminated box was no more than a painted mask, and she appeared in public for the last time at the great ball held on the following evening in her palace of the Elysée. Versailles was already humming with intrigues as to who would be her successor. Louis, however, was getting old and it would need a new face from a new world to rouse him from his lethargy.

In the following weeks, du Barry paid several visits to the ministry of war, to the special department devoted to Corsica which, since its annexation by France in 1769, continued to cost the country large sums in food supplies and ammunition. Most of these army contracts were in the hands of unscrupulous people like du Barry, who in the role of middleman reaped enormous profits. But in these days Jean-Baptiste was not so much concerned with his own affairs as in checking the whereabouts of Nicolas Rançon, who was still employed as storekeeper at army headquarters. The husband of Anne Bécu was now a sharp-faced, dried-up little man in his early forties, who had retained all the qualities of a high-class servant and prided himself on his integrity. By now both he and his wife had been forced to recognize that flighty, lazy Jeanne would never settle down to middle-class respectability, and that with her insane love of luxury she might run the danger of falling into prostitution. He was not entirely taken in by the plausible gentleman who went out of his way to cultivate his friendship by offering a dazzling future for his stepdaughter, but both he and Anne were sufficiently shrewd to settle matters with du Barry to their mutual satisfaction.

There are two versions as to how Jeanne Bécu and her mother first came to live with the Comte du Barry, both of which date from after Louis xv's death, when Jeanne was confined to the convent of Pont aux Dames and du Barry was making a desperate attempt to exonerate his conduct and save himself from prison. At this time he addressed a highly romanticized account to the secretary of state, Malesherbes, in which he wrote that, 'having a delicate son in need of attention, he had engaged a lady of his acquaintance, a certain Madame Rançon, to come and act as housekeeper, bringing with her a young daughter'.

The second version, which was slightly less edifying, was given by Anne Rançon when under strict interrogation by the police. In this statement she admitted that most of the furniture in the apartment belonging to her and her husband had been bought by Comte du Barry and her daughter, and that, while still a minor, Jeanne had gone to live with the count with the tacit consent of her parents and on the payment of a certain sum of money. It was not a pretty story. But Jeanne never seems to have raised any objection to being exploited in this way. On the contrary, throughout her mother's life she remained the most loving and devoted of daughters, and after her death continued to support her stepfather in 'gratitude for his kindness to her as a child'. Du Barry's offer was accepted by her not because she had any interest in him as a man, but because he was able to give her everything she had wanted since the days when as a child of six she had played with the crystal *flacons* and gilded brushes on Francesca's dressing table.

3

In the curious household set up by du Barry first in the rue St Eustache then in the rue Jussienne, the only one who appears to have been seriously involved was '*le roué*' himself, who for all his cynicism was in those first months so infatuated by his dazzling, golden-haired mistress that he could not bear to share her with any other man. He was delighted to find that the girl he had thought to be an uneducated little *grisette* had spent nine years in the convent of the Sacred Heart, that the pretty voice with the slight lisp spoke with the pure accent of the ladies of St Aure, that she enjoyed reading Shakespeare and, like every educated girl of her day, had a smattering of the classics and had heard of Cicero and Demosthenes. In spite of her extravagance she was able to keep accurate accounts and, if her spelling was bad, it was no worse than that of many a great lady at Versailles. Her years with Labille had taught her how to dress and to choose the soft pale materials most suited to her blonde beauty. So impeccable was her taste that not even a connoisseur like du Barry would have ventured to advise her on her clothes. Though at times he could be brutal and almost cruel, he was never mean and, in becoming his mistress, Jeanne Vaubernier entered into the world of expensive courtesans who, sparkling with diamonds, drove round Paris in elegant carriages. For the first time in her life, her mother was dressed in silks and satins with servants waiting on her orders, fitting into her new role with that natural dignity which all Fabien Bécu's children had inherited from their father. Nicolas Rançon had been promoted to be a collector of the salt tax (*la gabelle*) and spent most of the year in the provinces, and Anne Rançon's natural talents as a cook and her daughter's natural talents as a courtesan made life in the rue St Eustache so pleasant that du Barry regretted when necessity forced him to merchandise what he would willingly have kept for himself.

It is doubtful whether Jeanne had any feeling for du Barry other than a certain gratitude, but she knew so well how to flatter and cajole and thank so prettily for her gifts that she was able to satisfy his vanity with the illusion of love. Their brief honeymoon ended with the arrival in Paris of the count's fourteen-year-old son, who till now had been living with his mother at Levignac. Gentle, good-looking and delicate in health, Adolphe had none of his father's rumbustious personality and would have been utterly miserable in Paris had it not been for the warm welcome given him by Jeanne and her mother. For all her newly acquired sophistication, Jeanne was still very much a child at heart and preferred playing lotto with Adolphe, who was only six years younger than herself, to being endlessly educated by his father as to how to behave in the great world. The ambitions Jean-Baptiste had failed to realize in his own career were now concentrated on his son. The shy young boy from the provinces had barely been two months in the capital before his father was intriguing to obtain him a post as a page at Versailles. It would have seemed impossible for a man of du Barry's unsavoury reputation to realize such a place had it not been for the backing of the seventy-year-old Duc de Richelieu, one of the only men who was so close to the King that Louis was ready to forgive him every indiscretion and every betrayal, and whom neither the vindictive hatred of the Marquise de Pompadour nor the jealousy of the powerful minister Choiseul had succeeded in banishing from court. Great nephew to the cardinal, bearing one of the proudest names in France, the hero of countless battles and as many diplomatic triumphs, Richelieu destroyed many of his brilliant qualities by an incorrigible levity and a complete lack of morality which brought him into contact with debauchees like du Barry.

To get his son to court, du Barry was ready to sell him his twenty-year-old mistress, and we are told that Jeanne was paid no less than fifty *louis* for her complaisance. The whole of her vertiginous career may be said to have been based on her relationship with the old marshal who protected her from her first day at court and to whom she remained loyal up to the day of his death at the age of ninety-four. When he was old, lonely and forgotten by the world, Jeanne was one of the few who still had time to spare for the man who first opened for her the gates of Versailles.

Du Barry was a superb impresario and everything was done on a grand scale. Even the police reports pay tribute to his talents. Jeanne's first appearance in public as his official mistress was in a box at the *Comédie italienne* on the evening of 14 December 1764. 'The Marquis du Barry', writes Inspector Marais, erroneously giving him the title of Marquis, 'appeared on Monday night with his new mistress, Mademoiselle Vaubernier. She is a young woman of about nineteen years of age, tall, well-made with a noble carriage and the loveliest of faces. He will certainly try to barter her to his own advantage, for it is what he always does when he begins to tire of a woman. But one must admit him to be a connoisseur and his merchandise is always of the first quality.'

She was a sensation from the moment she appeared with him in public. To achieve his aims du Barry indebted himself still further by giving a splendid ball in the carnival week of 1765. By now Jeanne Bécu had become Mademoiselle Vaubernier, while her mother went by the name of Madame Rançon de Montrabé, and no one seems to have objected to these creations of the *'roué'*'s fertile fantasy. His dinners organized by Madame Rançon were excellent, and at the head of his table sat the prettiest and gayest courtesan in town. From a court plunged into mourning, decimated by death – the Marquise de Pompadour, the Dauphin and his wife all dying in a little more than a year – the young gallants flocked to du Barry's hospitable board. Before long it was noted that he was keeping his new mistress not only for his own pleasure, but in order to attract custom to his gaming rooms where she encouraged her admirers to lose thousands of *livres* a night in high play.

Towards the end of 1765 there appears to have been a rift in their *ménage*. Was it that du Barry, now that his son was at court, no longer approved of Adolphe's being on such friendly terms with his mistress, or was he jealous of the tender affection the two young people felt for one another? For Jeanne seems really to have loved the weak, charming boy who had such a boundless admiration for her. It was a pure, almost maternal love which a man of du Barry's character was unable to understand. Like so many others, he was convinced his precious son was being deliberately seduced. There were angry scenes till one day, without any previous warning, Jeanne left the rue St Eustache and moved to a small rented flat in the rue Montmartre.

Inspector Marais, who always kept a watchful eye, reports that 'Mademoiselle Vaubernier has at last left Monsieur du Barry. She was evidently tired of acting as a decoy at his clandestine gambling parties and, with the money she got out of Richelieu, has moved to an apartment in the rue Montmartre. She took all her possessions with her and had given no previous notice of her departure. Du Barry appears to have shown no great regret at her leaving, which is somewhat of a blow to the young lady's vanity. She is certainly a very pretty woman but is far too conscious of her beauty and is spoilt by her simpering affectations.'

Nothing is known of Jeanne's life in the rue Montmartre. But at the end of three months both she and Jean-Baptiste appear to have realized that they needed one another. Madame Rançon was probably the first to persuade her daughter to return, fearing that with her easy nature she might end in becoming too generous with her favours. For all his apparent indifference, du Barry had no intention of losing her whom he had been the first to recognize as *'un vrai morceau de Roi'*, one who if properly handled might end in the royal bed.

The King was lonely. There had been no successor to the Marquise de Pompadour whom he mourned not so much as a mistress but as a friend, and who for twenty years had filled Versailles with light and gaiety and laughter. A brooding melancholy now hung over the great palace. In the last years, death had taken a heavy toll of the royal family. Louis had lost his two favourite daughters, Madame Henriette and Madame Infante, followed by the eldest and most intelligent of his grandsons. Barely a year after the marquise's death both the Dauphin and his wife had succumbed to smallpox. The King loved his children and every death brought pangs of contrition and remorse, a fear of the Last Judgment, of what awaited him in the afterlife. In his loneliness he grew closer to his long-neglected Queen, but for all her sweetness and willingness to forget and to forgive, Maria Leczinska was unable to understand, still less attract a man whom even someone as brilliant as the marquise had judged to be *'impénétrable'*. Of all the women who had aspired to take her place, none had lasted more than a few weeks, and Lebel, his devoted valet who acted also as his pimp, was finding it increasingly difficult to supply the house in the Parc aux Cerfs with fresh young girls to stir his jaded appetites. Obsessed by the proximity of death, Louis paid fewer visits to this discreet little house in a quiet street in Versailles, which Madame de Pompadour had hired for her royal lover to protect his shabby little affairs from the eyes of his subjects.

Jean du Barry was determined that Jeanne would never become an inmate of the Parc aux Cerfs. To celebrate her return he acquired a grand new apartment in the rue Jussienne and the following year he took over the whole house, while Jeanne proved her willingness to cooperate in the expenses by extending her favours to two of the wealthiest of farmer generals. Du Barry showed no jealousy, beyond exercising his *droits de seigneur* by sleeping with her every night. It was an exhausting life, and an observant police inspector noted, 'The young lady is overdoing it. She has not the stamina to stand up to this sort of life. Before long she will be looking very tired.' The '*roué*' himself was too intelligent to allow Jeanne's delicate beauty to fade in entertaining men of no great importance, and by the end of 1766 the parties in the rue Jussienne had become quieter and more select. Du Barry, who was highly cultivated, numbered many poets and writers among his acquaintances. Marmontel, Collé and Crebillon *fils* were only a few of those in whose company Jeanne learnt not only to listen but to talk, to amuse by some funny story rendered all the more piquant when told in her soft, lisping voice. She was all things to all men, whether it was the Comte de Guibert, the most spoilt of all literary lions, famous for his love letters to Mademoiselle de Lespinasse, or the Prince de Ligne, the most fascinating of all European grandees who remained her friend to the end of her life. But she was still at her happiest with young Adolphe du Barry who, having graduated from a court page to a subaltern in the King's Infantry, had come to live with his father. Jean-Baptiste no longer objected to her friendship with his son and encouraged him to talk to her of Versailles, of court customs and behaviour, of the complicated laws of protocol and etiquette which made her laugh that fresh, childish laughter at once so fascinating and disconcerting in someone of her experience. She lived four years with du Barry before he allowed her to visit Versailles – always waiting for the propitious moment when, trained and polished to perfection, the woman whom he now regarded as his creation was ready to meet the King.

As a generous gesture he had handed over to his mistress the revenues accruing from his contract in supplying arms for Corsica. But the gesture was not quite so generous as it appeared. As minister of war, the Duc de Choiseul was determined to put an end to the enormous abuses in army contracts, most of which were in the hands of men like du Barry. The 'roué', to whom Choiseul had already refused a diplomatic post abroad, was aware that it would not be long before he was deprived of this highly lucrative contract. By handing it over to a beautiful young woman on the pretext that it represented her only source of income, he was acting on the assumption that someone as susceptible as Choiseul would be unable to resist her charms.

Etienne François de Choiseul was at the time the most powerful man in France, controlling the three ministries of foreign affairs, of war and of the marine; a man recklessly extravagant in his private expenditure and scrupulously honest in public life, who at the end of the disastrous Seven Years' War had directed all his tremendous energy to restoring his country's shattered prestige, in rebuilding the navy, reforming the army and negotiating the family pact between the Bourbon powers of France, Spain, Naples and Parma. With one aim in mind, he kept working for an eventual revenge on England who had deprived France of the greater part of her colonial empire and driven her crippled ships from the high seas.

In spite of an infinite capacity for work, he was at the same time a man of pleasure. One of his intimates wrote that he 'never knew of anyone who had such a way of making everyone round him seem happy and contented. When he came into a room it seemed as if he dived into his pockets and drew out an inexhaustible stock of fun and gaiety.' For all his intrinsic ugliness, women adored him. He had a pudgy face, a snub nose, thick lips and red hair which no amount of powder could conceal. But he had an elegant figure, bright smiling eyes and a charm which no one could resist. The little heiress whom he married when she was only fifteen, whose vast fortune he dissipated over the years and to whom he was unfaithful from the first month of his marriage, loved him to the day of his death and spent the rest of her life in paying off his debts. For all his faults he was a great statesman, a true patriot, ambitious both for himself and for his country. The only slur on his memory is the manner in which he came to power in denouncing to Madame de Pompadour a potential rival, one of his own relatives, a pretty young woman who had taken the King's fancy and who had been sufficiently foolish to take him into her confidence. The marquise, who was a good friend and a vindictive enemy, lost no time in destroying her rival. But Choiseul, or Stainville as he was called in those days when serving in the army, far removed from the seat of power at Versailles, was rewarded with the post of ambassador to Rome, the first step on the ladder which three years later would make him Duc de Choiseul and minister of foreign affairs. The death of the marquise, whom he had accepted as a necessity but despised as a *bourgeoise*, rendered him supreme both in the government and at court. He was at the apogee of power when, in the spring of 1768, he was asked by a friend to receive a young woman calling herself Jeanne de Vaubernier, who was already known to several of their acquaintances.

Even if one was as beautiful and self-confident as Jeanne, it must have been an intimidating experience on one's first visit to Versailles to be ushered into the office of the most powerful man in France. She came as a suppliant dressed in her simplest clothes, looking her most ravishing in a muslin gown cut low over her bosom, her pale gold curls escaping from a plain straw hat. But her beauty appears to have left the minister unmoved. He wrote, 'I found her only moderately pretty. There was a certain awkwardness in her manner which made me take her for a young woman from the provinces. Nor did I believe in her story of having confided the whole of her small fortune to an army contractor in charge of supplies for Corsica, who was now in danger of losing his job. I was kind, but in order to be rid of her I passed her on to Monsieur Foulon who was in charge of that department, at which the young lady did not seem to be very pleased.'

It is interesting to note that Choiseul, who was later to decry the King's mistress as having been a common streetwalker, should at their first encounter have regarded her as a shy and awkward young woman from the provinces to whom a great nobleman from Lorraine, whose mistresses were never less than duchesses, could never have been attracted but who nevertheless had nothing vulgar about her.

A few days later she wrote asking for a second interview. On this occasion she seems to have lost most of her shyness, but she made the fatal mistake of referring to du Barry, a name which till now she had carefully avoided, and the minister immediately recognized her to be a woman kept by the '*roué*' who at his instigation had come to ask him for money. He also suspected that she was trying to seduce him, but as he wrote in his memoirs, 'She was not at all to my taste.'

She may have failed with the minister but she triumphed with the King, for it was on leaving the ministry of war, escorted by one of her friends, for she had many at Versailles, that Jeanne de Vaubernier found her way to the state apartments at the hour when the King was going to mass. The royal family lived in public. Anyone decently dressed could wander into the palace and watch the monarch going to mass, or be present at the *couvert publique* while the King and the Princes of the Blood sat down to dine. It was a gloomy spring at Versailles. The Queen was dying and every day masses were being said for her recovery. The courtiers spoke in lowered voices and the smell of incense hung heavy on the air as the priests went by, with their acolytes swinging their censers. King Louis, surrounded by his daughters, passed across the gallery of mirrors barely glancing at the crowds pressing against the marble balustrades till he suddenly caught sight of a radiant young woman standing tall and straight, looking at him full in the face and daring to smile.

4

King Louis was bewitched at first sight of that lovely smiling face, so singularly pure and innocent, on which all her sordid experiences had not left a trace. That same evening he summoned his valet Lebel to discover the identity of the young woman he had noticed on his way to mass. There was no difficulty in finding her. Several of the courtiers who were already familiar with Jeanne de Vaubernier had noted her presence at Versailles. Lebel himself had once been on friendly terms with du Barry, but there had been a rift when the count had asked too high a price in providing for the King's pleasures, and the 'roué' played no part in the negotiations which brought Jeanne to the palace. The invitation was brought to her directly by Lebel and accepted with alacrity, as if she had been waiting for it for a long time.

A story is told of how Jeanne Bécu, a bastard born in a village in Lorraine, conquered the heart of the fifty-eight-year-old King of France. Ushered into the royal presence and having made the three curtseys required by protocol, she had gone straight up to him and kissed him full on the mouth. The story is probably apocryphal, but it would help to explain the extraordinary effect she had on Louis in the first twenty-four hours of their meeting. Even Lebel, who had administered to his master's secret pleasures for over twenty years, was shocked at his behaviour. The Queen was in her last agony in the very week in which Jeanne spent her first night with the King, who on the following morning told his friend and confidant the Maréchal de Richelieu, 'I am delighted with your Jeanne. She is the only woman in France who has managed to make me forget that I am sixty.' This leads one to suppose that Louis was aware that Richelieu had shared the favours of the fascinating Madame du Barry. Neither Richelieu nor Lebel had dared to tell him the truth. Jeanne had been passed off as a married woman of good standing who had indulged in one or two liaisons with important men at court and in the banking world. This, combined with a health certificate which implied freedom from venereal disease, was all that the King required for one of his passing affairs. But he now appeared to be losing his head over a woman who was able to give him sexual satisfaction such as he had never known, and he confessed to the Duc d'Ayen 'that he had discovered some pleasures entirely new to him', whereupon the duke, who never minced his words, replied, 'That, sire, is because you have never been to a brothel.'

On 25 June 1769 the Queen's death plunged the whole court into mourning and the King showed both sorrow and remorse over the death of a loyal and devoted wife. These were anxious days for a young woman living in seclusion in a small hotel in Versailles, not even daring to go to Paris for the day, always waiting for the hour when Lebel would come to take her to the palace. A natural sweetness of disposition, a genuine compassion for a melancholy old man haunted by death, combined with her talents and accomplishments as a court-esan, succeeded in rousing Louis from the depths of gloom to a mood approaching euphoria. Lebel began to be alarmed at his master's growing infatuation for someone whose humble antecedents could no longer be concealed. Paris was full of her relatives, most of them domestics in aristocratic households. It was well known that she had never been married to du Barry, who had a wife still living in Languedoc. Soon everyone at court would be aware that the King's mistress was the bastard child of a seamstress from a village in Lorraine. Le Parc aux Cerfs was where a woman of that class belonged. But Louis had no intention of putting her into that discreet little house on the outskirts of Versailles, which Lebel had directed for twenty years at the insti-gation of Madame de Pompadour. On the contrary, he was now talking of closing the Parc aux Cerfs and bringing his new mistress to Ver-sailles, where only a married woman belonging to the nobility could be admitted at court.

Lebel had no choice but to tell his master the truth. One morning at the royal toilette he confessed that not only had Madame never been married, but that she came from the lowest class of society. Louis was furious, but his anger was directed against the faithful valet for daring to cast aspersions on a woman whom he honoured with his love. Lebel was ordered to hold his tongue and to arrange at once for Madame to be married. The shock was so great for the old man who had spent a lifetime in his King's service that he was dead within a few weeks.

Jeanne's chief ally was the Duc de Richelieu who, as the King's friend and an intimate of du Barry, took a hand in the negotiations which led to the fraudulent marriage which made her into the Comtesse du Barry. The '*roué*' would gladly have married her himself, had Adolphe's mother not been still alive. But mouldering in Levignac was a brother called Guillaume who had been invalided out of the army after serving in the Caribbean and was now consoling himself with the bottle and occasional excursions to the brothels of Toulouse. He was small, fat and misshapen, but he would serve as husband to a woman who would never be required to share his bed. With the connivance of Richelieu and protected by the royal sanction, the '*roué*' used all his fantasy in composing a marriage contract of which every clause was a lie. With the consent of their old mother, who only asked for the wedding to be consecrated by canonical rites, and a handsome sum of money supplied by his brother, Guillaume du Barry set out at the end of July for Paris where the banns were already published, though he was not to see his future bride till the morning of the wedding on 1 September.

Jeanne had in the meantime followed the King to Compiègne, where she could be seen driving in a magnificent carriage with liveried footmen, all paid for by the '*roué*' who was staking his all on the biggest gamble of his career. People spoke of her as the woman who had infatuated the King, but no one met her during the six weeks that preceded the wedding, and life must have seemed very lonely for a young woman who was used to the brilliant parties of the rue Jussienne. The Duc de Choiseul, who had arrived in Compiègne a few days after the court, writes of a visit paid him by one of his colleagues who had come to tell him 'that there was a certain Madame du Barry at Compiègne with whom the King was said to have fallen in love and who was nothing but a prostitute kept by du Barry, who was now planning to marry her off to a brother with no other part to play than to give her his name and disappear at the earliest opportunity'. The two ministers deplored the fact that their King should have fallen so low and be behaving in a manner so unsuitable for his rank, his age and state of health. One could only hope it was no more than a passing fancy and that he would soon recover his senses. Choiseul, who immediately recognized her as the young woman who had come to his office, refused to believe that 'such a mediocrity could ever become a successor to the brilliant marquise'. But matters became more serious when the ambassadors, who had their spies among the lackeys and maids of *les petits appartements*, tried to discuss the situation with the minister, who was shocked to find how well the envoys of Spain and Austria were informed of his master's deviations.

By the time the court had moved to Fontainebleau everyone had become aware that the King had fallen so desperately in love that he refused to listen to either criticism or advice. A marriage so scandalous that, without royal protection, it would have landed the perpetrators in the galleys, was celebrated in Paris in the little church of St Laurent in the early morning of 1 September 1768. The contract, in which three years were taken off the age of the bride, described her as being the twenty-two-year-old daughter of Anne Bécu, called Cantigny, and of Jean-Jacques Gomard de Vaubernier (deceased), while the putative father, the ex-monk known as Brother Angel, now serving at St Eustache, appeared at the wedding in the role of an uncle, wearing a smart brown suit with gold buttons and elevated by du Barry to the rank of King's almoner. Both Monsieur and Madame Rançon were present under their new names of Monsieur and Madame de Montrabé.

The marriage contract made it clear that the husband should have no right over the income of his wife. There was to be no *communité de biens*. The bride was to be responsible for all household expenses including servants' wages, carriages and horses and, what was the most farcical claim of all, was to pay for the education of any children born from the marriage. That she was already a woman of substance was made clear in a detailed list of her possessions which added up to a sum of no less than thirty thousand *livres* consisting of diamonds, laces, embroidered gowns and personal linen, including twenty-four corsets – a formidable list for a young woman who only a few years ago had been a shopgirl at Labille's and which, in the wording of the contract, was entirely the result of 'her own earnings and economies'.

With her gay, superficial nature Jeanne probably looked upon the whole of the marriage contract as a joke. But for all her dissolute life, the nine years spent in the convent of St Aure had left their mark. She was still religious at heart and must have had certain qualms of conscience as she stood beside the repulsive little man to whom she was to be tied in holy matrimony. She might never have had the courage to go through with the ceremony had not Jean-Baptiste reminded her that her lover was King of France by divine right and that his will was law. The husband, who was not even allowed to touch her, had consoled himself with copious libations of brandy and could barely stagger down the aisle. But the '*roué*', who had carried out the biggest coup of his career, was in the best of moods. However much he had had to borrow, it would not be long before he would have unlimited access to the royal treasury.

An hour after the wedding the new Comtesse du Barry had rejoined the King at Compiègne. She travelled in a coach emblazoned with the family arms, a triumph of her brother-in-law's fertile imagination, for which he had borrowed the armorial bearings of the Irish Barry-more family, to whom he claimed to be related, and joined them to a mythical coat-of-arms belonging to the bride's family of Gomard. The result was a showy and glittering piece of work centred round the Barrymore motto, '*Boutez en avant*'. Though Jeanne was not yet living at the château, she could be seen driving out in public and behaving with all the effrontery of 'a woman kept by a powerful lover'. Every day her presence was becoming more and more necessary to Louis. The doctors might say she was too young for a man of his age and made too many demands on his health, but it was noted that he had never looked so well and that all his apathy and lassitude had gone. The great ladies who had run the court since the death of Madame de Pompadour – the Princesse de Beauvau, Madame de Boufflers, and the most arrogant of them all, the Duchesse de Gramont, who was Choiseul's sister – now found that the King was becoming every day more indifferent to their presence. Choiseul, who till now had looked upon the new favourite as being no more than a *passade*, allowed himself to be dragged into a turmoil of mischievous female intrigue directed by his sister, a woman of immense conceit, who, in spite of having neither looks nor charm, had aspired to the role of royal mistress and, given Louis's loneliness and weakness, might even have succeeded had it not been for the radiant smile of a young woman seen on the way to mass. The frustrated anger of this proud, embittered virago was eventually to contribute to her brother's downfall.

It was a time when reputations were destroyed by scurrilous rhymes and pasquinades, when poisoned darts were concealed in frivolous lyrics. Maurepas, who had been one of Louis's favourite ministers, suffered twenty years of exile for mocking Madame de Pompadour. Choiseul's greatest mistake was in resorting to this type of weapon to ruin a woman whom he feared not for herself but because she was supported by his arch-enemy, the Maréchal de Richelieu. It would have been far more effective to have laid before the King the reports of the minister of police, which contained the whole of the Comtesse du Barry's sordid past. Even the doting Louis might have quailed on reading the lists of hairdressers and silk merchants who numbered among his predecessors, the details of her life as the concubine of du Barry.

What had been no more than whispered rumours at Compiègne grew into a crescendo at Fontainebleau. Unable to exist without his mistress, Louis found lodgings for her in the château. Here she was even lonelier than at Compiègne, for not even the King dared go against protocol to the extent of inviting to the royal hunts a woman who had not even been presented at court.

Du Barry wisely and deliberately kept away from Jeanne, sending her instructions by relays of messengers, the most frequent of all being the son whose regiment was stationed at Fontainebleau and who, thanks to his beautiful aunt, was destined to have a brilliant career at court. But Jean-Baptiste's cleverest move was in bringing his young sister from Languedoc to act as companion to the friendless Jeanne. Claire Françoise, commonly known as Chon, was plain, intelligent and extremely cultivated. In Toulouse she had enjoyed a certain literary reputation by contributing poems and articles to the local press. But with neither looks nor dowry she had little to expect from the future, till by a surprising twist of fate she was sent to guide her new sister-in-law on her perilous rise to fame. Shrewd and witty, with a *naïveté* which was largely feigned, she managed to amuse the King, and within a few months this unknown young woman from the provinces had become a popular guest at the royal supper parties.

The two sisters-in-law had a lot to learn from each other. Chon saved Jeanne from committing many a social error, teaching her to restrain her natural exuberance, to behave in public as a lady rather than as a courtesan, and to keep her salacious sallies for the intimacy of *les petits appartements* where Chon delighted the old King with her shrewish wit. Jeanne on her side gave confidence to her plain sister-in-law, imparting to her certain talents in which she proved herself an apt pupil, so that before long she had found herself lovers among the most hardened libertines at court. These two women with such disparate characters grew into loyal and devoted friends. Chon was equally loyal to her brother, protecting his interests and never forgetting that it was he who had brought her from the obscurity of the provinces to the limelight of Versailles.

Of all the artists who painted the royal favourite, even to immortalizing her dog and her little Indian serving boy, none ever seems to have taken any interest in Mademoiselle du Barry. Contemporary descriptions, which are mostly malicious, say that she was small and slightly hunchbacked with a pointed face and long nose, resembling her brother, her redeeming features being her expressive eyes and the delightful smile which made that consummate rascal of a '*roué*' so difficult to resist. In the years to come, the great Duc de Choiseul was to find the favourite's sister-in-law a far subtler opponent than the simple-minded Jeanne.

But in the autumn of 1768 no one, least of all Choiseul, could have believed that the Comtesse du Barry could ever become *maîtresse en titre*. She was seen coming out of her lodgings in the Court of the Fountains. No one met her but everyone talked about her, and scurrilous verses, which did not even spare the King, passed from mouth to mouth. Autumn at Fontainebleau was always a time when a bored, disorientated court living in cramped quarters in a draughty old château indulged in malice and vituperation. But never had scandal reached so low a level as now, when the chief minister of France allowed the police to publish the filthiest exudings of the gutter press attacking both the favourite and the King. An old madrigal sung in the streets of Paris on the life of a courtesan, known as 'la Bourbonnaise', was revived and adapted with clear references to the past of a certain countess who, born a peasant girl, had come to Paris where she had shared her favours with lackeys and with hairdressers till she found her way to court. The popularity of 'la Bourbonnaise' was such that before long it appeared on the stage in the form of a burlesque so coarse and vulgar as to bear no resemblance to the woman it was intended to libel, but not too vulgar to be learnt by heart by the elegant ladies of Versailles and repeated to the King's daughters, who were horrified to hear that their beloved father was spending his nights with a woman who was little more than a prostitute.

But this campaign of defamation organized by Choiseul had the opposite effect to what was intended. All that was best in Louis reacted to the falseness of the horrible allegations brought against a woman whom he judged to be sweet and modest, and with whom every day he was falling more deeply in love, and the first shock to his court came with the announcement that he intended to bring his mistress to Versailles and to have her officially presented.

5

At court and in town people spoke of nothing else but of the future presentation of a Madame du Barry whom the King had installed at Versailles in the face of bitter opposition from Choiseul. But the powerful minister had many enemies. Libertines like the Duc de Richelieu, and the so-called *dévots*, a religious group at court to which the Dauphin belonged, who had never forgiven Choiseul for the expulsion of the Jesuits, were ready to make common cause to bring about his downfall. The Duc de Croy, one of the few men at court genuinely devoted to King Louis xv, wrote in his journal: 'It is terrible to think that humanity has come to a pass when envy and personal hatred have rendered people blind to the important issues at stake, when the royal governess, Madame de Marsan, sister to the Prince de Soubise, and the young prince's tutor, the Duc de la Vauguyon, should be ready to welcome the advent of a Madame du Barry if it brought about the disgrace of Choiseul.'

Jeanne's position during her first months at Versailles was not entirely enviable. Financially she was still dependent on du Barry. The carriages, jewels and clothes with which she was so liberally supplied remained unpaid for up to the time when he could reclaim the money from the royal treasury. In Versailles she was lodged in a small apartment adjoining the chapel which had formerly been that of Lebel, the King's valet. There was no room here either for her sister-in-law or servants, who were housed in a small house in the rue de l'Orangerie, rented in her name. Here she was able to entertain some of the poets and artists who had frequented the rue Jussienne. The Prince de Ligne has left us a description of the charming, animated hostess who received with such elegance and grace and never in any way betrayed her humble origins. But at Versailles she remained completely ostracized, and the women who passed her in her gilded *chaise* being carried to the King's apartments deliberately turned their backs.

Neither Choiseul nor his sister, the proud and vindictive Duchesse de Gramont, would accept the fact that a peasant girl from Vaucouleurs in their home province of Lorraine had captured the King's heart. The most scurrilous of lampoons, all of which had to pass the censorship of the minister of police, were known to have been commissioned by Choiseul. Fearing that some of these were so pornographic as to offend the ears of Mesdames de France, special verses were composed, calculated to bring the princesses to the side of a minister they had hitherto detested. They gave them details of an affair so shameful that they were prepared to welcome the overtures of the Austrian ambassador, who hinted that the only solution for their father's future happiness and a respected old age would be for him to marry the Archduchess Elisabeth, one of the Empress Maria Theresa's unmarried daughters, the cleverest and most beautiful of them all until a virulent attack of smallpox had spoilt her looks.

Against all these intrigues, Jeanne had no weapon other than her beauty and her charm. To amuse the King required endless patience and inexhaustible reserves of gaiety and good humour. She might lack the brilliance and versatility of her predecessor, but she had a natural sweetness of disposition which enabled her to give him warmth and affection such as he had never known. The orphan who had become King at five years old had never experienced the normal pleasures of a happy childhood.

The Duc de Croy, who had known him over the years, wrote: 'He is more in love than he has ever been. He seems to be rejuvenated and I have never seen him in better spirits, extremely good-humoured and far more outgoing than he has ever been.' He was unable to tear himself away from his lovely young mistress and thought only of the time when he could present her openly to the world. But the weakness and indecision which was a fundamental part of his character, his inability to make up his mind, and the counter-influences to which he was being constantly subjected made him put it off from day to day. There were many obstacles in the way. The most difficult of all was to find a lady of title ready to sacrifice her reputation by presenting Madame du Barry. Those who were willing were so outrageous in their demands as to shock the usually unshockable Richelieu. In the end it was the old Duchesse d'Aiguillon, wanting to get her son back in favour with the King, who succeeded in unearthing an impoverished relative buried in the provinces, so crippled by debts that she was unable to live at Versailles. On the payment of these debts and the promise of promotion for her two sons, one of them in the army, the other in the navy, the Comtesse de Béarn was ready to incur the odium of her peers by befriending the former Jeanne Bécu.

January 25 was the day fixed for the presentation, and on the 24th Madame du Deffand wrote to her English friend Sir Horace Walpole: 'They say that tomorrow will be the day when a petticoat will perhaps determine the destinies of Europe ... But I refuse to believe in all that they say – they may overcome the greatest obstacles and in the end be held up by shame.' Which was exactly what happened, for at the last moment Madame de Béarn lost her nerve, and on the excuse of a sprained ankle took to her bed. A far more serious obstacle occurred two days later when the King went out hunting and fell from his horse, hurting his arm so badly that at first it was thought to have been broken. The accident took place at the beginning of Lent, at a time when the Lenten sermons disturbed Louis's uneasy conscience and the sins of the flesh weighed heavy on his mind. In the first days he was well enough to preside at his council and receive the Ash Wednesday blessing from the Archbishop of Rheims. But later the contusion spread and he was confined to his room for ten days, during which not even Richelieu dared to bring Jeanne into his room for fear of meeting the royal princesses who never left their father's bedside.

Choiseul and his party rejoiced to see the priests and the princesses regain their ascendancy over the weak, vacillating King who even went so far as to discuss with Madame Adelaide the possibility of marrying again. Jeanne was in despair waiting for Richelieu to bring her to her lover's bedside. Everything hung on the presentation. Without it she was no more than any other girl who had passed through the Parc aux Cerfs. She knew such moments of misery that she was ready to go back to her old life rather than remain at Versailles without the King. Then Louis recovered, more amorous than ever, ready to forget the exhortations of the priests and the advice of his daughters.

'He still loves my lady with the same passion. She is not yet presented. However, it is generally expected that she will be,' wrote Voltaire's niece, Madame Denis, in one of those chatty letters which kept her uncle informed of the latest events in the capital. But for the time being the court was not so much taken up with the presentation of Madame du Barry as with the forthcoming marriage of the King's cousin, the young Duc de Chartres, to Mademoiselle de Penthièvre, the richest heiress in France. Her exclusion from all the brilliant wedding festivities, in which she would have loved to shine, made Jeanne painfully aware of the ambiguity of her position. On du Barry's advice she resorted to tears, the weapon which a man in love finds so difficult to resist. Caresses and passionate entreaties were all part of a technique which overcame Louis's last hesitations. Barely a week after the royal wedding he announced to his gentleman-in-waiting, the Duc de Richelieu, that Madame du Barry was to be presented on the evening of 22 April. 'I am opening my letter, dear friend, to tell you that Madame du Barry is to be presented on the Sunday after Easter. I can assure you the news is authentic,' wrote Madame Denis to Voltaire. But to the very last, people refused to believe it, and at Versailles they were laying bets for and against the presentation. Foreign ambassadors filled their despatches with news which could affect their country's relationship with France, and the Comte Mercy d'Argenteau, who was particularly incensed at having his plans for the King's remarriage come to nothing, wrote to the Austrian chancellor: 'It is a scandal that Maréchal de Richelieu should lend himself to such a sordid intrigue.' The marshal, who had become Jeanne's greatest ally, had been entrusted by the King to order her court dress and to present her with a royal gift of diamonds worth a hundred thousand *livres*.

That evening Versailles was crowded. However great the scandal, no one had kept away. Beyond the courtyards, outside the gilded gates, were hundreds of sightseers who had come out from Paris to witness the triumph of a little *grisette*. In the royal apartments no one dared to speak aloud. Even Richelieu looked nervous, for the King kept looking at his watch. Madame was already ten minutes late. There was a frown on this handsome face and in five minutes the most impatient of men would be cancelling the whole presentation. Choiseul's supporters were already hoping that the lady had lost her nerve and dared not face up to a hostile court, when there was the clatter of horses' hooves arriving in the Cour de Marbre and the sound of soldiers presenting arms as Madame du Barry alighted from her carriage, a vision so radiant that the crowds gasped in admiration. Calm and unruffled, she ascended the grand staircase and, with head held high, she passed through the curious crowds, outwardly indifferent to the hostile looks and the whispered comments.

Richelieu had ordered a dress fit for a queen with enormous panniers of silver and gold cloth bespattered with diamonds and a train of inordinate length which she managed with as great an ease as she did the three complicated curtseys decreed by court etiquette. Proudly she appeared before the King, sinking to her knees as gracefully as a lovely swan. Even Madame de Béarn, who by now had conquered her fears, looked pleased at presenting someone so perfect and so sure of herself. Louis himself was completely transformed. His face was aglow with happiness and he might have been a young lover presenting his bride. For the extraordinary thing about Jeanne du Barry was that, for all her sordid past, she still managed to look as innocent as any virgin, with a skin so delicate it hardly required any rouge, teeth of a dazzling whiteness in a small, naturally scarlet mouth, blue eyes made all the softer by their long dark lashes, and a smile so sweet and open that only envy could inspire hatred of her. Even the disapproving princesses were momentarily so subjected to her charms that they received her more graciously than might have been expected, while the young Dauphin, who rarely noted anything in his journal other than the record of his hunting trophies, was sufficiently impressed to write under the entry for Sunday, 22 April: 'Presentation of Madame du Barry.' Even Choiseul might have been disarmed by her beauty, had it not been for his sister's bitter envy. But the sight of the King's happiness aroused in Béatrice de Gramont a vindictive desire for revenge. As the most powerful woman at court she was determined that the royal mistress should never be allowed to forget that she was born Jeanne Bécu.

In Paris, Jean-Baptiste du Barry was celebrating the most successful gamble of his career. He himself had no entry to Versailles, but his beloved son was in continual attendance on his lovely aunt and would now be admitted to the intimacy of the greatest of kings. Tomorrow Chon du Barry, the little spinster from the provinces, would accompany her sister-in-law to mass in the royal chapel, where they would occupy the places once reserved for the Marquise de Pompadour. From now on the girl he had discovered when serving behind a counter at Labille's, whom with infinite patience he had educated and trained as a delightful companion and the most accomplished of courtesans, would take her place as the King's *maîtresse en titre* at the most civilized court in Europe. Who of his creditors would now dare to present him with their accounts? What jeweller would ask him to settle the bills for the diamonds which the new Comtesse du Barry had worn with such *éclat* at Compiègne and Fontainebleau? Tonight the King had presented his mistress with jewels worth one hundred thousand *livres*, only a foretaste of what there was to come. Du Barry was a patient man who knew how to wait. He would not hand in his own accounts till later in the year.

On Monday, 23 April 1769, the Comtesse du Barry took her place as Louis's official mistress, a position which gave her privileges and powers of which she may not yet have been aware. Seated in the royal chapel, she was surprised to see the number of bishops included in the King's suite. Still innocent of politics, she did not realize that the clerics and the *dévots* who hated Choiseul were among her staunchest supporters. In her new position she was permitted to assist at the *grands couverts* both of the Dauphin and of his aunts and to have a place at the King's card table. But no one took the place beside her and no one addressed her a pleasant word. No court lady accepted the invitations to her parties in the rue de l'Orangerie and Choiseul's coterie, led by his sister, his wife and the Princesse de Beauvau, deliberately absented itself from Versailles. In public the countess made a point of ignoring these insults, of adopting an attitude of calm disdain, but there were many tears in the privacy of the King's apartments, calculated to make Louis all the more loving and chivalrous on her behalf. His reaction to the attitude of his courtiers was to order the master of his household, the Duc de Noailles, to install Madame du Barry in the most intimate of all the *petits appartements*, the one immediately above his own to which he had direct access by a private staircase. The scandal of putting his mistress in the rooms where his daughter-in-law, the Dauphin's wife, had died in the previous year brought criticism from the loyalest of his courtiers. But criticism only made him the more obstinate, the more determined to impose Madame du Barry on his family and his court.

Barely a month after the presentation, it was announced that His Majesty was giving a supper party at the château de Bellevue, the most charming of all the pleasure houses built by Madame de Pompadour. The supper was said to be in honour of the new favourite and eight ladies of his court had been invited to make her acquaintance. The royal invitation was an order no one dared to refuse, and those who had been selected were mostly old friends of the King. There was Madame de Flavacourt, one of the famous Neslé sisters, four of whom had at one time or the other been his mistress. There was the Maréchale de Mirepoix, who in the past had befriended Madame de Pompadour and, as the most inveterate gambler at court, was grateful to the King for always paying her debts. Madame de l'Hôpital and the Princesse de Monaco, mistresses of the Prince de Soubise and the Duc de Condé, came with their lovers, both of whom aspired to sit in the Grand Council and whose ambitions till now had been frustrated by Choiseul and, strangest of all, there was Choiseul himself, for Louis was a man of habit who hated change and still hoped that his minister and his mistress might end in becoming friends.

Vandals of the Revolution have long since destroyed the rococo gardens Madame de Pompadour laid out with such loving pride. But on the night of the King's supper party the gardens of Bellevue, with the cascades of roses climbing over marble balustrades and the fountains playing in pools of waterlilies, must have seemed the perfect setting for a reconciliation. The guests, while waiting for the King who had been to mass to celebrate the *Fête-Dieu*, wandered across the lawns, each little coterie keeping strictly to itself, with the Duc de Richelieu as always in assiduous attendance on Madame du Barry while the Duc de Choiseul ostentatiously ignored her. At the end of an hour it was noted that more and more people were drifting in the direction of the lovely young woman who, in a diaphanous white gown with pearls and roses in her hair, made every other woman present look over-rouged and overdressed. The King had eyes for no one else. From the moment he arrived he never left her side, escorting her round the gardens, sitting beside her at supper, making her the centre of every conversation. In the light of his admiration she glowed and sparkled, relaxed and happy, completely at her ease. Those who saw them together realized that this was no passing infatuation on his part, but a deep and serious love. When supper was over, he sat down to cards and asked who was ready to play at *vingt-et-un* with Madame du Barry, a game of which she was particularly fond. The first to reply was Madame de Flavacourt, who had spent all her life at Versailles and had learnt how to trim her sails to every breeze. She was readily seconded by the Duc de Richelieu, who with all the gallantry of an old courtier called out that he was always at the disposition of Madame du Barry.

The King played his usual game of whist with the Duc de Choiseul, who for all his apparent serenity appeared this evening to be lacking both in spontaneity and wit, taking little part in the gaiety and laughter which surrounded the favourite. On the following day, while the King honoured Madame du Barry by attending her *levée* in her new apartments, the duke left for a short holiday on his property in Touraine. What was supposed to be a clever move, a tactful way of showing his disapproval of His Majesty's behaviour, turned out to be a mistake, for Richelieu profited by his absence to introduce Madame du Barry to his nephew, the Duc d'Aiguillon.

6

Emmanuel Armand, Duc d'Aiguillon, had in his youth been so unfortunate as to fall in love with the most fascinating of the five Neslé sisters, who as mistress to Louis XV was created Duchesse de Châteauroux. Versailles was not a pleasant place for a young man who had presumed to be a rival to the King, and the disappointed lover adopted a military career. After distinguishing himself both in Italy and during the Seven Years' War, he was created governor-commandant of Brittany. A brilliant victory gained at St Cast in repulsing the English off the French coast made him into one of the heroes of the day. But his popularity did not last for long. Cold and arrogant with all the pride and self-sufficiency of the Richelieus, d'Aiguillon showed no tact in dealing with the tough, independent Bretons. In forcing them to adopt taxes imposed by Versailles, he offended the susceptibilities of the local magistrates, who rejected them in the *parlement* of Rennes. When the King reversed their decree, the *parlement* replied by dissolving itself and the magistrates, led by the attorney-general and his son, followed by the armed forces of the whole province, rose against the governor, accusing him of despotism and of corruption and even going so far as to deny him the victory of St Cast, claiming it had been won by the brave Breton soldiers while he hid for safety in a flour mill. D'Aiguillon replied by arresting the chief magistrates and forming a new *parlement*. But this in no way helped to solve the situation. The Bretons refused to recognize it, and after four years of stalemate the King, acting largely on the advice of Choiseul, restored the old *parlement* and recalled d'Aiguillon.

The proud, disappointed man who returned to Versailles labelled as a failure was filled with a bitter hatred of Choiseul, a convinced parliamentarian who had chosen to support the magistrates against the representative of the King.

He arrived at Versailles in the summer of 1768 when Jeanne du

Barry was making her first uneasy debuts at Compiègne and Fontaine-bleau and was in desperate need of friends. Richelieu, who had been one of the few to support her from the very beginning and believed in her star, recognized her as a powerful ally in bringing his nephew back into favour. Six months later, when she was established as *maîtresse en titre*, holding her first *levées*, d'Aiguillon was among the most assiduous of her courtiers. Soon there were rumours that 'Mon-sieur le duc was sharing my lady's favours with the King'. Nothing could have been further from the truth. Even had they been so inclined, neither would have dared to arouse the jealousy of the ageing monarch. Jeanne, who really loved her sexagenarian lover, thought of nothing else but of keeping him happy and amused, while d'Aiguillon, however tempted, was at once too cold and too ambitious to embark on a career so fraught with danger. But d'Aiguillon had a mother known as the 'fat duchess', a woman of immense ability and charm, who advised him to pay court not to the favourite but to her plain little sister-in-law, who for all her lack of looks was brilliantly intelligent and well equipped to deal with the intrigues of Versailles. A plain woman would always be grateful to a lover, while her kind-hearted sister-in-law would only be too delighted that her 'dear little Chon' had found an admirer in the nephew of Maréchal de Richelieu and would do all in her power to further his interests with the King. Louis was the first to appreciate Chon's intelligence and would often invite her to his *petits soupers*. Dandling her on his knees, he would laugh at her caustic accounts of provincial politics, teasing her on what he called 'her radical opinions'.

Within a year the penniless spinster from Toulouse had become a leading figure in the cabal which was eventually to bring about the downfall of Choiseul. At first she counselled prudence. It was only when all the countess's friendly overtures had been rebuffed, when the charming letters she dictated to Jeanne, reminding the minis-ter of the help he had promised in assisting her administrator in Corsica received cold and discourteous replies, that Chon du Barry began to take an active part in d'Aiguillon's fight against Choiseul.

The minister had returned from holiday in Touraine to find the Comtesse du Barry included among the few intimate friends invited

by the King to join him in what was known as *les petits voyages**
to the pleasure houses of Marly and Choisy. In both places the apartments formerly occupied by the Marquise de Pompadour were restored
for the new favourite, the works being carried out by the minister
of fine arts who, somewhat ironically, happened to be brother to the
late marquise. Neither Choiseul nor his sister could control their indignation at seeing the countess driving in the royal carriages and sitting
at the King's table. But though Louis could command his guests to
a supper party, it was more difficult to impose his mistress on the
intimate life at Choisy. Most of the women continued to ignore her,
and even some of the men excused themselves from playing cards
with her on the grounds that they were short of funds. The theatrical
performances put on for the first time since the Queen's death did
little to enliven the atmosphere. It was generally known that the choice
of the plays had been left to Madame du Barry, who in a laudable
but mistaken effort to emulate her predecessor as a woman of culture
and refinement had chosen a repertoire derived mostly from the
classics, such as Racine and Molière, interspersed with a few insipid
modern comedies, which bored everyone except the King who, though
usually the most impatient of audiences, was now ready to sit through
the heaviest drama of Racine, providing he had the lovely countess
at his side. Every day he was falling more deeply in love and even
Choiseul began to take alarm, openly venting his spite when the court
moved to Compiègne.

Here life was far easier for Jeanne than at Choisy. Riding out with
Louis in the forests, or driving herself in an elegant phaeton, she could
forget the acid looks, the veiled insults. Accompanying him on military
manoeuvres, she revelled in the open admiration of the young officers.
The whole of the royal family, including Mesdames, were present
at these manoeuvres, which were more of a military fête designed
to initiate the young princes in the arts of war. But in spite of their
presence, the King would ride up to his favourite's carriage and bare-
headed, hat in hand, engage her in conversation. Many of the older
officers present were saddened at seeing their King forfeiting his dignity
in what they thought was an obsessive and senile passion. No one was

* *Petits voyages* were short journeys to his various pleasure houses undertaken by the King
to distract him from his boredom. They were extremely expensive as they entailed taking
the court.

more saddened and more indignant than Choiseul who, as minister of war, was in attendance on the monarch.

The countess was triumphant. The fact that the youngest du Barry brother was serving as captain in one of the regiments on parade and that his colonel was the Chevalier de la Tour du Pin, whom she had known in the old days in the rue Jussienne, made her feel that for once she belonged to this brilliant gathering instead of being made to feel unwanted and despised. To complete her triumph, her brother-in-law's regiment paid her the same military honours as they did the King, an act which enraged Choiseul, who insisted, rightly, that a regiment should pay royal honours to the King only. When the countess invited the officers of the regiment to a dinner the unfortunate colonel found himself in a predicament as to whether it was better to offend the rising favourite or the minister. To resolve the situation he sent his sister to Choiseul to ask him whether he should accept the invitation. All she got was a rude and angry reply that her brother 'could do as he pleased', upon which the chevalier allowed his young officers to dine with Madame du Barry while he, accompanied by his lieutenant-colonel and his major, went to dine with the minister. In these circumstances it might have been wiser had the countess allowed the whole matter to drop. But elated by success she wrote to Colonel de la Tour du Pin expressing the desire to be invited to dine in camp. Again the unfortunate colonel sent his sister to the Duc de Choiseul for his advice, only to get an angrier and even ruder reply to the effect that he would have nothing to do with the matter. But by now the chevalier was tired of his rudeness and, assured of the King's approval, invited Madame du Barry to a dinner at which the entire regiment was present. Included among the guests was none other than the Maréchal de Richelieu, the one man whom Choiseul both hated and feared. This was such an act of open defiance that the colonel's sister completely lost her nerve and left Compiègne rather than assist at the dinner.

Choiseul, who was renowned for his imperturbality and calm, now gave way to such uncontrollable fury as to say the most outrageous things, not only of the colonel and his regiment, which he accused of being slovenly, but also going so far as to attack the commander-in-chief Baron Wurmser, who reported this to the King. Louis, who had been delighted at having his beloved countess publicly honoured by his officers and had been particularly gracious to the Chevalier de La Tour du Pin, was incensed at his minister's behaviour and determined to show him that it was the King and not his minister who was the master. In a stern but moderate letter, showing that this was not the first time he had had trouble with Choiseul on the subject of Madame du Barry, he wrote:

'I have given you my word to tell you all that I hear about you and that promise I now fulfil. You are said to have reprimanded Wurmser, I do not know why. You are said to have reprimanded the Chevalier de La Tour du Pin, because Madame du Barry had dined at the camp and because the majority of the officers had dined with her on the day of the Review ... You promised me I should not hear any more in connection with her.

'I speak to you in confidence and as a friend. The public may inveigh bitterly against you. Such is the fate of ministers, specially when they are believed to be opposed to their master's friends. But nevertheless the master is well satisfied with their work and yours in particular.'

It was an amazingly tolerant letter, considering that by now the King was well aware that it was Choiseul and more particularly his sister who were responsible for the filthy lampoons attacking one whom he considered to be the sweetest and most generous of women. No man and in particular no monarch enjoys having himself referred to as *un vieux paillard* (an old lecher), or knowing that such verses were circulating round his capital.

Choiseul realized he had gone too far, and in a letter expressing his gratitude and devotion towards the best of sovereigns, he defended himself 'against the malicious fictions of those who surround Madame du Barry and whom you know as well as I do have specially marked me out in their desire to do me injury. Were I not assured of the goodness of your heart and your discernment concerning the nature of your court, I should be horrified at the evil which has been attributed to me.'

After defending himself against all the accusations brought against him, he ended his letter: 'I have but two aims in life, to serve you well and to please you. If you will deign to bear in view that I owe everything to you, that I have never served anyone but you, nor wish to serve anyone but you, and that I serve you for love and the most zealous love which is far more than ambition or talent.'

Louis accepted this letter as coming from a devoted servant, and throughout the year Choiseul continued to be in attendance at all *les petits soupers* at Compiègne and Fontainebleau. But it was the Duc de Richelieu who was now the leading figure at court. 'The marshal has been made years younger by his present position. He seems to tread on air which is indeed his natural element,' wrote the court physician, Tronchin, half in mockery, half in admiration of this sprightly old man who, regardless of his grey hairs, continued to woo the royal favourite. The loves of his youth, such as the Duchesse de Valentinois and the Princesse de Talmont, were persuaded to accept her invitations. When the King's cousin, the Prince de Condé, who aspired to succeed Choiseul at the ministry of war, gave a summer fête at Chantilly in honour of King Louis and his new mistress, the list of guests was handed to the Duc de Richelieu, who as first gentle-man-in-waiting deliberately struck out the names of the Duchesse de Gramont and the Princesse de Beauvau and those who had followed their lead in insulting Madame du Barry.

With her happy, easy-going nature Jeanne was at a loss to under-stand the reason for this bitter animosity. From her earliest youth she had subjugated men by her beauty and it piqued her vanity to think that a notorious womanizer like Choiseul should have failed to appreciate her charms. Her brother-in-law who, however discreetly, was still in the background of her life giving her shrewd if sometimes unwanted advice, now offered to act as an intermediary in contacting Choiseul's nephew, the young Duc de Lauzun, one of the gayest and most fascinating of the libertines who had frequented the rue Jussienne and paid court to the lovely Mademoiselle Vaubernier. The '*roué*' who now considered himself the equal of all his former clients, arranged a secret meeting in the forest of Compiègne in which he warned Lauzun 'that the Comtesse du Barry had no wish to quarrel with his uncle, that on the contrary she had the greatest admiration for his talents. But if ever the day should come when he would force her to be an enemy, then he would suffer for it, for the King was far more in love with her than he had ever been with the Marquise de Pompadour.' Choiseul, who had already had a warning from the King, might have listened to his nephew, but unfortunately Lauzun spoke to him in the presence of Béatrice de Gramont, and the vindictive duchess assailed him as the most despicable of renegades in consorting with creatures like the du Barrys.

Wise old Madame du Deffand, one of the Choiseuls' most devoted friends, wrote to Horace Walpole, 'It is grandpapa's [Choiseul] fault that he does not do as he likes with the du Barry. I cannot believe that his conduct has been right or that his pride has been sensible. In my opinion Mesdames de Gramont and de Beauvau have been unwise counsellors.' Curiosity to see the reigning favourite had brought Horace Walpole from London to Paris, where a place in the royal chapel at Versailles gave him the opportunity of seeing Madame du Barry at close quarters seated on a tribune immediately below the King. He was surprised to find her so different from what he had expected. 'There is nothing bold, assuming or affected in her manner. She is pretty when you consider her, but so little striking I would never have asked who she was. She was without rouge or powder, almost without having *fait la toilette*.'

The casualness of her attire was characteristic of Jeanne, who on gala occasions would appear in wonderful creations costing thousands of *livres*, but in ordinary daily life would wear the simple, light-coloured gowns which became her fragile colouring. When riding or driving out with the King she would adopt masculine clothes, the plumed hat, the grey silk jacket over an open waistcoat showing a lace fichu, the costume in which Drouais painted her for the *Salon d'Automne* and which is one of the most delightful of all her portraits. To appear in masculine clothes appealed to her love of dressing up, a taste which remained with her from her earliest childhood when Dumonceaux painted her, dressed as a cupid. In contrast to the Marquise de Pompadour, whom Nattier and Boucher immortalized as the queen of fashion in exquisite clothes which reflected her perfect taste, Jeanne is more often depicted *en déshabille*. She would arrive at the King's intimate supper parties impersonating Flora, the goddess of flowers, with garlands of myrtle round her waist and roses in her hair, her golden curls falling about her shoulders in charming disarray. Hours would be spent in achieving this youthful and seemingly effortless appearance, and there were times when even the King was kept waiting. But the result was so enchanting that the enamoured King was ready to wait for the woman whose very smile made him forget that he was sixty years old.

'She is here to stay,' said the old Duc de Croy after witnessing a curious scene one evening at Compiègne when Louis dropped a snuffbox on the ground and Madame du Barry swiftly knelt down to pick it up, whereupon the King was heard to murmur, 'Madame, it is for me to assume that position and for all my life.'

A few weeks later Louis presented the château of Louveciennes to the Comtesse du Barry. Apart from diamonds and gala gowns it was the first gift he had given to the woman who had been his mistress for over a year. The château was small, but the situation was delightful and its value was enhanced by the fact that it was crown property where former owners had all been relatives of the King. They had been Mademoiselle de Clermont, granddaughter of Louis xiv by the Duchesse de Bourbon, and the Comtesse de Toulouse, aunt to the present King, whose heir the Duc de Penthièvre had handed it over to his only son, the dissolute Prince de Lamballe, who had died there at the age of twenty. Since then Louveciennes (or Luciennes as it was called) had reverted to the crown, coveted by many but given to none; till one summer evening when Jeanne was out driving with the King and they came to the little château bathed in the evening sunlight, its windows looking out over the wide, wooded valley of the Seine. In a moment of tenderness, when Louis became again the young lover, he handed over the keys and title deeds which made Jeanne Bécu the owner of a house which had once belonged to a granddaughter of the *roi soleil*.

7

In the late autumn of 1769, when the court had returned to Versailles, the old Duc de Croy wrote in his journal: 'I observe that by degrees more and more people are ready to see the countess. She has been given the "Cabinet" rooms which formerly belonged to the late Madame la Dauphine, all of which give her the advantage of being treated as a lady of the court. She with everyone else is present at all the entertainments, and one has become accustomed to it. She has gained much, but she appears to have no aptitude for intrigue. She loves dress and to be seen everywhere, without showing any desire to interfere in state affairs. Her manner to the other ladies seems respectful and she never ventures too far.'

But the gentle, pliable little countess had changed more than the old duke had reckoned with. Certain events at Fontainebleau had contributed to this change. After going from triumph to triumph, an incident had occurred which, trivial in itself, wounded her more than any of the scurrilous verses which had attacked her in the past. A Comte de Lauraguais, a popular figure at court and a nephew of Choiseul, had had the ingenious idea of bringing a beautiful young woman to Fontainebleau and introducing her to his friends as the Comtesse du Tonneau. People were quick to see the allusion when it transpired that the *soi-disante* countess was a prostitute from Sarah Gourdan's celebrated establishment. At the same time there appeared a brutal caricature of the reigning favourite, wearing full court dress, seated on a barrel, which could be called either a *baril* or a *tonneau*.

The proud arms of the Barrymores blazoned on her carriages could not spare the Comtesse du Barry the humiliation of being identified as a common prostitute. And nothing was more calculated to amuse the bored and disgruntled courtiers with nothing to do while the King and his friends went out hunting day after day. In the time of Madame de Pompadour, Lauraguais's brutal joke would have earned him a *lettre de cachet*, a decree of banishment without trial signed by the King. Now he was merely told to absent himself from court and take a holiday in England. But behind Lauraguais Jeanne recognized the hand of Choiseul, and she deliberately abstained from attending all public functions so long as the minister remained at Fontainebleau. Instead of appearing at the theatrical performances which were such a feature of court life, she remained quietly in her apartments which gave out on the Court of Diana. And Louis, who was bored without her, would leave after the first act and return to have supper with his mistress and a few intimate friends, the inevitable Richelieu and his nephew who, with the Countess's help, was winning his way back to favour. D'Aiguillon had not long to wait before a post fell vacant which gave him direct access to the King. To be colonel-in-chief of the Light Horse and captain of the Royal Bodyguard were two of the most coveted positions at court. Left vacant by the death of the Duc de Chaulnes, it was immediately claimed by Choiseul for one of his relatives. But the protégé of Madame du Barry was chosen by the King and, what was worse, her protégé was Richelieu's nephew, the hated d'Aiguillon.

This was the first of a series of setbacks which showed the once omnipotent minister that his star was on the wane. The situation became more serious when two of the cleverest and most unscrupulous men in the government, the chancellor Maupeou, whom Choiseul himself had brought to power, and the new finance minister, the Abbé Terray, began to pay court to the King's favourite. Choiseul's old friend Madame du Deffand warned him that his conduct had been unwise, 'for though La du Barry was nothing by herself, she was a very useful stick for others to lean on', and by the time the court had returned to Versailles, he had unbent to the extent of soliciting a meeting with the countess. But it was too late. 'Her ladyship no longer conceals her hatred of him and the conversation he had with her was a mistake on his part as it resulted in nothing,' wrote Madame du Deffand, sad at seeing her brilliant friend behaving in a manner so unworthy of his talents.

By now Jeanne had consolidated her position and her intrinsic kindness and willingness to help others less fortunate than herself gained her many adherents. A young woman, guilty of infanticide when the baby she had failed to register during pregnancy was born dead, secured a reprieve largely owing to her intervention. The moving letter written to the chancellor and signed in her name was in all probability dictated by Chon, whose epistolary talents had already gained her fame in Toulouse. On another occasion Jeanne saved the life of a young guardsman who, suffering from a bad attack of homesickness, had deserted from his regiment, taking with him his uniform and horse. He was sentenced to death, whereupon one of his officers took pity on him and applied for help to his commander-in-chief, the Duc d'Aiguillon, who told him that the only person who could help him was the Comtesse du Barry.

In his memoirs the officer, a certain Monsieur Belleval, describes being introduced by the Duc d'Aiguillon to the celebrated beauty, who made so great an impression on him that he almost forgot to mention his petition. 'I can still see her carelessly seated or rather reclining in a large easy chair, wearing a white dress with wreaths of roses. She was one of the prettiest women at a court which boasted so many, and the very perfection of her loveliness made her the most fascinating. Her hair, which she often left unpowdered, was of a beautiful golden colour and she had so much that she scarcely knew what to do with it all. Her wide blue eyes looked at one with an engaging frankness. She had a straight little nose and a complexion of a dazzling purity. In a word, I like everyone else fell immediately under her charm.'

In those first years before the corrupting influence of power and the constant flattery and adulation had contrived to spoil her essentially simple character, Jeanne du Barry must have been the most delightful of women, distributing her smiles to all alike, whether it was a simple lieutenant or a peer of the realm. On hearing Belleval's petition, she promised to speak to the King. She kept her word, for the next day one of her footmen brought him the message to tell him that he was expected at her apartment on the following evening. This visit was even more frightening than the first, for in a small crowded room he saw the King leaning against the fireplace. And Louis, even at his most benign, could be a very awe-inspiring figure. But the countess, in that light, childish voice that seemed to hold no fear, called out to him, 'Sire, here is my guardsman come to thank Your Majesty.' A smile lit up the handsome, melancholy face and Louis said, 'You can first thank the Comtesse du Barry, and you must tell your protégé he must blot out his fault by a zealous attention to duty.' The reprieve was signed that very evening, and when it reached the regiment every officer and soldier drank a toast to the King's new mistress, which can hardly have pleased the Duc de Choiseul who was still acting as minister of war.

Louis could be kind, but he was not merciful by nature and those who transgressed found it hard to obtain a pardon. A crown case brought before the *parlement* of Paris caused considerable excitement among the nobility, when criminal proceedings were lodged against a Comte and Comtesse de Louesne who, poor and crippled with debt, had been threatened with eviction from their crumbling château in the Orléanais. Rather than submit, they had defied the authorities and resisted arrest with the old countess, gun in hand, standing beside her husband. After two days they had been forced to capitulate, having killed both a bailiff and an officer of the mounted police. Now, after a year in prison, they had been sentenced to be beheaded and not all their daughters' tears could bring a pardon from the King. But the couple had a powerful friend in the Comtesse de Béarn, the shabby old lady who had earned the gratitude of Madame du Barry in having dared to defy the hostility of Versailles in introducing her at court. The royal favourite now offered to intervene with the King, though even Richelieu warned her she might fail. At first Louis listened to her in a stony silence and only unbent when she fell on her knees, refusing to rise till he had given in to her petition. Then he raised her from the ground and in a voice which held only tenderness replied, 'Madame, I am delighted that the first favour you should ask of me should be an act of mercy.'

This unusual act of clemency on the part of the King brought many people to the side of the Comtesse du Barry who, in contrast to her predecessor, was good rather than ambitious. The Comte d'Espinchal describes her as being 'gentle in company and an excellent friend, always sweet and obliging'. She was lavishly generous towards the women whom self-interest made into her friends. There is a story told of her having solicited the King for the revenues of 'les loges de Nantes', a block of shops on the ramparts of the port of Nantes, to be given to the Maréchale de Mirepoix, only to be told it was impossible as the revenues had already been allocated to a certain Madame du Barry. Needless to say, the old maréchale, who

51

was among the most faithful of the countess's *soupeuses*,* was amply rewarded for her complaisance.

Richelieu, one of the few who could claim to know the King, noted that Louis was so much in love that this girl from the Paris streets had it in her power to be the uncrowned queen of France. But for the time being Jeanne wanted little else than to enjoy her good fortune. For the first year Jean du Barry had taken it upon himself to pay for his sister-in-law's establishment. But when he presented his account he had considerable difficulties in getting paid. Louis did not like to be reminded that he owed his mistress to the Comte du Barry. The bills were paid, but for the time being the '*roué*' was advised to absent himself from Paris.

Now that she was officially recognized as the royal mistress, Jeanne received a monthly allowance of two hundred thousand *livres*. The money, paid out to her by the court banker, was in the following year, 1771, raised to two hundred and fifty thousand *livres*, rising to three hundred thousand *livres*. Yet in spite of these enormous sums she was constantly in debt, what with the maintenance of a large household, the sixteen footmen and as many maids, for whom there was no room at Versailles and who had to be accommodated in her *hôtel* in the rue de l'Orangerie; the stabling of her carriages and horses, and above all the staggering figures of the bills she ran up with the fashionable dressmaker Madame Sigly. Whether it was one of her simple white gowns or the court dresses of gold and silver tissue embroidered in paillettes and pearls, there was not one which did not cost well over a thousand *livres* – a *livre* was the equivalent of 350 francs today. Each skirt and petticoat had to be flounced with the finest lace; each pair of slippers had to have jewelled buckles to match her gown. Jewels were an obsession with her, for at heart she was still the peasant girl whose gold chain is her most treasured possession. Whereas Madame de Pompadour had a passion for acquiring houses, those ravishing little châteaux not one of which survives today, Jeanne du Barry had a passion for acquiring jewels of every colour, shape and size, a passion which in the end was to cost her her life and lead her to the guillotine.

The legendary diamond necklace which brought about the scandal

* *Soupeuse* was the name given by their enemies to those court ladies who by their compliance to La du Barry were invited to the King's supper parties.

in which the innocent Marie Antoinette was unwittingly involved was originally intended for the Comtesse du Barry and would undoubtedly have been given to her by the doting King had he not died before it was completed.

Among the eaves and gables of Versailles, immediately above the royal apartments, are the series of small panelled rooms which were known as *les petits appartements*. It is here that the King of France led his private life far removed from the show and glitter of La Salle des Glaces. Here he had his library and his kitchens, where it amused him to cook little dinners for a few friends. Here were his stores of sweetmeats and his aviaries, his telescope placed on a little balcony from where he could watch the comings and goings below in the Cour de Marbre. Here we find the suite of rooms which had once belonged to his beloved daughter-in-law, Marie Josephe de Saxe, and which, to the horror of his daughters, he had handed over to the Comtesse du Barry. These narrow, low-ceilinged rooms with their delicate gilding have still a certain atmosphere of intimacy. We can see the alcove from where a secret staircase led directly from the royal apartments to the countess's bedroom, which the infatuated Louis would sometimes climb as often as twenty times a day.

During her five winters at Versailles, most of Jeanne's life was spent in those small panelled rooms in which she realized the dreams she had cherished since, as a child of six, she had left the luxury of Francesca's bedroom for the austere convent cell of St Aure. Everything she remembered from those days was faithfully reproduced: the taffeta hangings and the soft carpets, the glittering chandelier and gilt-topped bottles on the dressing table. But the chandelier was now of rock crystal and the glass bottles were topped in gold, while the mirror which reflected her lovely face was a masterpiece by Roettiers de la Tour, the greatest goldsmith of the day. Chased in the purest gold, decorated with the countess's device of myrtle and of roses, surmounted by a crown, it created a sensation when first exhibited in his workshop. But there was more criticism than praise, for even by the standards of Versailles it was judged to be excessively extravagant, and by order of the King the toilet service was never completed.

In many ways Jeanne's taste was as faultless as that of her predecessor. From an early age she had lived with men of culture and discernment. When still working as a shop girl she had had a friend in the young artist Adelaide Labille. Du Barry may have corrupted her, but he had also refined her. Every piece of furniture in her rooms, from the rare lacquer cabinets to the tables of rosewood and of white satinwood inlaid with plaques of painted porcelain, was perfect. Every picture, from Greuze's *La Cruche cassée* to the landscapes of Fragonard and Vernet, was chosen with taste. Even the bronze firescreen and door handles were chiselled by that master craftsman Gouthière. There may have been a hint of the *parvenue* in the richness of the décor, in the sumptuous golden bed gilded by Cagny, in the gilding which covered so much of the panelling, but the general effect was voluptuous, sensual and intensely feminine, calculated to appeal to an old man who himself admitted 'that his senses would never give him peace'. Here Louis found at once the delights of a brothel and the gaiety of a schoolroom. For Jeanne du Barry was that enchanting mixture of being at once a child, a whore and a loving, tender woman comforting him in his trouble, chasing away his melancholy, giving him back his energy and youth.

It must have been infuriating for a man as brilliant as Choiseul to see the King, who smiled so rarely, laugh wholeheartedly at some puerile joke when made by Madame du Barry, or note her childish grimaces when she found herself his partner at whist. It must have been even worse for the royal princesses, and in particular for Madame Adelaide, who adored her father, to find themselves excluded from the little visits to Marly and to Choisy because they had failed in politeness to the countess.

The visit of the crown prince of Sweden in the early months of 1770 brought Jeanne her first real triumph at court. The young prince and his handsome blond equerries were lionized by all the great ladies of Versailles. His Egeria* was the Comtesse d'Egmont, daughter of the old Maréchal de Richelieu, but in no way sharing her father's taste for the new countess. On the contrary, she was an ardent supporter of Choiseul and was bitterly resentful when the prince, acting on the advice of his ambassador, paid court to the reigning royal favourite. The enthusiasm rose to fever heat when, on his father's sudden death, Gustavus became King of Sweden. But the French alliance and subsidies to carry out his future plans were sufficiently important to delay

---

* Egeria was an Italian nymph whose worship was connected with that of Diana.

his return to his own country, and during the weeks spent in Paris there were many intimate suppers in *les petits appartements* at which Jeanne acted as the most charming of hostesses as well as the most helpful of allies. On leaving the country, Gustavus presented her with a diamond collar for her pet dog, a miniature greyhound, and she in return gave him one of her portraits by Drouais, a gift which infuriated the Comtesse d'Egmont to such a degree that she tried in vain to prevent him from accepting it:

> *Lisette ta beauté seduit*
> *et charme tout le monde.*
> *En vain la Duchesse rougit*
> *et la princesse en gronde.*
> **Chacun sait que Venus naquit**
> *de l'écume de l'onde.*

> (Lisette your beauty enthralls
> and charms the whole world.
> In vain the duchess sees red
> and the princess becomes enraged.
> Everyone knows that Venus was born
> from the froth of the tide.)

But Choiseul himself could afford to ignore the favourite's growing popularity, the old friends deserting him to assist at her *levée*. Never had he felt more sure of himself than in this spring of 1770 when the whole of France was preparing to celebrate a royal wedding, the marriage of the Dauphin, the King's grandson, and Marie Antoinette, daughter of the Austrian Empress, Maria Theresa, which would cement the alliance between Habsburg and Bourbon, and end all those hereditary feuds which had torn Europe in half for the past two centuries. Smiling imperturbably, his nose in the air, Etienne de Stainville, Duc de Choiseul, the architect of the family pact, still saw his position as impregnable. Even the King recognized him as such by giving him the honour of being the first to welcome the young Austrian archduchess on her arrival at the outskirts of the forest of Compiègne.

8

With trembling hands Jeanne du Barry opened the envelope containing the invitation to the royal supper party at the château de La Muette. For the past weeks she had been living in anguish for fear she would be excluded from the list of guests bidden to meet the young archduchess on her arrival at the French court. These included the royal family, the Princes of the Blood, the ladies-in-waiting and a few of the highest nobility in the land. Her enemies were already crowing over her discomfiture, and even some of her well-wishers had advised her to leave Versailles rather than stay and face the humiliation of being excluded from a wedding which promised to be of an unparalleled magnificence. Though his treasury was empty, King Louis was determined to show his fellow sovereigns that the French court still led the world in elegance and taste. The workmen who were busily completing Gabriel's exquisite gold and turquoise theatre at Versailles might not have been paid for months, but they had created a unique setting for the wedding of the century.

With characteristic optimism Jeanne du Barry had ordered a series of beautiful dresses for this great occasion. But in the end her courage might well have failed her had it not been for the encouragement of the Maréchal de Richelieu, who told her that in running away she would be abdicating from a position she had barely won. Still more insistent was the marshal's nephew, the Duc d'Aiguillon, dependent on her help in his struggle with the Breton *parlement*. The King himself, vacillating and uncertain, a prey to melancholy, had need of his mistress's vitality and strength to see him through these long and anxious weeks where, in Paris, the *parlement* was in open revolt against the crown, and at Versailles there was open criticism of the Austrian marriage. Even the bridegroom, Louis Auguste, appeared to resent a wedding arranged by Choiseul, who had been his father's enemy. But the rapturous welcome given to the fourteen-year-old bride from the moment of her arrival in France showed that the people themselves looked upon the royal wedding as the harbinger of prosperity and peace, bringing an end to the scandals and disorders which had defiled the image of monarchy in the past years and destroyed the reputation of the King.

'I have the honour to inform you that the King has included you in the list of ladies invited to La Muette on the fifteenth of this month [May] to meet Madame la Dauphine. If for any reason you are unable to be present, I beg you to inform me of it. I am with respect, Madame, your most humble and dutiful servant, Le Duc d'Aumont.'

This letter, signed by a holder of one of the *grands charges*, the most important positions at court, usually hereditary to certain families, set a seal on Jeanne Bécu's vertiginous career which was to last for the next four years.

Up to the day of the wedding no one believed that Louis would defy the conventions to the extent of introducing his low-born mistress at what was primarily a family gathering. The Austrian ambassador went so far as to assure his Empress that such a thing would never happen. But among the last to arrive that evening at La Muette, driving up in the largest and most ostentatious of carriages and glittering with jewels, was the Comtesse du Barry, insolently beautiful, outwardly so sure of herself but inwardly frightened, not out of fear of competition from some rival beauty, but on account of the fourteen-year-old princess with the porcelain skin and laughing eyes with whom the old King appeared to be delighted from the moment she alighted from her carriage and, running quickly towards him, had dropped gracefully at his feet in the most perfect of curtseys. People spoke of nothing else but the new Dauphine, of her delicacy and charm, and the favourite would have been very near tears had it not been for the precious invitation she had taken such pains to acquire.

Never had she dressed so carefully as this evening, choosing from among her dresses a glorious creation of silver tissue spun with gold and spangled in rubies. Never had she spent so many hours before her mirror, for tonight she had to show the world that at the age of twenty-seven she could still defy comparison. Her triumph was complete and even her enemies were forced to admit that she was still the loveliest woman in the room and that the little Dauphine was no more than a pretty child. Surrounded by his family, the King continually allowed his eyes to stray to the far side of the room where his mistress sat among the holders of *les grands charges* and *les dames aux tabourets*,* none of whom would have spoken to her had they met her anywhere else than at the King's table, and all of whom noted his concupiscent glances and the look she gave him in return, her aquamarine eyes half closed in a secret smile. The Duc de Croy, one of the few who really loved his King, was saddened to see him give way so openly to a senile infatuation. Even the little Dauphine was heard to ask her mother's ambassador who was the lady sitting at the far table who seemed to be a friend of the King, whereupon Comte Mercy, who was wishing not for the first time that his Empress had been more explicit in warning her daughter on the situation she would find at Versailles, replied, 'Madame, that is the Comtesse du Barry. She helps to amuse His Majesty.' 'She is very pretty,' said the Dauphine in a light, indifferent tone before going on to talk of other things.

But it was not long before Marie Antoinette had been enlightened as to the countess's role at court. She was at all the wedding festivities – at every supper, at every ball, enthroned in her box at the opera, surrounded by admirers which, according to the master of ceremonies, did not entirely please Madame la Dauphine. She even had to suffer her presence at those interminable card games which were part of the court ritual, where the poor little bride had to endure hours of boredom playing *cavagnole* and *lansquenet*, but where etiquette was such that the countess did not dare to address a word to her unless she was spoken to first. Only a few weeks after her wedding, Marie Antoinette wrote to her mother: 'The King could not be kinder and more full of attentions. I love him dearly, but it is pathetic to see how weak he is with Madame du Barry, who is the silliest and most impertinent creature imaginable. She played cards with us every evening at Marly. Twice she sat beside me, but she never spoke to me and I made no attempt to speak to her, though when necessary I have done so.'

It was not difficult for the shrewd old Empress to guess that outside influences had been at work to make her daughter speak in these terms of a woman she hardly knew. However much Maria Theresa

---

* Court ladies, mostly duchesses, who had the right to sit on a stool in the presence of the King. Both the Marquise de Pompadour and the Comtesse du Barry had the honour.

might deplore the advent of Madame du Barry, she was prepared to accept her in the same way as she had accepted the Marquise de Pompadour when the French alliance became necessary in the interests of her country.

The Austrian ambassador blamed Mesdames as potential trouble-makers, in particular Madame Adelaide, who loathed the woman she described as her father's 'whore'. No one had been more strongly opposed to the Austrian alliance and no one had hated Choiseul more bitterly than she. But now she was prepared to welcome the pretty little Dauphine, whom fundamentally she disliked, because she represented the only hope of getting the King away from Madame du Barry. And the lonely girl, who was finding marriage so different from what her mother had led her to expect, saw in her husband's maiden aunts her only friends in a cold, inimical court. Childish amusements, games and donkey rides were planned for her entertainment, and the King's perfunctory visits to his daughters became longer and more frequent when his charming little granddaughter-in-law was there to amuse him. Optimistic by nature, spoilt from her earliest childhood, Marie Antoinette thought she would have no difficulty in persuading Grand-papa to get rid of that 'impertinent creature'. But 'the impertinent creature' had talents of which she was completely unaware, talents she was prepared to put into effect the moment she felt her position to be threatened.

Till now the Comtesse du Barry had been a gay, carefree young woman who only thought of making the old King happy. In this role, her enemies, and most of all Choiseul, had underestimated her poten-tialities. When the Dauphin's marriage restored his ascendancy, the minister used all the means in his power to destroy the Duc d'Aiguillon. But he was reckoning without the Comtesse du Barry, who from her gilded bed directed the policy of the King, infecting him with the energy and determination to espouse the cause of d'Aiguillon against the Breton magistrates who had dared to have the documents for his defence burnt by the public hangman in the square at Rennes.

To the fury of Choiseul, the Duc d'Aiguillon was included in the list of guests invited by the King to join him in *les petits voyages* to Marly and Choisy. The invitation, which he owed entirely to Madame du Barry, drew a letter of violent protest from the minister, to which Louis replied in a tone surprisingly mild for a Bourbon aristocrat:

'With regard to Aiguillon, how can you imagine that he could take your place? I like him well enough, but what good could he do, when he is so hated ...? You manage my affairs well and I am satisfied with you. But have a care of those in whom you confide and who give you gratuitous advice. I have always hated that kind of thing and now detest it more than ever. You know Madame du Barry. I am pleased with her. And her, too, I am always advising to have care of those whom she confides in and of her advisers. You may be sure she has several. She has no feelings of hatred for you. She recognizes your talent and bears you no grudge. The denunciations against her have been frightful and for the most part unfounded ... But such is the way of the world. She is very pretty and she pleases me and that should be enough.'

Louis was well aware that it was Choiseul, or rather his sister, who was responsible for the fiercest and most scurrilous of the attacks, which did not always spare his august person. But he was a man of habit who hated change, and he recognized the work done by Choiseul in re-establishing his country's prestige after the disaster of the Seven Years' War. At Choisy and at Marly he had hoped to have friendly faces around him. But neither the Dauphine nor her ladies-in-waiting were prepared to accept the position given to his favourite. To amuse the young bride the King had arranged for the Comédie Française and the Théâtre des Italiens to perform in the little theatre of Choisy. But Marie Antoinette lost all pleasure in these entertainments when she heard that the programmes were chosen by the Comtesse du Barry and that some of the very best seats in the theatre were reserved for her and her friends. One evening the countess arrived accompanied by her two intimates, the Maréchale de Mirepoix and the Duchesse de Valentinois, to find their places taken by some of the Dauphine's ladies, who not only refused to move but indulged in sarcastic remarks at their expense. It might have been wiser for Madame du Barry to have ignored the incident, one of the ladies in question being the Comtesse de Gramont, sister-in-law to the fierce and vindictive Béatrice de Gramont. But for the first time one finds her reacting in a manner very different from her usual conciliatory behaviour. With angry tears she complained to the King that both she and her friends had been insulted. And Louis, who would have preferred to ignore what he regarded as a storm in a teacup, was forced to punish the offending countess and have her sent into exile.

Jeanne du Barry was to pay for her petty triumph in making an enemy of Marie Antoinette. From now on the Dauphine never gave her a friendly look or addressed her a single word, till finally Louis was forced to intervene on behalf of his injured favourite. Humiliated in her pride, the gentle, laughing countess became brazen and assertive in flaunting her power and in working unceasingly to bring about the dismissal of Choiseul, whom she mistakenly believed to be responsible for the Dauphine's attitude towards her. That year the atmosphere at Compiègne and Fontainebleau was rife with intrigue, the various factions using the favourite for their own purposes.

Everyone knew that Choiseul was backing the parliamentarians, that both the Princes of the Blood and the general public were on their side, and that the Duc d'Aiguillon would have been lost without the help of Madame du Barry. She who was usually so frivolous and lazy, interested in little else but her dresses and her jewels, now listened for hours on end to the legal details of a case she did not begin to understand. But whether she understood or not was a matter of complete indifference to the wily politicians who only wanted her to work upon the King. Self-interest, fears for the future, gave her a hitherto unsuspected eloquence. So well did she succeed that in the end Louis took the momentous decision to confiscate all documents connected with the trial and forbid the *parlements* from making any further attacks on the Duc d'Aiguillon.

On 3 September the firing of cannon announced His Majesty's arrival at the Paris *parlement* and the summoning of a *lit de justice*,* at which Louis ordered a suspension of the trial and severe punishments for all who dared to disobey him. The session was remarkable for the absence of the Duc de Choiseul and the presence of Madame du Barry, who sat in a box in the role of a presiding deity.

Her protégé had triumphed, but the Duc d'Aiguillon had emerged from the trial as the most unpopular man in France, an unpopularity in which she shared, for the personal attacks against her had never been so virulent as now, when the grateful duke presented her with a superb cabriolet, known as a *vis-à-vis*, exquisitely painted and gilded and costing no less than fifty-two thousand *livres*. The outraged

---

* A solemn session of the *parlement* held in the presence of the King seated on a divan or a raised dais.

Parisians reacted with an insulting song, in which a passerby enquired, 'What is this brilliant *vis-à-vis*? Is it the chariot of some goddess or of some princess?' 'No,' says a voice in the crowd, 'It is the cart of the laundress who has whitewashed the infamous d'Aiguillon.'

Whether the King objected to his mistress receiving such an extravagant gift, or whether through her own good sense, the *vis-à-vis* was never seen either at Compiègne or Fontainebleau. Exhausted by her efforts on behalf of the Duc d'Aiguillon and her political sessions with the chancellor Maupeou, the countess spent the greater part of the summer leading a quiet life at Louveciennes, superintending the alterations being carried out by the court architect, Gabriel. The King was more enamoured than ever, but she had not yet succeeded in getting him to dismiss Choiseul.

Of all those who hated Choiseul, no one hated him so bitterly as her brother-in-law du Barry, who had never forgiven the arrogant duke for having blocked his career in the foreign office. To destroy the duke, who threatened the future of his sister-in-law in a position vital to his interests, had become the dominating obsession of a clever, unscrupulous man who had never achieved a greatness he believed to be his due. In the lower echelons of the foreign office were men who suffered from the same grievance. There was Favier, a writer of talent, and a one-time agent of King Louis in the *correspondance secrète* he carried on unknown to his ministers. And, more important still, there was the Abbé de la Ville, chief clerk of the foreign office, in charge of all the agreements and negotiations made by Choiseul, often without consulting his colleagues. Disappointed in their ambitions, these two men were ready to collaborate with the '*roué*' at a time when Choiseul, in order to render himself indispensable to the King, had embarked on a dangerous and imprudent policy which could well lead his country into war. In the summer of 1770 a quarrel between Spain and England regarding the future of the Malvinas or Falkland Islands, a small group of windswept islands far out in the south Atlantic, provided France, through her dynastic alliance with the Bourbon King of Spain, Charles III, with an opportunity to interfere. Not only would this enable her to avenge herself for the humiliations inflicted by the Seven Years' War, but it would also restore the power of the Duc de Choiseul, the only minister to whom the rebellious *parlement* would vote the necessary subsidies for war and who could count on popular support throughout the country. Encouraged by Choiseul, the King of Spain adopted a high-handed attitude he could ill afford and England replied in kind. The situation was becoming serious and Choiseul, acting as minister of war, began to mobilize the army. But the last thing Louis wanted was a war. The glories of Fontenoy belonged to the past: his defeat at Rosbach by the armies of Frederick of Prussia was still fresh in his mind. Both the finance minister, the Abbé Terray, and Maupeou threatened to resign if Choiseul remained in office. But the most insistent of all was his lovely mistress, who in floods of tears besought him to get rid of a man who was out to destroy the country for his own ends. In confidence she told him of a high-ranking official at the foreign office who could vouch for the treachery of Choiseul and was in possession of certain documents which proved that the whole Falklands affair had been deliberately instigated by his minister. She assured him that a letter to his cousin the King of Spain was all that was needed to make King Charles give up his claims to the islands, rather than to drag Europe into a war.

Touched by her concern, impressed by her sagacity, Louis listened to her far more than to his ministers. In his memoirs, Talleyrand gives a largely apocryphal account of a secret meeting arranged by the du Barrys in which the Abbé de la Ville visited the King in disguise and showed him certain despatches written by Choiseul to the foreign office in Madrid. Whether or not this was true, it is certain that it was Jean du Barry, with the help of his clever little sister Chon, who instructed the royal favourite as to the exact wording of the letter she was to dictate to the King. We have a picture of King Louis, who was an awkward correspondent, sitting down at his mistress's writing desk (a priceless piece of furniture, made of white satinwood inlaid with plaques of Sèvres porcelain), which he had recently given her out of the royal collections, while the Comtesse du Barry, wearing one of her beautiful négligés, stands behind him enveloping him in the heady scent of her perfume, her voluminous breasts escaping from her corsage, her golden curls stroking his cheeks, dictating to him word for word the letter she had learnt by heart.

Small wonder if the King was lost in admiration of a woman who after a night of love could compose such a letter. The du Barrys, both brother and sister, were brilliant correspondents, and the letter addressed to the King of Spain was a masterpiece of diplomacy well calculated to make King Charles have second thoughts and prefer giving up his claims to a cluster of barren islands rather than to risk losing the friendship of his cousin.

9

Before this letter went to Spain, the King sent for the Duc de Choiseul asking him to render an exact account of the situation. As calm and self-confident as usual, the duke informed him that all was well and that his army would be fully mobilized by January. Unable to control his rage, Louis exploded, 'Monsieur, have I not told you that I did not want a war?' And, without giving him time to reply, he dismissed him from his presence. On the following day, 23 December 1770, du Barry's letter was sent off to Spain, the messenger entrusted with this confidential mission being none other than Madame du Barry's hairdresser. It was an age when hairdressers were more trusted than ministers, and it would continue to be so twenty years later when Marie Antoinette was to give the crown jewels of France to be taken out of the country by the court hairdresser, Leonard.

King Charles of Spain was hardly in a position to refuse his royal cousin's plea for peace. The letter began: 'Your Majesty must be aware that the spirit of independence and fanaticism has spread in my kingdom. I have so far been patient and gentle. But now I am driven to extremity, my *parlements* having so far forgotten themselves as to dispute my sovereign authority which I hold from God alone. I am resolved to be obeyed at all costs. War under the present circumstances would be a terrible evil for me and for my people. But my great regard for Your Majesty would make me forget all else but you. My ministers are no more than my instruments. Should I find cause to change them, be assured there would be no corresponding alteration in the relations between us. As long as I live, we are united. If Your Majesty can without detriment to your honour make some sacrifice for the sake of peace, you will do humanity a great service and me in particular.' How du Barry must have enjoyed inserting the line, 'My ministers are no more than my instruments.' How delighted he must have been to hear that on Christmas Eve the King had signed a *lettre de cachet* sending the Duc de Choiseul into exile, a letter of no more than four lines commanding him to place the resignation of his positions as secretary of state and superintendent of the posts in the hands of the Duc de la Vrillière, and to retire until further orders to his property of Chanteloup.

The duke brought the news to his wife as she was sitting down to dinner, and the charming little duchess, who in spite of all his infidelities had always adored her husband, reassured him with a smile, saying, 'Your dismissal is no reason to spoil a good dinner.' And by the end of the meal husband and wife were calmly making plans for their journey to Chanteloup. But while Choiseul accepted his loss of office with his usual equanimity, feeling throughout the country was one of indignation and dismay. For eleven years he had ruled the destinies of France, admired and respected by people in every walk of life. No sooner was the news made public than Versailles became deserted, with friends and relatives flocking to Paris to the Hôtel de Choiseul to offer him sympathy and help. The whole of the rue de Richelieu was blocked with carriages trying to reach the door. When the duke left Paris, the route was lined with well-wishers cheering him on his way. His downfall became a triumph in which the King and his mistress were held up to shame.

But in her gabled rooms in the palace of Versailles the Comtesse du Barry was at last at peace. Maupeou, d'Aiguillon and Terray were at her feet, her *levées* were crowded with sycophants, and the fashionable poets wrote poems to her beauty. When the King was worried and harassed over the formation of a new government, she was the only one who could put his mind at rest, suggesting a name he might have forgotten, eradicating another which at some time in the past had given her offence. In Paris her name was anathema, but at Versailles she reigned supreme. There were animated suppers in the *petits appartements* at which she glowed with happiness and pride, where conversation sparkled and the wine flowed freely – too freely in the opinion of the royal doctors, for Louis's digestion was no longer that of a young man and his Bourbon appetite was taking a toll of his health. That, and what they considered to be his excessive love life, led the court physicians to regard the Comtesse du Barry as being too young for the King. An older woman might be more suited to a man whose sexual appetites were a strain on the heart. Others, like the Duc de Croy, maintained that they had never seen the King in better health, more energetic and alert. His squalid escapades in the Parc aux Cerfs belonged in the past, and though the Choiseul cabal had attempted to attract his wandering eye with a certain Madame Pater, a foreign beauty who had taken Paris by storm, she had been unable to compete with the irresistible fascination of a mistress whose talents were as varied as those of Jeanne du Barry.

The visit of the crown prince of Sweden, which took place early in 1771, brought her to the zenith of her power. The sixteen-year-old Axel Fersen, who was in the royal suite, was so entranced by her beauty that he barely noted the pretty little Dauphine whose lover he would later become. Marie Antoinette resented the attentions paid to the King's mistress, and to having to submit to her presence at all the festivities held in honour of the Swedish prince, who carried his enthusiasm for the countess to a point that his ambassador had to warn him that, in view of King Louis's age, it might not be long before there was a new king in France with a queen who detested La du Barry. The fall of Choiseul had been a terrible blow for the Dauphine, who had looked upon him as her only friend in France. Her mother advised her not to compromise herself in any way, writing to her: 'I admit I am very upset. But whatever reason the King may have had is none of my affair, still less of yours. But never forget that your marriage was made by Choiseul and that you must always be grateful to him. Knowing you to be so straightforward and honest, I fear this blow is going to hit you very hard. But do not let yourself be involved in any faction, and above all try to remain neutral.'

It was not easy to remain neutral for an impulsive fifteen-year-old girl with her full share of Habsburg pride. Not a day passed that she was not provoked by the insolence either of Madame du Barry or of one of her friends. The Dauphin's former tutor, who was one of the favourite's most devoted adherents, had encouraged him to attend the King's hunting parties at St Hubert, and the shy young man had enjoyed the free and easy atmosphere of the suppers where his grandfather was always in the best of moods and the Comtesse du Barry the most delightful of hostesses. But his aunts lost no time in telling him of the true origins of a woman who had a pernicious influence over their beloved father, after which the young prince could never be persuaded again to attend a supper at St Hubert.

The countess took her revenge in calling him a 'mannerless lout'. She even allowed herself to make disparaging remarks about the little Dauphine, describing her as 'that red-haired child' (*la petite rousse*) who neglected her toilette. For in those days the future Queen of Elegance was still a tomboy who tore her dresses in romping with the children of her maids. It was worse when the countess dared to make witty jokes about the Dauphin's matrimonial shortcomings and a marriage which after nearly a year was still unconsummated. All of these remarks, exaggerated a hundredfold, were brought to the ears of the Dauphine, who conceived such a violent hatred for Madame du Barry that she refused to listen to her mother's ambassador when he begged her to say a few polite words to the lady who was a friend of the King's.

Left to herself, the countess might have been more discreet in her behaviour, but she was now entirely in the hands of the Duc d'Aiguillon, who forced her to assert her position, reminding her that the Marquise de Pompadour had not only been made *une dame au tabouret* but a lady-in-waiting to the Queen, and that even the haughty Madame Adelaide had ended by accepting her. It was at his suggestion that the favourite asked the King to have her invited to the weekly balls given by Madame la Dauphine. But when Louis asked his grandson's wife to have Madame du Barry included among the guests, Marie Antoinette replied that it would be difficult for her to do so as she always invited the aunts, who in such an event would refuse to come. Louis, who disliked embarrassing situations, would have been relieved at her refusal had it not been for the tears and scenes made by his beloved mistress.

The political situation in the spring of 1771 made him more than ever dependent on her. The fall of Choiseul followed by the reassertion of royal authority, the suppression of the *parlements* and the exile of the magistrates had ended in the installation of what was known as Maupeou's *parlement*, a measure so unpopular that the chancellor's effigy was burnt in public, while the Princes of the Blood and several of the peers abstained from appearing at the solemn *lit de justice* held in the great Salle de Gardes at Versailles. Speaking from a throne of purple velvet embroidered with fleur-de-lys, the King addressed the Assembly in tones reminiscent of *le roi soleil*, commanding them to conform to his orders, to assume their duties in the new *parlement* and to have nothing further to do with the exiled magistrates. His speech ended with words which reverberated through the hall: 'My mind is made up and I shall never change.' Watching from a gallery, Madame du Barry smiled down on her lover. And, noting her presence, the Austrian ambassador wrote to his Empress, 'The authority of the countess is such that nothing like it has ever been seen before.'

Nevertheless, King Louis continued to resist her efforts to have the Duc d'Aiguillon appointed as foreign minister. It was only six months later that she finally obtained his unwilling consent. Even then there were those who maintained that d'Aiguillon had never been properly nominated, that the royal favourite had sent him to thank the King for a place he had never been given, and that Louis had ended in accepting him on these terms. Many believed that Louis regretted banishing Choiseul and might even have recalled him, had it not been for his presumptuous behaviour, the insolent manner in which he and his friends flaunted their opposition to the throne. Life at Chanteloup, his property in Touraine, was on a princely scale, with never less than four hundred guests, a hundred lackeys to serve them and two theatre companies to entertain them. Braving the King's displeasure, who gave but a grudging consent, nearly half of the nobility of France travelled to Chanteloup to show allegiance to the fallen minister. From all accounts, life with the Choiseuls was far more amusing than at Versailles. But many returned the poorer, having lost a position at court or the governorship of a province, for Louis was not a man to forgive such flagrant disloyalty to his person.

Ignoring his own mistakes and the folly of his behaviour in having allowed himself to be dominated by his sister, Choiseul saw himself as the victim of royal ingratitude. One is shocked at the bitterness and pettiness of memoirs which a statesman, who had been so great in his prime, dictated in exile. They are one long diatribe against the sovereign he had once professed to adore. Although Louis never saw these memoirs, the stream of vitriolic verses which continued to pour out of the gutter press, the coarse and unjust calumnies which attacked his favourite could all be traced back to the Choiseuls and in particular to Béatrice de Gramont. Since her brother's fall from power, the duchess had become so obsessed by her hatred of La du Barry that she was willing to circulate the foulest tales at her expense. One hears of the King's mistress receiving the papal nuncio and the grand almoner of France at one of her *levées* and rising to receive them from her gilded bed 'as naked as Venus coming out of the sea'. We are told of her entertaining another prince of the Church by asking him to assist her in holding her golden urinal, of spanking one of her ladies in the presence of the King who took much pleasure in her action – stories which no one who knew either the King or the countess would have believed, but which her enemies were only too ready to repeat. The Duc de Croy and the Marquis d'Espinchal were among those who testified to the purity of the countess's language and the elegance of her manners. The Duc writes that 'whereas the Marquise de Pompadour, in spite of her culture, would in speaking betray her bourgeois origins, the Comtesse du Barry had no difficulty in assimilating the accents peculiar to Versailles.' Never would she have dared to address her royal lover other than as 'Sire'. Nor would Louis, who was so jealous of his 'divine prerogatives', have ever allowed the slightest familiarity.

All that was best in him – his pride, his chivalry and love – rose in defence of his mistress. And in view of the continual attacks against her, it is not surprising that, at the end of 1771, he decided to make the presumptuous duke resign from his position as colonel-general of the Swiss Guards – a post which was usually regarded as a sinecure providing a large and steady income. His reckless extravagance in the past year had brought Choiseul to the verge of bankruptcy, and the threatened loss of a handsome income made him lose all dignity and self-respect. Writing to the King, he offered his resignation at the price of an enormous compensation of no less than four hundred thousand *livres*, plus a yearly pension of thirty-five thousand *livres* and his recall from exile. He also asked for a pension to be given to his wife, whose large fortune had been dissipated in keeping up the various embassies in which he had served his country. These demands struck the King as being so outrageous that he never even troubled to reply, while his ministers, and in particular the Duc d'Aiguillon, were only too delighted to have Choiseul become a bankrupt. But the duke was fortunate in having honest, disinterested friends ready to champion an unpopular cause. One of these was the Comte de Châtelet who, when the King and his ministers refused to grant him an audience, was sufficiently bold to approach the royal favourite whom he used to meet in the days when she acted as du Barry's hostess in the rue

Jussienne, where she was already known for her kindness and generosity.

He found her to be amiable and approachable, ready to receive him and to listen to him with tolerance and understanding. Speaking of the man who had done his best to destroy her, she showed a lack of malice, a willingness, even an eagerness to forgive, referring to Choiseul as someone she had never meant to injure, that on the contrary she would have been enchanted to have him back. In the beginning she had done her best to warn him against the foolishness of his behaviour in attacking her, not on account of herself but as the object of the King's affection, and that therefore it was the King whom he had offended. The soft voice, the lovely smile and caressing eyes ended in persuading the friend of Choiseul that both she and the duke had been the victims of their entourages. The count, who was an experienced courtier, flattered her vanity by telling her that only someone so beautiful could be so kind. And she ended in offering to espouse the cause of her former enemy. Was she really so open-hearted, so ready to forgive? Or did she hope that in showing generosity towards Choiseul she would succeed in conciliating the Dauphine, the one person by whom she longed to be accepted, from whom she would have been only too happy to receive a smile or a few words?

It was difficult for King Louis to come to a decision and, having made up his mind, it was even more difficult to make him change it. He was annoyed to have his mistress come to plead the cause of a man whom a year ago she had begged him to dismiss. The treasury was empty and the marriage of his second grandson was going to run the country still further into debt. Yet here was Madame du Barry asking him to award enormous sums in compensation to a man she was supposed to detest. Cold and unresponsive, he listened to her in silence, before telling her abruptly that she was wasting his time. But the countess's vanity was at stake and she was determined to succeed where anyone else would have failed. Time after time she returned to the charge. They quarrelled and King Louis was frightening in a rage. But Jeanne du Barry was never so fascinating as when she lost her temper, turning on him like an angry cat and with blazing eyes accusing him of ingratitude and meanness towards a man who in the past twelve years had done so much for his country. When the anger was spent she wept and was gentle and tender, telling him

71

to be magnanimous and to show that His Christian Majesty of France knew how to forgive. When their rage was over and they were both at peace, they ended in making love. Louis gave way, and the Duc de Choiseul received a pension of sixty thousand *livres* and a capital sum of three hundred thousand *livres* in compensation for the loss of his position as colonel-general of the Swiss Guards, which was now given to the King's youngest grandson, the fifteen-year-old Comte d'Artois.

Both Paris and Versailles were full of praise for the Comtesse du Barry. But no word of thanks reached her from Chanteloup, where the proud, embittered duke, who resented her intervention, wrote in his memoirs, 'Neither I nor Madame de Choiseul thought it necessary to thank her. The injustice and specially the harshness of our treatment exempts us from gratitude.' Nor did the Dauphine make the slightest sign of appreciating her generosity. It was only later in the year that Marie Antoinette was to obey her mother in recognizing 'the lady who was a friend of the King'.

10

The marriage of the King's second grandson, the Comte de Provence, to a princess of Piedmont gave Madame du Barry the opportunity of revenging herself on Marie Antoinette and asserting her position by arranging for the wedding to be in every way as magnificent as that of the Dauphin's. The master of ceremonies had to consult her on every detail, from the display of fireworks to the choice of plays and operas to be performed during the festivities. She chose the jewels the King was to give the bride, while the respective households of the young couple were made up entirely of what at Versailles were known as *Barriens* (supporters of Madame du Barry).

With the Duc d'Aiguillon at the foreign office, she was even beginning to interfere in the posting of ambassadors abroad. Baron de Breteuil, who was one of the ablest diplomats, had his appointment to Vienna cancelled for no other reason than that he had failed to pay her court, while the so-called *dévots*, who, given their hatred of Choiseul, had always been on her side, had one of their clan, the inept and frivolous Prince Louis de Rohan, appointed instead. Though already accredited to the Church, the young prince's dissipations were such as to shock the pious old Empress Maria Theresa. The Empress's letters to her daughter were full of complaints, embittered by the fact that her son and co-ruler, the Emperor Joseph II, and her chief minister Prince Kaunitz were both amused at his wit. They were not so much amused as that it suited them at the moment to have a superficial and ignorant French ambassador in Vienna and an inexperienced minister like the Duc d'Aiguillon in Paris.

It was the year of the first partition of Poland, when the ambitious young Emperor and the unscrupulous Prince Kaunitz were forcing Maria Theresa into becoming a partner in crime with the Empress of Russia and the King of Prussia, the two people whom she disliked and despised the most. Though her fundamentally noble character revolted against the spoliation of an innocent people, she was at the same time too much of a statesman to allow Russia and Prussia to take over a country which bordered on her frontiers. Against her will she ended in putting her signature to the secret treaty which gave Austria the rich province of Galicia. All this took place without informing France, who was Poland's oldest ally. King Louis had not only had a Polish wife, but his father-in-law, the ex-King of Poland, still reigned at Nancy as Duc de Lorraine. There had even been a time when his cousin the Prince de Conti had been a candidate for the elective throne of Poland, and a large part of Louis's *correspondance secrète* was devoted to Polish affairs. He was always in favour of a free Poland, maintaining that the disappearance of what he called the 'Royal Republic' would result in the destruction of French influence in Eastern Europe. But in a country given over to anarchy, which was neither a monarchy nor a republic, where the only sovereign authority resided in the collective wishes of a people forever quarrelling among themselves, there was little hope of any effective help being given by an ally five hundred leagues away.

Nevertheless, there was general indignation when the first news of the secret treaty became known in France. It was an unpleasant task for even the most accomplished of diplomats to persuade King Louis that the Empress Maria Theresa had been acting in good faith. Comte Mercy's position was rendered all the more difficult owing to the fact that Austrian troops had been the first to invade Polish territory, by occupying the German-speaking district in Galicia inhabited by Swabian settlers. King Louis was not impressed by the argument that the territory had formerly belonged to Austria, who had leased it out to the Jagellon kings of Poland and had never received it back. Relations were further strained by the arrival in Paris of a leader of the Polish nationalists who succeeded in interesting the Comtesse du Barry in his country's tragic plight. Jeanne may have barely heard of Poland, but her treatment at the hands of Maria Theresa's daughter was sufficient to make her sympathize with the handsome Pole who spoke so eloquently of Russian tyranny and Austrian hypocrisy. She listened 'visibly moved', and spoke of Poland to the King, who, in spite of his indignation, knew how little France could help a country which did so little to help itself.

Maria Theresa was the first to admit 'that France had a just cause for complaint'. And she wrote to her ambassador, 'that in the circumstances the most important thing of all was for her daughter to win the favour of the King by her attentions and her tenderness. She should seek to divine his wishes, offend him in nothing, and *above all* treat the favourite well.' But now, at this crucial time, an obstinate sixteen-year-old girl was acting directly against her mother's wishes in refusing to address a civil word to the Comtesse du Barry.

The situation came to a head shortly after the royal wedding when the court was already at Compiègne. The Duchesse de Valentinois, the favourite's intimate friend, had become mistress of the robes to the young Piedmontese princess and was holding a grand supper in her honour. But the queen of the evening was not the insignificant little princess, nor even the pretty Dauphine, but the King's mistress, aglitter with diamonds, seated in a place of honour between the Sardinian ambassador and the papal nuncio, who were outvying one another in paying her court. The Austrian ambassador who was present wrote: 'This was the first time I found myself in that woman's presence and I thought it my duty to observe a greater discretion than my colleagues. I did not begin to feel at ease with the lady until we had exchanged a few words.' But who could resist the countess when she turned her aquamarine eyes in your direction and addressed you in that soft, childish lisp, outwardly so modest, yet so supremely sure of her powers to fascinate? Comte Mercy may have been too much of a diplomat to expatiate on her charms to his imperial mistress, but he was very ready to accept when d'Aiguillon came to him with a message from the King inviting him to meet him on the following evening at the Comtesse du Barry's as he wished to speak to him in private.

The King had not yet arrived when the Duc d'Aiguillon brought him to the countess. They found their hostess reclining on a sofa, wearing one of those diaphanous white gowns she affected when receiving at home. She was simple and straightforward, taking him immediately into her confidence, speaking to him of the Dauphine not with bitterness but with sadness, complaining of the wicked people who were deliberately making trouble, inventing the foulest lies that she, who had the greatest admiration for the charming little princess, had dared to speak of her with disrespect. Her blue eyes filled with tears when she spoke of her enemies at court, people to whom she had never done the slightest injury, and Mercy realized she was too naïve to grasp that her greatest crime in the eyes of the ladies of Versailles was that she had been born Jeanne Bécu.

No sooner had the King arrived than she left the room with the Duc d'Aiguillon. Louis seemed nervous and apprehensive and, in the slow, embarrassed manner of one who hated explanations, he began to speak of the Dauphine, whom he loved as if she were his own child but who had allowed herself to be misled by the prejudice of certain older people, who unfortunately included Mesdames. All he demanded was for Madame du Barry to be treated in the same way as any other lady who had been presented at court. And, with the charm he could assume at will, he begged Comte Mercy to act for once as his ambassador, rather than that of the Empress.

Nevertheless, it was to take Comte Mercy many weeks before he succeeded in convincing his rebellious charge that 'that creature' was too important to be ignored. Mesdames had succeeded in convincing her that the King did not want his family to be on friendly terms with his mistress, and it was only after several weeks that Marie Antoinette, under pressure from her mother's ambassador, finally consented to speak to Madame du Barry.

This took place after one of her evening card parties, when she was in the habit of going round the room bidding every one of her guests goodnight. Comte Mercy, who accompanied Madame du Barry, was among the first to arrive. Unfortunately Marie Antoinette had also confided in her aunts, and Madame Adelaide was determined that Mercy's plans should fail. Just as the Dauphine had come to where the countess, already smiling in anticipation, was about to make her curtsey, Madame Adelaide rushed up and in her loud, strident voice called out, 'Hurry, we are late! The King is waiting for us at my sister Victoire's.' Taken by surprise, Marie Antoinette completely lost her head and, turning on her heels, practically ran out of the room, leaving the countess speechless with anger and mortification.

All eyes turned in her direction, and there were whispers and sniggers behind painted fans. A few commiserated, but the majority were delighted at her discomfiture. Comte Mercy was angry and embarrassed and the King was in a rage. At a small supper party held by Madame du Barry, which had been meant to celebrate her triumph and at which she made a brave attempt to keep back her tears, Louis turned to Comte Mercy and with an icy sarcasm said, 'Your advice does not seem to have been much of a success. I see I shall have to come to your assistance.' After which he did not address him another word.

His daughters may have been right and Louis might have preferred to have kept his mistress apart from the Dauphine. He loved his family but he resented any infringement on his private life, and his egotism was such that he would refer with tenderness to the Queen, who had been so tolerant and understanding of his weaknesses. Left on her own, Jeanne du Barry would probably have made no effort to force herself on the royal family. But behind her was the Duc d'Aiguillon, whose whole position depended on her influence and who kept telling her that her predecessor the marquise had been accepted even by the Queen and had taken part in the meetings of the Grand Council. Hence the tears and scenes, the determination to assert herself, even as to the right of choosing the Dauphine's ladies-in-waiting and reading the letters written by her to the King.

That autumn at Fontainebleau she insisted on building herself a pavilion in the private garden reserved for the royal princesses, and in having her young nephew, Adolphe du Barry, appointed chief equerry to the King, a post which the great families such as the Noailles had hitherto looked upon as one of their prerogatives. In her brilliant, lonely life her young nephew was one of the only people Jeanne really loved, for whose sake she was ready to put up with the incessant demands for money made by his father, the attempts at blackmail in reminding her that her fat drunkard of a husband was still living in Toulouse and might claim his marital rights. The 'roué' with his card debts and his women was a continual drain on her finances and was heard to say in public 'that it was his brother-in-law the King who would have to pay'.

Fortunately Jeanne had one of those light, volatile characters which evaded unpleasant issues. Hunting with the King in the forests of Fontainebleau, surrounded by his admiring courtiers, she could forget du Barry and his sordid attempts at blackmail and the studied rudeness of the Dauphine, who in spite of the admonishments of Comte Mercy and the scolding letters of her mother, continued to ignore her presence.

'What good reason can you have for not having done what Mercy told you was desired by the King? You should not think of the du Barry in any other light than that of a lady who has been admitted to court and to the society of the King.' The harassed Empress was at a loss to understand the obstinacy of a hitherto docile daughter. But Marie Antoinette was too proud, too much in awe of her formidable mother to tell her of a certain supper party held by the Comtesse du Barry at which the Duc d'Aiguillon had regaled the guests with a letter he had received from the French ambassador to Vienna. In a witty description of the negotiations over the partition of Poland, the Prince de Rohan had made fun of the pious old Empress 'qui prenait en pleurant', and while weeping over the sorrows of that unfortunate country had ended in taking for herself the greater share of the spoils. No one, it appears, had laughed so heartily as the hostess. But none of the guests would have dared to repeat the story, had it not been for the Comte de Provence, sly and two-faced, always ready to make mischief. That d'Aiguillon should have dared to read such a letter in front of 'that woman' and her friends incensed Marie Antoinette to such a degree that from now on she swore she would never address another word either to the minister or the King's favourite.

Comte Mercy, who had certainly heard the story, must have hoped against hope it would never reach the Dauphine, and as a perfect diplomat he was determined to ignore it by continuing to pay court to the countess. He wrote, with a certain complacency, 'The woman receives foreign ministers on Sunday afternoons. I am the only one to have daily access even when the King is present.' He was amused at the light, flirtatious tone she adopted in conversation, and before long she was taking him into her confidence, complaining of the unkindness of the royal family, her difficulties in coping with the King's religious fears, his growing fits of melancholia. 'I hope to make use of this woman, if only Madame la Dauphine will be good enough not to frustrate my schemes by any inconsiderate action.'

But the autumn went by with Marie Antoinette remaining as obdurate as ever, and it was only her mother's scoldings which finally drove her into submission. On 1 January 1772 she consented to speak to Madame du Barry, this time without informing the aunts. It was a day when Versailles was crowded with courtiers come to offer their good wishes for the New Year, when the Dauphine's apartment was full to overflowing with a long queue of ladies passing along the gilded balustrade of what had once been the old Queen's bedroom. Among them was the Comtesse du Barry, her face pale under her rouge, nervous that she might be courting yet another humiliation. All eyes turned towards her, as the Dauphine stopped in front of her, looking her full in the face, saying in a loud, clear voice, 'There are a lot of people today at Versailles.' Blushing with pleasure, with shining eyes, the countess curtseyed almost to the ground. But Marie Antoinette never even smiled, and when Comte Mercy came to congratulate her she cut him short, saying, 'I have spoken to her once, but that woman will never hear my voice again.' She was barely sixteen and she had already learnt to hate. Nor had she any love or respect left for the King, who was so pleased on account of the few words she had spoken to his mistress. She could not bear being fondled and taken on his knees in the same way as he probably fondled his mistress. But everything had to be endured now that her mother, half against her will, was beginning to treat her as an adult and, fearing for the Austro-French alliance, was writing to Comte Mercy: 'The ill will of the favourite might have the most dangerous consequences, and this must at all costs be avoided. We are assured that England and the King of Prussia want to win over the du Barry. But you should know better than us if this is so. Every possible means must be taken to prevent these evils and troubles to the monarchy and the country. And only my daughter, with the help of your counsels and knowledge of the place, can render such a service to her family and her country.'

Jeanne du Barry may have been completely unaware of the important role she played in the diplomatic correspondence of the time. For a short while her kind heart had been moved by the plight of Poland. But she was too frivolous to sustain any serious interest for very long, too occupied in furnishing the classical white pavilion which Ledoux was building for her in the gardens of Louveciennes, too busy with her dressmakers and jewellers to spare much time for politics. Such time as she had was devoted to the romantic young King of Sweden, who, with the help of French subsidies and King Louis's brilliant ambassador, the Comte de Vergennes, had carried out a *coup d'état* which established his authority and freed his country from the corruption of rival factions. It flattered the favourite's vanity to refer to Gustavus III as her protégé, and both the King and his ambassador, Count Creutz, were wise enough to foster her illusion. Many years later, when the storms of revolution had destroyed her home and plundered her possessions, the countess's heirs still treasured among the few things which were left, a perfumed glove box given her by the grateful Swedish king.

11

1772 and 1773: years of triumph and years of folly in which a peasant girl from Vaucouleurs virtually ruled France. Who can blame her if she indulged in every extravagant whim? In Maupeou's *parlement* the sovereign's will was law, and the sovereign was at her feet. Many a state secret was discussed behind the gilded shutters of the rooms occupied by the royal favourite. Many a time the King would leave her bed at daybreak to take the secret staircase which led back into his room. If he did not go hunting, he would look in at her *levée* on his way to mass. She never dared go out for long, for she did not know when he would suddenly appear, in need of sex or sympathy, or just to rest for a while in peace.

From early morning her ante-chamber would be crowded with suppliants and sycophants, tradesmen and jewellers. As she lay in her perfumed bath, her waiting women would already be reading to her the petitions and begging letters which came with every post. Back in her room, wearing one of her exquisite morning gowns tied with ribbons and bordered with the finest Brussels lace, her small bare feet thrust into satin slippers, she would drink the hot chocolate brought to her by Zamor, the little Indian servant given her by the King. From Bengal, he was very dark, and artists delighted in using him as a foil to her blonde beauty. We see him in one of the most charming of her portraits, the one by Gautier Dagoty, which shows her at her morning toilette drinking her chocolate, before commencing on what for her was the most serious business of the day – the art of making herself into the most beautiful woman at King Louis's court. The dressing table has been wheeled to where the morning sunlight is at its cruellest, for no blemish must be left unseen. She is no longer the artless little *grisette* who could tumble out of bed with flushed cheeks and tangled curls. She is now a mature woman in her thirtieth year who has to cherish and preserve her beauty. In Dagoty's portrait the great blue eyes look out from under the curved black eyebrows; the little mouth is about to break into a smile. It is a far better likeness than all the insipid Hebes and Floras painted by Drouais, for it shows her for what she was – the loveliest and most expensive of courtesans.

The tradesmen who crowded the ante-chamber knew that if any jewel or object was sufficiently costly and sufficiently rare, Madame would never be able to resist. When she was young and unsophisticated she delighted in covering herself with diamonds, but her taste had developed with the years. At a fête at Fontainebleau she had appeared in a mauve dress covered in gold spangles, her hair piled high under a heavy coronet of amethysts and gold, a masterpiece copied from Byzantium by the court jeweller, Aubert, that made the princesses in their family heirlooms look ordinary and insignificant. She was the only one at court to wear jewels in various colours, mixing rubies and emeralds, pink and grey pearls. The jewellers who tempted her with their wares knew that, however long they might have to wait, the bills in the end would be settled by the court banker.

The tradesmen gave way to the courtiers, who were admitted while the hairdressers were still putting the final touches to her *coiffure*, and gossip and compliments filled the powder-scented air. But now there were more serious matters to attend to, for every important man in France came to her *levée*, ministers and *intendants* from the provinces, bankers and *fermiers généraux*, bringing her their plans and projects, seeking her help or offering her advice. She was always ready to listen, even when she did not understand, always ready to smile and to encourage. She was more at home with the arts than with politics, and in the past years had become a patron of writers and of artists. Her education at St Aure, her association with du Barry and his friends had developed her natural taste for literature and history, enabling her to praise and criticize with taste and discrimination. Poets and dramatists, aspiring academicians, were assiduous in attending her *levées* and many of them owed to her their generous pensions. She was even prepared to battle with the King on behalf of a protégé too closely linked to the *encyclopédistes*, the contributors to the *Encyclopédie* published between 1751 and 1772 under the direction of Diderot and d'Alembert, a link which was incompatible with the patronage of 'His Christian Majesty'. Voltaire's niece, Madame Denis, was one of the many to enlist her support in obtaining permission for her uncle to return to France, and the King's refusal did not prevent the countess from asking the court banker, when passing through Switzerland, to visit Monsieur Voltaire and give him two kisses on her behalf, one on each cheek – a characteristically frivolous gesture which earned her immortal verses which began:

> *Quoi deux baisers sur la fin de ma vie*
> *Quel passeport vous daignez m'envoyer*
> *Deux c'est trop d'un adorable Egérie*
> *Je serais mort de plaisir au premier.*

He writes that he has taken the liberty of kissing her picture.

> *Vous ne pouvez empêcher cet hommage*
> *Faible tribut de quiconque a des yeux*
> *C'est aux mortels d'adorer votre image*
> *L'originel était fait pour les dieux.*

These verses, which travelled across Europe and were even appreciated by the mysogynist King of Prussia, succeeded in pleasing King Louis, who for all his disapproval of Voltaire was delighted at this tribute paid to his beloved mistress.

To please the Comtesse du Barry was to please the King, whether it was with the box of perfumed gloves sent to her at Christmas by the King of Sweden, or the ship launched by a merchant of Bordeaux and called *La du Barry*, with the Barrymore motto *'Boutez en avant'* intertwined with the fictitious arms of Gomard and Vaubernier painted on its prow. Jeanne was immensely proud of the ship which she adopted as her own, with the crew becoming her protégés. Her birthday was always celebrated on board with a splendid feast supplied at her expense, while a small watercolour of *La du Barry* battling in heavy seas took pride of place among the treasures of Louveciennes.

But Louis was growing old. His obsession for his mistress alternated with religious doubts and the qualms of an uneasy conscience. The sudden death of old friends, two of them in his presence during a game of cards, filled him with such a terror of the future that for days he would keep away from Madame du Barry, who would wait in vain for the sound of his familiar step on the little staircase. But he always came back, as avid as ever for her caresses and at the same time more ashamed of his own weakness. The rival she feared more than any of the beautiful women whom her enemies were always placing in his path was the King's youngest daughter, Madame Louise, who in becoming a Carmelite nun had obtained an enormous influence over her father. He believed her to have taken the vows in order to save his immortal soul, and every two or three weeks he would drive out to her convent, which by special dispensation he was allowed to visit at all hours of the day. Much of the time was spent in prayer, but in the depths of the Carmelite convent there were powerful influences at work persuading Madame Louise to encourage her father to marry the recently widowed Princesse de Lamballe. Born a princess of Savoy-Carignan, Marie Thérèse de Lamballe, who was barely nineteen, could hardly be looked upon as a suitable bride for the sixty-three-year-old King, but as sister-in-law of the Duchesse de Chartres and friend of the young Dauphine, she had the support both of the clergy and of the royal family. For a short while King Louis played with the idea of making this pretty young widow into the Queen of France. The favourite took alarm. There were jealous scenes which only served to irritate her royal lover, and tears which for once left him unmoved. Her wise little sister-in-law told the countess she was making a mistake. She was there to amuse the King, not to make scenes. He would soon be bored with the sad little princess who, in an unhappy marriage to a dissolute husband, had conceived a loathing for every form of sex.

Jeanne wept, but she kept her tears to herself, and before long King Louis was confessing to his old friend, the Duc de Richelieu, that now that his sexual powers were failing the only woman who could still give him satisfaction was the Comtesse du Barry, and the duke, who was one of the few to whom everything was permitted, dared to suggest that His Majesty should emulate his great-grandfather who had died in an atmosphere of sanctity as the husband of Madame de Maintenon. Louis had always had a horror of morganatic marriages. It was only after many years that his cousin the Duc d'Orléans had succeeded in obtaining his grudging consent to his marrying his mistress, a widow of impeccable morals and a good social background. Even so, she had been denied the title of Royal Highness and the right of calling herself the Duchesse d'Orléans. Yet now Richelieu had dared to suggest that the former Jeanne Bécu should become the morganatic wife of the King of France. He not only made the suggestion but was listened to by the King, who consulted with Madame Louise, who in turn consulted the austere and saintly Christophe de Beaumont, Archbishop of Paris.

Forgotten were the tears. In a euphoric mood, the favourite already saw herself as the Queen of France when Guillaume du Barry, whose existence she had completely forgotten, suddenly arrived from Toulouse, reminding her that, apart from the division of their property, he was still her legal husband in the eyes of the law, and that not even the most obliging of ministers or the most tolerant of bishops would accept the principle of divorce. Guillaume du Barry was not only an embarrassing presence, he was also an extremely expensive one who, failing the payment of a handsome settlement, threatened to appear at Versailles. D'Aiguillon and Maupeou might encourage her in the illusion that an annulment could be procured in Rome, but Cardinal Bernis, French ambassador to the Holy See, was not inclined to further the ambitions of a Madame du Barry, and His Majesty would be embalmed in the crypt at St Denis long before the lawyers of the *Sacra Rota* had begun to discuss the possibility of his mistress's annulment.

Guillaume du Barry returned to Toulouse the richer by several thousands of *livres* and as a chevalier of the Order of St Louis, a decoration for merit he had earned by blackmail. His wife consoled herself for her thwarted ambitions in looking for a suitable bride for her nephew Adolphe. The choice was limited, for none of the great families were willing to ally themselves with a du Barry, whose name would fall into opprobrium no sooner than the King was dead. The young viscount would have to be given a very handsome settlement before even the poorest of the nobility would consent to a daughter having the '*roué*' as a father-in-law. With his habitual effrontery, Jean du Barry enlisted the favourite's support in asking for the hand of the King's daughter by the lovely Miss Murphy, once the most famous of all the inmates of the Parc aux Cerfs. The husband of a royal bastard would continue to retain a certain position even under another reign. But Louis's passion for his mistress did not extend to the du Barrys. Acting on the advice of the girl's guardian, he declined the offer and the family had to satisfy themselves with a penniless relation of the Prince Rohan de Soubise, a seventeen-year-old girl of such astounding beauty as to rival that of her aunt. Brought up in the provinces, Hélène de Tournon arrived in Paris totally unaware of the circumstances of her marriage, and ignorant of the fact that the bridegroom's handsome settlement, of which twelve per cent interest was to be paid out monthly, was supplied by the King's mistress. Her indifference and contempt for her handsome young husband, who was entirely servile to his aunt, and the ingratitude with which she later treated Madame du Barry can be explained by the humiliations she was made to suffer during her first months at court.

The wedding itself, which surpassed her expectations, took place in the private chapel at Versailles. As chief equerry to His Majesty, Adolphe du Barry was honoured in having his marriage contract witnessed by the King and the whole of the royal family. It was a strange document in which the signatures of Mesdames de France were followed by those of Jeanne du Barry, born Gomard de Vaubernier, no mention being made of Jeanne Bécu, and of Comte Jean du Barry, with the whole list of spurious titles he had added to his name. But the most shocking of all was to see the King of France talking amiably to a man with a reputation as unsavoury as that of the 'roué'. Wearing a magnificent dress of silver lace given her by her new aunt, who had also supplied the whole of her trousseau, Hélène de Tournon was so ravishingly lovely as to create a sensation at court and win her the concupiscent glances of the old King. Malicious courtiers took note and mentioned it to the favourite who, with a certain cynicism replied, 'Anyway, we would be keeping His Majesty in the family.' Unfortunately the remark was repeated to the Dauphine, who was led to believe that the countess was following in the steps of Madame de Pompadour in producing her young niece for the pleasure of the King. Marie Antoinette, who was prepared to believe the worst of the person she called 'that woman', gave the countess and her niece an icy reception when they presented themselves at Compiègne. Orders were given not to invite the Vicomtesse du Barry to any of her balls, or include her in her hunting parties. Excluded from the young life which revolved round the Dauphine, in the constant company of her husband's aunt and of the elderly women who formed her court, the proud unhappy girl grew to detest both her husband and her benefactress.

There was still another du Barry to be married. The 'roué' had a younger brother, a highly respected army officer by the name of

Comtesse du Barry by Jean-Baptiste Greuze

Louis xv by Maurice Quentin de la Tour

Madame de Pompadour by
Maurice Quentin de la Tour

Le Duc de Choiseul by
Carle van Loo

Bust of Madame du Barry by Augustin Pajou

'*La Tasse de Lait*' by Louis Lassalle.
'After milking a cow Madame du
Barry dressed as a milkmaid offers
some milk to Louis xv at Marly.'

Madame du Barry by Jacques Fabien Gautier d'Agoty

Madame du Barry as a page by François-Hubert Drouais

Corner of a room in Les Petits Appartements de Madame du Barry at Versailles

The oval vestibule at the Pavillon du Barry:
scene of the inaugural supper in September 1771

'Le Souper à Louveciennes 1771' by Moreau le jeune

above Henry Seymour by Jean Pierre
Lemoine

above right Le Duc de Brissac by Louis
Carrogis de Carmontelle

Madame du Barry – one of her
favourite pictures – by Madame Vigée-
Lebrun

Madame du Barry by Madame Vigée-Lebrun

Below: Journey from Varennes Return of the royal family to Paris on 25 June 1791

Bottom of page: The Last Mass at the Tuileries by Hubert Robert

Nicolas, known as the 'honest du Barry'. Having neither charm nor looks, he might have spent his career in some obscure garrison town if his sister-in-law had not chosen to include him in her family. The promise of being appointed as lady-in-waiting to one of the princesses persuaded the parents of a wealthy heiress, a Mademoiselle Funel, to become allied to a du Barry. The bride was not pretty, but she brought with her a large dowry which included the prestigious vineyards of Château Margaux, to which the King added a further sum of over five hundred thousand *livres* and the right for the bridegroom to assume his father-in-law's title of marquis. At the marriage of the Comte d'Artois in November 1773, Nicolas du Barry was made captain of the Swiss Guards, while his wife became lady-in-waiting. Twenty years later at the revolutionary tribunal, one of the chief accusations brought against Jeanne Vaubernier, wife of du Barry, was that of having squandered the country's money on herself and her family.

While furthering the interests of the du Barrys, Jeanne did not forget her own more humble relatives. Hélène Bécu, the only member of the family who had befriended her pregnant sister and her little girl on their arrival in Paris, was given a handsome pension, while the mother who had allowed her to be debauched by du Barry was cherished and protected to the end of her days. Having assumed the more elegant name of Madame de Montrabé, Anne Bécu was now living in the aristocratic convent of St Elisabeth, the same place in which her so-called niece, the charming Betsi, was being educated at the countess's expense. When the King was out hunting for the day, Madame would drive into Paris to the convent of St Elisabeth where, given a papal dispensation by her friend the papal nuncio, she was permitted to visit her mother and the pretty little girl who, in her white serge uniform, reminded her of her own childhood at St Aure. Only then there had been no loving aunt to spoil her with cakes and sugar plums, no nun with a lovely voice who by order of the Mother Superior was sent to entertain the privileged visitor. Betsi, her blue eyes shining with excitement, would scramble on to Jeanne's knees and amuse her with her artless prattle while she and her mother spent happy hours reminiscing on the past, the days in Francesca's kitchen, the parties in the rue Jussienne. Laughing and crying at the same time, they remembered the hardships and the fun. While Anne admired her daughter's lovely clothes, Jeanne would ask for the recipe of some country dish which she thought might please the King. Chatting with her mother, the Comtesse du Barry forgot the cadenced accents of Versailles and reverted to the language of the streets, so that, one evening after returning to the palace, when she was sitting at the King's table and losing at cards, she suddenly burst out in a loud clear voice, *'Mon Dieu, je suis frite!'* The courtiers smiled their thin, malicious smiles, and one was heard to whisper, 'Her mother being a cook, she certainly should be able to fry.'

12

In the autumn of 1773 Comte Mercy wrote to the Austrian Empress: 'King Louis is so completely given up to Madame du Barry that he is becoming more and more isolated from his children who can give him neither consolation nor advice, while he can expect no attachment of fidelity from the bizarre kind of people by whom he is surrounded and who are the friends of Madame du Barry.'

At the opening of the new bridge at Neuilly, one of the few public ceremonies attended by the monarch, the favourite sat beside him in the royal coach, while neither the Dauphine nor his daughters were invited. It was the countess's revenge for the humiliating reception Marie Antoinette had given to her nephew Adolphe's wife.

In November, the wedding of the King's youngest grandson, the sixteen-year-old Comte d'Artois, gave her yet another opportunity to triumph over the family. Madame Adelaide, who would have liked to organize the festivities, was told by her father that all the arrangements were in the hands of Madame du Barry. With impeccable taste allied to a reckless extravagance, the countess planned a series of fêtes, each more beautiful than the last, in which the younger Vestris, the most famous dancer of the day, performed for the first time, and the lovely sixteen-year-old actress Mademoiselle Raucourt entranced the King and the court in her performance as Dido, Queen of Carthage. Gabriel's blue and gold theatre was once more turned into a glittering stage for the wedding banquet, and the star of the evening was again the reigning favourite rather than the insignificant little Italian bride, a younger sister to the Comtesse de Provence.

Adulated and hated, fawned on and despised, Madame du Barry took her place at the royal table to which only the family and the Princes of the Blood had hitherto been admitted. But tonight the King had thrown all discretion to the winds, and his mistress sat opposite him in the middle of the table, where an eyewitness described her 'shining like the sun in a dress of cloth of gold covered in jewels worth over five million *livres*. She and King Louis appeared to be entirely absorbed in each other, giving each other loving looks, smiling and making signs, His Majesty occasionally pulling a comic face as if by this extraordinary behaviour he wanted to prove that, despite all rumours to the contrary, the Comtesse du Barry was still the reigning favourite.'

Earlier in the year, he had paid her the honour of spending the night at Louveciennes. The château was small, but dinners and fêtes took place in the newly completed pavilion designed by Ledoux in the neo-classical style which had replaced the rococo. Constructed in the form of a Roman temple with columns and a carved pediment, it was built in a garden on the banks of the Seine, its windows looking out to the distant spires of Paris. In the symmetry of its lines and the perfection of its decoration, the Pavilion du Barry, as it is still called today, proves the countess to have been a worthy successor to Madame de Pompadour. The high vestibule, faced in grey marble with a ceiling by Boucher and a gilded minstrels' gallery, was sufficiently large to serve either as a banqueting hall or a small theatre. Madame might be demanding, capricious and difficult to please, but she succeeded in inspiring artists and craftsmen to some of their finest work. The golden dinner service, gilt candelabra and doorhandles by Roettiers de la Tour, the armorial bearings and bronze fire screens chased by Gouthière were among the best examples of French decorative art.

Enormous sums were spent on Louveciennes to serve as yet another pleasure house to distract a world-weary monarch, where after a day's hunting he could come and rest in one of the smaller salons while the countess played to him softly on the harp or amused him with the antics of her little blackamoor. Zamor played a large part in the life at Louveciennes, the house and mistress he was later to betray. The countess adored him, stuffing him with sweetmeats, dressing him in the most extravagant of costumes in velvet and in satin with plumed caps and jewelled earrings. She even went to the lengths of having him christened, with her as godmother and a Prince of the Blood, the Comte de la Marche, standing in as godfather. People spoke of the orgies of Louveciennes, of little blonde peasant girls brought in to frolic and make love to Zamor for the pleasure of the old King, who to amuse his mistress gave her blackamoor a pension and appointed him as governor of Louveciennes, calling in the solemn-faced chancellor to affix his seal on the documents. Small wonder if the Empress Maria Theresa, on hearing these stories, enquired of her ambassador as to whether it was true that King Louis had taken to drink, and that the royal doctors were worried over the gradual failing of his powers and blamed the Comtesse du Barry. Louis was putting on so much weight that he was having difficulty in mounting his horse. But he still insisted on hunting several days a week, and his Bourbon appetite did full justice to the dinners of Louveciennes, where Salanave, the countess's chef, was considered to be one of the best in France.

The younger Moreau has left us a vivid sketch of the first dinner to be held in the pavilion. It shows the glittering luxury of the décor, with the ceiling by Boucher lit by the gold and crystal candelabra on the elaborate table centre, with the countess's servants in their gold and scarlet liveries waiting on the guests, assisted by His Majesty's Swiss Guards. One sees the faithful steward supervising the service and Zamor, in his feathered cap, frisking round the table playing with a greyhound. Madame du Barry, on what must have been one of the proudest days of her life, sits beside the King, her little head held high, her white dress cut low over the bosom. But what strikes one most in Moreau's sketch is the bored, melancholy expression on Louis's face. His mistress has never been more powerful, more sure of his affection, but none of her desperate efforts to amuse him could cure him of the lethargy brought on by age. Underlying the laughter and gaiety of a woman who never dared to look tired was the growing fear that the Church might triumph over her in the end.

This fear reflected on a character which, having been easy and compliant, had become arrogant and overbearing, so that no one dared to refuse her slightest wish, and even artists were beginning to complain of their most generous patron. When visiting Vernet's studio she had admired a seascape he had already sold to a foreign client, but he was forced to cancel the order and to sell her the picture, albeit at an exorbitant price. At the great Crozat sale she outbid the ambassador of the Empress Catherine.* But not every artist submitted to her

* This was the sale of one of the most important art collections in France, made by the father of the Duchesse de Choiseul.

whims. Fragonard was one who refused to comply, and she ended up losing what is generally recognized to have been his greatest master-piece – the panels entitled *The Progress of Love* which are now installed in the Frick Museum in New York. These had been commissioned for one of the smaller salons at Louveciennes. There were four – 'The Pursuit of Love', 'The Rendezvous', 'The Love Letters', 'The Lover Crowned' – enchanting allegories set against a background of the misty blue gardens beloved of Fragonard, where Cupid casts his shafts from behind marble columns covered in cascades of roses, and courtiers disguised as shepherds make love in a world of eternal spring. Sensuous and earthy, frivolous and gay, patron and artist would seem to have been completely in tune. Then something went wrong. It was said that the countess wanted the young lovers to resemble herself and the King, but that Fragonard refused to play the role of sycophant. Little is known except that the panels were declined and that the artist was paid an indemnity of eighteen thousand *livres*. Fragonard kept his paintings and sent them to his home in Grasse, where over a hundred years later they were discovered by the art dealer Joseph Duveen.

Vien, a fashionable painter in the neo-classical style and a friend of Ledoux, was now given the commission. But in his hands 'the pro-gress of love in the heart of young girls' became a cold, academic work with none of the nostalgic magic with which Fragonard evoked the delicate flavour of an age of which the Comtesse du Barry was the reigning deity.

'All that she wants is flattery. She can never have enough,' was the advice which Chon du Barry gave to her lover the Duc d'Aiguillon. And, following this advice, the most unpopular man in France had risen to the post of foreign minister. After four years of power the favourite was still in constant need of reassurance. The walls of Louve-ciennes were crowded with her portraits; no adulatory verses were too insipid to gain her praise. Even her fêtes, which according to Comte Mercy 'were carried to such an indecent pitch of luxury as to insult the poverty of the people', never had a ballet or a *tableau vivant* in which the beauty of the hostess was not the central theme.

Louveciennes and its pavilion were barely furnished before she had acquired another house, a large villa at Versailles in the avenue de Paris, in which to keep her ever-increasing staff of servants. It was here, in the carnival of 1774, that she held the most legendary of all her fêtes, in which over a hundred actors from the three theatres of Paris performed for the benefit of no more than thirty guests. There were the usual intimates, Richelieu, d'Aiguillon, her young nephew with his wife, and the various middle-aged duchesses who, having nothing to expect from the future, were ready to prostitute themselves as her ladies-in-waiting. Only the King was notably absent. With the approach of Lent and the severity of the Lenten sermons, His Majesty was spending more hours in his daughter's cell than in the *petits appartements* of Versailles. Neither Madame du Barry nor her niece was included in the exclusive carnival balls held by Madame de Noailles in honour of the young princesses. A misguided attempt to ingratiate herself with the Dauphine had ended in failure. The countess had dared to suggest that if Marie Antoinette desired a certain pair of earrings valued at over seven hundred thousand *livres* she had only to tell her and she would see that the King gave them to her for Christmas. The Dauphine replied coldly but politely, thanking Madame for her kind intentions, saying that she 'already possessed sufficient jewellery and had no need of any more' – a reply which delighted her mother.

'My daughter's refusal to accept a gift through the mediation of the favourite is just as it should be,' wrote Maria Theresa to Comte Mercy. 'It is a matter of which I am very particular, and I do not know how to forgive the Empress of Russia for having accepted and even displayed the superb diamond given her by her subject Count Orloff.' Yet when the Franco-Austrian alliance was still in the making, Maria Theresa had been ready to exchange letters and presents with Jeanne Poisson, Marquise de Pompadour.

The countess consoled herself in giving gifts worth hundreds and thousands of *livres* to those she regarded as her friends. The most expensive items shown in the yearly exhibition of Sèvres porcelain held before Christmas at Versailles were earmarked for the Comtesse du Barry. A favoured actress received a gown costing no less than six thousand *livres*, and the King was presented with the somewhat unsuitable gift of a suit of patterned silver, entirely embroidered in lilac sequins. But in spite of the extravagance and wanton luxury, the endless fêtes and card parties, life at Versailles must have been of a stultifying boredom for a woman who had grown up in the streets of Paris and savoured to the full the excitement of a large city. For someone of her temperament it must have been difficult to resist the attentions of men sufficiently brave or sufficiently bored to risk incurring the jealousy of the old King. Her nearest neighbour, quartered above her in the attics of Versailles, was the captain of the Royal Guards, the Duc de Cossé. A handsome man in his early forties, of immense wealth, famous for his amatory exploits, he could not have been an easy neighbour for a woman insatiable for love. To please him the countess succeeded in having his wife appointed as mistress of the robes to Marie Antoinette – an appointment resented by the Dauphine, though time was to prove the proud young duchess, who detested Madame du Barry, to be utterly devoted to her mistress. But in spite of his admiration for his beautiful neighbour, the duke was too much of a courtier and Madame du Barry too careful of her position to indulge in anything beyond the mildest flirtation.

In recent months the countess's visits to Paris had been curtailed, after rioting crowds attacked her carriage. The royal whore, as she was known, had become as hated as the Pompadour, being held responsible for the unpopularity of the government, the shortage of bread and the growth of unemployment. Neither Louis nor his ministers made any attempt to curb her extravagance, so deplored by Comte Mercy. Having spent a fortune first on Louveciennes, then on her new villa on the avenue de Paris, she was now kept busy in arranging a library which vied with that of the greatest scholars of the day, in which every binding was of exquisitely tooled Moroccan leather with gilt edging and the du Barry arms stamped in gold on the covers. It was a curious collection for, apart from a natural love of history and of the plays of Shakespeare, one feels she was more interested in the bindings than in the contents. It is difficult to imagine her reading for pleasure Locke's essay *Concerning Human Understanding*, which was to be found next to the pornographic novels of Restif de la Bretonne.

It was the time when the whole of Paris was discussing the Goezman trial – the quarrel between Pierre-Augustin Caron de Beaumarchais, watchmaker, playwright and pamphleteer of brilliant talent and dubious reputation, and Councillor Goezman, a corrupt magistrate in Maupeou's *parlement*. Beaumarchais lost his case, but his famous *Mémoires* written in his own defence were sold at every street corner in the capital, and the playwright condemned by the courts became the idol of Paris. With biting satire Beaumarchais had dealt a drastic blow at an already weak and vacillating government. But Madame du Barry was so entertained by the *Mémoires* that she ordered a part of them to be dramatized and performed at Louveciennes where the King was said to have been present. Nevertheless, the judgment of the courts prevented the Comédie Française from presenting the *Barbier de Seville* and not even the King's all-powerful favourite dared to speak in the author's defence.

Beaumarchais was famous but down-and-out, the cost of the trial having deprived him of most of his fortune. But in eighteenth-century France clever adventurers were rarely unemployed for long. The end of the Goezman trial coincided with the outbreak of a scandal which threatened to be damaging for the royal favourite. A notorious blackmailer, resident in England, called Théveneau de Morande, had produced an obscene publication entitled *The Secret Memoirs of a Woman of the Town: the Adventures of the Comtesse du Barry from the Cradle to her Bed of Honour*. The author, who was said to have been one of the countess's former lovers, demanded the payment of five thousand *louis* in cash and a pension of four thousand *livres* for himself, to revert after his death to his wife and son. Failing this, the appalling document, giving a lurid and detailed account of the countess's early beginning in a Parisian whore house, would be distributed all over the Continent. The news was shattering to a woman desperately striving after respectability, still living in the illusion that she might become the morganatic wife of the King of France. In tears she went to d'Aiguillon and to the minister of police, imploring them to have the libellous pamphlet suppressed and the scoundrel brought to justice. But the British government was powerless or unwilling to intervene beyond assuring the French ambassador that nothing would be done to prevent their agents from kidnapping, drowning or even killing the miscreant, providing it was done in secret. An attempt to carry this out ended in ignominious failure, with Théveneau rousing an East End mob on his behalf and the agents of the French minister of police being thrown into the Thames.

But the minister, Monsieur Sartine, had friends in unexpected quarters, and one of these was Beaumarchais. Two weeks after he had been sentenced by the courts, the playwright was entrusted by the King with a secret mission to England – an outlaw hunting an outlaw. One was a genius, the other a squalid blackmailer, and Beaumarchais succeeded where d'Aiguillon and his ambassador had failed. The money finally paid to Théveneau was half the sum originally demanded, and the existing volumes were burnt in the presence of Beaumarchais. But the negotiations were long and drawn out. By the time the playwright returned to France to claim his reward, the old King was dead and Sartine was not prepared to present Louis XVI with a large bill on behalf of Madame du Barry, who was now a prisoner of state in the convent of Pont aux Dames.

13

The Paris carnival had never been so brilliant as it was in 1774, when the Opéra ball was honoured for the first time by the presence of the royal princes. The summer before, the Dauphin and Dauphine had made what was known as *la joyeuse entrée* into the capital and taken it by storm. Now that Marie Antoinette was the idol of Paris, there was no longer any need for her to be jealous of the royal mistress. Madame du Barry still ruled supreme at Versailles, but this year she found little pleasure in the carnival festivities. Courtiers and ambassadors wrote of the brilliant fête held in her new villa in the avenue de Paris, but the King's absence spoilt it for her. Many believed that her day was coming to an end; there was talk of potential rivals, of a beautiful Dutchwoman who had reappeared at Versailles, an intimate friend of Choiseul, and with whom the King was said to have been enamoured in the past. But the countess had no serious rival other than her lover's growing infirmities allied to an uneasy conscience and a growing fear of death. The Lenten sermons held fresh terrors. Last year in Holy Week an audacious young preacher, the Abbé de Beauvais, had thundered from the pulpit, denouncing the corruption of the court in which he did not hesitate to attack the King's favourite as another 'Queen of Sheba'.

'Solomon, satiated with voluptuousness, exhausted by his efforts to revive his withered senses, has found a new pleasure in the vilest dregs of human corruption.' Small wonder that Madame du Barry and the Duc d'Aiguillon would have liked to banish the offending abbé to some provincial monastery in the farthest part of the country. But King Louis, who was genuine in his religion, considered the abbé had only done his duty in saying what he believed. On leaving the chapel at the end of one of his severest sermons, the King had turned to his old friend the Maréchal de Richelieu and said to him in one of his rare flashes of humour, 'The preacher seems to have thrown a good many stones into your garden,' whereupon the irrepressible marshal replied, 'Yes, sire, and he threw them so hard that many ricocheted into the park of Versailles!'

The abbé was created a bishop, his superiors hoping this might cool his ardour. But Holy Week of 1774 saw him back in the pulpit, preaching on the morality of the gospels. Seated in her place of honour in the royal chapel, Madame du Barry heard this inspired preacher utter a prophetic warning: 'In forty days Nineveh will be destroyed.' Superstitious and frightened of the future, a constant reader of the various almanacs giving their predictions for the year, she read in one of them that 'a great lady of a certain court will play her last role in the coming April'. In her present mood it was hard for her to retain the gaiety and insouciance with which she tried to dispel the King's depression. All the efforts to amuse him, the jugglers and the clowns, the burlesque operettas and farces imported from Paris failed to remove the brooding melancholy from a face which had forgotten how to smile.

Easter went by and the King did not go to confession. His mistress had triumphed over the priests, and with the coming of spring his one desire was to escape from Versailles and spend a few peaceful days in her company. At Choisy and Marly there had to be a court: the only place which was really private was Le Petit Trianon, the pavilion built by Gabriel in the middle of the famous botanical gardens which had given the King so much pleasure in the past. Originally designed for Madame de Pompadour, it was only finished after her death, and it was not till recent years that it had become a favourite retreat for the old King and his mistress. Here they could dine in privacy and dispense with servants, thanks to a mechanical device which brought fully laden tables from the kitchens direct to the dining room. On fine spring days they could breakfast in Bouchardon's Temple of Love or visit the greenhouses and savour the first strawberries, of which over forty varieties were grown at Trianon. In former years Louis had taken great pride in the rare fruits and plants celebrated botanists had brought him from the Indies and Antilles, and giant pineapples from his hothouses had been sent as gifts to his fellow monarchs. But now he had lost interest in his hothouses and his aviaries. The gardens full of blossoming trees, the flowerbeds laid out with jonquils, tulips and narcissi were no more to him than a place where he could rest with his young mistress whose warmth and vitality gave him the illusion of youth. But at heart he knew that he was finished. To one of his doctors he confessed, 'I am growing old and it is time I reined in the horses,' to which the doctor replied, 'Sire, it is not a question of reining them in. It would be better they were taken out of harness.'

On the way to the Trianon, they passed by a funeral. Madame du Barry shivered and crossed herself, but with his morbid interest in death the King insisted on stopping to examine the coffin. It was that of a young girl, but no one told him what she had died of, and only later it was discovered that she had been a victim of smallpox.

The first few days at Trianon were spent in idyllic seclusion with only one gentleman in attendance, the Duc d'Aumont, who was an old friend of Madame du Barry and supported her in the following weeks when she was accused of keeping the King's illness a secret from his family. On the morning of 27 April Louis awoke feeling unwell, but, being better by the afternoon, he insisted on going out by coach to follow the hunt. A few hours later he returned shivering and feverish, and the countess, who knew him to be an alarmist over the slightest sign of illness, did her best to comfort and reassure him. Later she sent him to sleep in his own room, but by the middle of the night he felt so ill that he woke her and asked her to call for his physician. Doctor Lemonnier arrived and found he had a high fever, but agreed with Madame du Barry in regarding it as no more than a passing indisposition, and that it was wiser to keep him quietly at Trianon rather than risk taking him back to the confusion of Versailles. D'Aiguillon, who had meanwhile been summoned by the countess, was of the same opinion, though he was concerned with himself and his future rather than with the health of his sovereign. But a King's illness could not be kept a secret for long. Madame Adelaide had no sooner heard the news than the royal surgeon, La Martinière, was sent to Trianon. Here he was shocked to find the monarch being attended only by the physician-in-ordinary, his mistress and his valet. In words which admitted no denial he declared, 'Sire, it is at Versailles that one has to be ill.' And the King, who by now was too ill and frightened to disagree, allowed himself to be bundled into a cloak over his dressing-gown and carried into a carriage, thereby exposing himself to the cold and forfeiting what might have been his only chance of recovery.

At Versailles nothing was ready, and Louis was taken to the apartment of Madame Adelaide before he could be moved into his own room. But no sooner was he settled in bed and had got rid of what appeared to be the entire faculty of medicine, which now filled an already crowded room, than he asked for Madame du Barry, and neither his doctors nor his daughters dared to refuse him.

Blamed for what the King's courtiers described as her neglect, and ignored by Mesdames, Madame du Barry was quietly crying in her apartment when she was called upon to act the role of heroine. While his daughters continued to nurse their father by day, Madame du Barry took their place at night. But by the following day the King's condition had deteriorated to such an extent that the doctors, who knew him to be in for a long and painful illness, decided to bleed him. When the first attempt was unsuccessful, they immediately tried a second time, thereby reducing him to such a state of weakness that he kept tossing and groaning, asking every doctor in turn – and by now there were no less than fourteen in his room – to tell him the true nature of his illness. By the evening of the second day, smallpox had declared itself, but no one dared to tell him for, having had a slight attack when he was young, he believed himself to be immune. His daughters, neither of whom had ever had smallpox, remained bravely at his side, and the countess had perforce to follow their example. It must have been terrifying for a woman whose very existence depended on her beauty to expose herself to an illness which could destroy her lovely face. There were times when she longed to escape, when she was heard to say, 'I displease his whole family. No one wants me here. Please let me go.' But those to whom she appealed, like Richelieu and d'Aiguillon, had too many interests at stake to allow her to go, and with a sublime courage she forced herself to go in to the room already filled with the sweet, sickening smell of sweat and of decay. Taking her place by the camp bed to which for comfort and convenience they had brought the King, she would sit in silence, stroking his hot and feverish forehead and at times, in a last flicker of lust, he would stretch out a wasted arm to pull at her bodice and fumble with her breasts.

On the night of 3 May she saw for the first time a terrible eruption on his hands. Louis saw it at the same moment and cried out, 'It is the smallpox,' and no one had the courage to deny it. At first she thought she was going to faint. Then, making the bravest gesture of her life, she took his scarred hands and kissed them. By now the whole of the royal family, with the exception of Mesdames, had been banished from the sick room. There was a general exodus of courtiers who till now had prided themselves on the right of entrée. But with a supreme egotism the King still wanted his mistress to remain. D'Aiguillon and the so-called *dévots* were doing all in their power to keep him alive and postpone the time of confession. The Duc de Croy, one of the few devoted courtiers who, risking contagion, carried out his duties to the end, wrote of the unedifying spectacle of the rival parties squabbling in the sick room, of the old Archbishop of Paris, who was sick with gallstones, having been summoned by Madame Adelaide and forcibly prevented by Richelieu from approaching the King's bed, and of the Duc de Fronsac threatening to throw a little *curé* from Versailles out of the window if he as much as dared speak of confession.

By the evening of 4 May, the King knew he was dying, and the thought of death brought memories going back thirty years, when as a young man he had fallen dangerously ill when visiting his troops at Metz. His mistress in those days was the beautiful and imperious Duchesse de Châteauroux, who had insisted on accompanying him to the front and refused to leave him. The King was thought to be dying, but the stern Bishop of Soissons refused to give him the sacraments unless the duchess was dismissed. She left in ignominy, and by a miracle the King recovered to make a triumphal return into the capital, welcomed by jubilant crowds who hailed him as 'Louis the well beloved'. But on the very night of his arrival he went incognito to the rue de Bac where his mistress was hiding. The duchess demanded the punishment of her enemies, and in particular the bishop, before she returned to Versailles. The weak and infatuated Louis gave way and, in surrendering to her, forfeited the affection of his people. But Madame de Châteauroux had little time in which to enjoy her victory, for within a week she had fallen ill of a malignant fever and a few days later she was dead.

Louis had never forgotten what was called the 'Scandal of Metz', and at midnight on 4 May, when his mistress as usual was sitting beside his bed, he suddenly said, 'If I had known before what I know now you would never have been allowed to come to me. From now on I owe myself to God and to my people. Tomorrow you must leave. Tell d'Aiguillon to come and see me at ten o'clock in the morning. You will not be forgotten. Everything that is possible will be done for you.' She neither cried nor remonstrated, and went quietly out of the room. But on the threshold she fainted and had to be carried back to her apartment, where she lay all night sobbing with the pent-up grief of days. The following morning the Duc d'Aiguillon went to the King, who in a calm and lucid voice gave him the instructions to arrange for the countess's departure, and the duke, who knew he had nothing to expect from the new reign, displayed a loyalty foreign to his nature and offered to take her under his protection and bring her to his castle of Reuil, no further than a few leagues from Versailles. Lodged in the ancestral home of the Richelieus, full of memories of the great cardinal, Jeanne with her youthful optimism could still delude herself in the belief that the King would recover and call her back to Versailles. But the fact that d'Aiguillon made her leave in a hired carriage, so as to avoid the insults of the crowds waiting outside the gates, filled her with uneasy premonitions for the future. That same evening, only two hours after her departure, the King called for his chief valet and asked for Madame du Barry. On being told she had left he said, 'What, already?', and tears were seen pouring down his cheeks.

The next morning he was better and there was as yet no talk of confession. Madame du Barry was not yet abandoned by courtiers who believed in her return. But among those who had no such illusion was her brother-in-law Jean-Baptiste, who had already packed his bags in preparation for a flight across the frontier. Though they had barely met since Adolphe's marriage and she had finally refused to give way to his incessant demands for money, he now arrived at Reuil offering to accompany her abroad. For all his cynicism he may still have cherished a certain affection for the woman whose vertiginous success had justified his career of lechery and pimping, and whom he still regarded as an asset who would help to smooth his passage in a life of exile. The countess had a far more disinterested offer of hospitality from the Prince des Deux Ponts, the ruler of one of those small independent states lying between Germany and France. A charming, cultivated man who spent half the year in Paris, he had known Madame du Barry long before she became the royal mistress.

In accepting the prince's offer she might have spared herself the humiliation of becoming a prisoner of state. But with her sanguine nature she never thought the young King would condemn the woman his grandfather had loved. Nor could she ever have imagined that, in his fear of death, the King himself would send her to prison on the orders of the priests.

On the morning of 7 May Louis was ready for the confession he had not made in over thirty years. The solemn procession of the Holy Sacraments, carried by the Cardinal de la Roche Aymon, grand almoner of France, attended by courtiers in full regalia and preceded by a galaxy of priests and bishops, passed from the chapel through the state apartments and the gallery of mirrors till it came to the so-called Dauphine's staircase leading to the royal apartments. Behind the procession walked the Dauphin and Dauphine and the rest of the royal family, followed by the ministers of state. For fear of contagion, only two of the princes, the Prince de Condé and the Duc d'Orléans, who had already had the smallpox, were allowed to proceed beyond the head of the staircase leading to the royal apartments. It was a privilege that both of them, who cordially detested their royal cousin, would willingly have forfeited. For by now the atmosphere in the sickroom had become so pestilential that the old Archbishop of Paris practically fainted on reaching the threshold of the room to read aloud the public confession – the final humiliation the priests had exacted from the King in which Louis begged the pardon of God for having transgressed and brought scandal on his name and promised that, should God in his mercy give him back his health, he would dedicate himself entirely to the welfare of his people.

For two days he lingered on, his body putrefying, his mind calm and lucid to the end. Those who were praying in the council chamber saw him across a vista of rooms, lying on his camp bed, his face covered in pustules, swollen and dark as if he were a Moor. In those last two days the grand almoner never left his side, and on the morning of 8 May he sent for the Duc d'Aiguillon to give him his last orders. The priests had triumphed in the end. To save his immortal soul the cardinal had forced the dying King to dictate the *lettre de cachet* which sent the Comtesse du Barry as a prisoner of state to the abbey of Pont aux Dames.

14

At a quarter to three in the afternoon of 10 May 1774, the impatient crowds who for the past two days had been watching the light of the flickering candle in one of the central windows of the palace of Versailles, saw it suddenly go out. In the *oeil de boeuf*, the room next to the King's bedroom, ushers threw open the doors and the lord chancellor announced: 'Gentlemen, the King is dead.' There followed a great noise of scuttling feet as ambitious courtiers pushed and clawed their way to be among the first to congratulate the new King.

So ended a reign of nearly sixty years. But out in the spring sunshine there was hardly a single tear. Forty days of prayer had been ordered throughout the country, but the churches remained empty, and the few who really loved the old King were shocked by the gay, holiday atmosphere in the streets of Versailles. By four in the afternoon the sixteen state coaches were already underway, taking the royal family away from the infected atmosphere of Versailles. It was decreed that for the first nine days they were to remain in seclusion at Choisy without seeing any of the courtiers who had been in contact with the late King, while the aunts, who had nursed him to the end, were put into quarantine. Seventeen people who had been on duty in the palace were already known to have died of smallpox, and such was the fear of contagion that none of the courtiers who came to pay homage to Louis Auguste was permitted to kiss his hands. No one gave a thought to the woman who night after night had sat with the old King, breathing in the infected air of the sick room, and to whom no one had had the courage to say that the *lettres de cachet* sending the Comte du Barry to the château de Vincennes and the Comtesse du Barry to the Abbaye de Pont aux Dames had been dictated by King Louis and not by his successor.

Even Marie Antoinette flattered herself it was her husband who had dispatched 'that creature to a convent', writing to her mother in one of her first letters as Queen of France: 'The King expects a lot of changes from the new regime. Everyone with the name of du Barry has been banished from court. The King owed it to the people of Versailles who, when the late King was dying, attacked the carriage of Madame de Mazarin, one of the favourite's most intimate friends.' The old Empress was shocked at her daughter's vehemence towards an *'unfortunate creature* who had lost everything and was more in need of pity than anyone else'. But there were few among the sycophants of Versailles – even among those who had called themselves her friends – who felt any pity for the fallen favourite. When she left for the Abbaye de Pont aux Dames on the evening of 12 May, she travelled in a closed coach under an escort of mounted constabulary, with only one maid and such luggage as could be carried in the coach.

At the same time a hearse, accompanied by over three hundred horsemen, was driven out of a side entrance of Versailles and taken in all haste to the royal burial ground of St Denis. In the past two days only the priests had remained to hold vigil by the putrefying corpse of the King who had once been known as Louis *le bien-aimé*. In the end labourers from the town of Versailles were forcibly commandeered to place the body in a leaden coffin packed with aromatic herbs; and even so the stench was so overpowering that the pages escorting the hearse had to cover their faces. Only a few devoted courtiers, among them the old Duc de Croy, followed in closed carriages. Outside St Denis the cortège ran into a drunken crowd of merrymakers who greeted the mourners with jeering cries of *'Taiout! Taiout!'* in imitation of the late King's hunting cries. And already on the following day they were singing in the streets of Paris the first of a series of ribald ditties besmirching his memory

Louis a rempli sa carrière
Et fini ses tristes destins
Tremblez, voleurs, fuyez, putains,
Vous avez perdu votre père.

It was already morning when Jeanne du Barry arrived at Pont aux Dames and saw the grim old abbey emerging from the woods. All night she had wept with the abandon of a child, having gone back over the years to when, as a little girl of six, she had left Francesca's sunlit villa by the Seine for the convent of St Aure. The nearer she approached the abbey, the more she was appalled by the sadness and the gloom. Built in Carolingian times, half of the vast edifice had been allowed to fall into ruin. Courtyards opened out on courtyards, dark, dank places where the spring sunshine barely penetrated. On crossing the threshold, the poor woman gave way and cried out in despair, 'How sad it is. Why have they brought me here?'

Awaiting her in her parlour, surrounded by her nuns – fifty of them in all, including twenty lay sisters – was the abbess, a large, formidable-looking woman with a stern, unsmiling face. The nuns, and in particular the novices, hardly dared to look in the direction of the notorious Comtesse du Barry. When they glanced at her through lowered lids, they saw to their surprise a beautiful woman dressed in black with a sad face and a smile of an almost angelic sweetness. The abbess, Madame de la Roche Fontenelles, was polite but cold, telling her to wait while her rooms were being prepared. Soup was served her in an earthenware bowl. The thought of Zamor bringing her her morning chocolate on a golden tray brought on another fit of tears. Her rooms in the remotest part of the convent were reached by a series of long dank corridors, rooms which were little better than cells, with a hard narrow bed on which the exquisite linen being unpacked by her miserable, little maid looked strangely incongruous. What had she done to be imprisoned in such a place? What crime had she committed other than to have been loved by a king? There was a moment of blind panic when she wanted to scream aloud, followed by another flood of tears. Then, overcome by exhaustion, she fell on to her bed and slept the heavy, dreamless sleep of a child. It was late afternoon when she woke to find a shy young nun summoning her to evening prayers. And suddenly she felt at peace, as if she were again the little girl at St Aure, and Versailles was a dream which had never been.

There was no change of government in the first nine days of the new reign, during which the King remained at Choisy and the friends of the former favourite had the unpleasant task of carrying out the terms of the *lettre de cachet*. The Comtesse du Barry was guilty of having possessed *le secret du Roi*, of receiving confidences it was dangerous for her to know. The convent in the lonely woods of Brie was a place to which for centuries ladies no longer in favour at court were sent to spend months, even years of penitence. But d'Aiguillon, who was hated by the young Queen and had nothing to hope from the future, did all in his power to mitigate a punishment so little deserved. Chon du Barry, who had been too closely associated with her sister-in-law and too much involved in the intrigues of Versailles to be allowed to accompany her into exile, was nevertheless permitted to superintend the dismantling of *les petits appartements* at Versailles and to select a certain amount of furniture to be forwarded to Pont aux Dames. Only the simplest and plainest of things were to be chosen – a comfortable bed, a couple of upholstered chairs, an Aubusson rug to cover the stone floor, a painted screen to shield her from the draughts. The treasures collected during five years as royal favourite – the lacquer cabinets, the satinwood and rosewood tables and writing desk inlaid with plaques of painted porcelain, the chairs and bed carved by Lanoix and gilded by Cagny, the golden clocks and rock-crystal chandeliers, the numberless pictures by Greuze and Drouais, Vernet and Fragonard – were all moved to Louveciennes or to the villa in the avenue de Paris of Versailles. There they were carefully catalogued by Montvallier, the countess's steward, with detailed lists for her lawyers, who already in the first weeks were being assailed by her creditors.

A wagon-load of furniture and the permission to have another maid was all d'Aiguillon could do before he was himself dismissed from office. With no friend in power, her brother having fled the country and anyone with the name of du Barry forbidden to show themselves at Versailles, poor little Chon had no other choice than to return to her family home at Levignac.

In the first euphoric weeks of the new reign, when the Parisians had at last a Queen of whom every Frenchman could be proud, the woman whose name a month ago had been on everybody's lips appeared to have been completely forgotten. The princesses, who had been sent into quarantine, had all in turn succumbed to smallpox and by a miracle survived. The superb health inherited from her peasant forebears, which throughout those early years in Paris had kept her immune from any form of venereal disease, protected Jeanne du Barry from catching the virus. But those last weeks of struggles and intrigues, and her genuine grief over King Louis's death had reduced her to such a state of exhaustion that she had now neither the energy nor the will to rebel, and the stern old abbess was surprised at the docility with which she obeyed the convent rules.

Louis XVI had decreed that there should be masses and funeral orations throughout the country in memory of his grandfather. Dressed in the deepest mourning, Madame du Barry sat at the back of the chapel of Pont aux Dames, when the almoner attached to the abbey delivered his oration in praise of a monarch who had been so denigrated in his lifetime. Seeing the tears pouring down her lovely face, every nun in the congregation included her in her prayers. Within the first weeks her sweetness and simplicity had won all hearts. On the fine summer days she could be found in the garden picking flowers for the chapel or gathering fruit in the orchards. When it rained she would be working in the stillroom, bottling and pickling preserves – anything which would prevent her from dwelling on a future she did not dare to contemplate. What she dreaded most was to hear that Choiseul was back in power – that proud, uncompromising aristocrat who had shown no gratitude for the generosity of a Jeanne Bécu. But the first news that came through from the outside world told her that the young King had chosen as his chief counsellor the seventy-three-year-old Comte de Maurepas, who was to be lodged in her former apartments at Versailles. Whatever pang she may have felt at the thought of those lovely gilded rooms being taken over by an old man and his raddled wife were counterbalanced by the immense relief on hearing that Choiseul was to be kept out of the government, and that it was only with the utmost reluctance that Louis Auguste, who had an unconquerable aversion for the presumptuous duke, had been persuaded by the Queen to allow him to return to Paris.

Maurepas, who had been an able minister in his youth, had fallen out of favour for having composed a lyric insulting Madame de Pompadour. After over thirty years of exile, he was still the charming, witty man to whom nothing was serious, but who had sufficient judgment to introduce men of real merit like Turgot and Vergennes into the new government. A relation of d'Aiguillon by marriage, he felt no enmity towards La du Barry. But time would have to elapse before the young King and Queen could forgive the former favourite the slights inflicted by her vanity and pride.

So Jeanne stayed on at Pont aux Dames, while summer turned to autumn. The months went slowly by, though it was reported 'that she was very happy in her convent and the nuns were enchanted with her'. Even the stern abbess ended in becoming a friend, and those two women, so disparate in character and upbringing, spent many hours together, with Madame de la Roche Fontenelles falling more and more under the fascination of a woman whom few were able to resist. But however assiduous in her prayers and devout in her behaviour, the countess's interests were strictly of the world. She worried over her possessions, the pictures and furniture gathering dust at Louveciennes; the jewels for which she had such an obsessive passion, where every ring and necklace held a memory of passionate nights at Versailles and Fontainebleau after which an enamoured King would add yet another gem to a collection said to be one of the largest in the world. But now her lawyer was pressing her to sell some of her magnificent diamonds to satisfy her most pressing creditors; and the first visitor allowed her at Pont aux Dames was her notary, in order to negotiate the sale of two diamond-and-ruby *parures* so grand they could only be worn at court; and for all her optimism Jeanne did not envisage a speedy return to Versailles. As yet she did not know whether she would be allowed to retain the income she received from the revenues on the shops in Nantes and on the Hôtel de Ville, both of which the late King had given her for life. Nor did she know when or if she would be allowed to return to Louveciennes, though with her customary generosity she continued to pay the servants and the interest due on the settlement made on Adolphe du Barry.

A young man with little to recommend him other than a gentle disposition and a handsome face, allied to a frenetic passion for gambling he had inherited from his father, Adolphe du Barry now found himself without employment, having resigned his commission and being forbidden to appear at court. This was the ultimate humiliation for his wife, who as time went on was finding it more and more irksome to be married to a du Barry. In view of her husband's devotion to his aunt and the fact that he was looking after some of her affairs, special permission had been given for the viscountess to visit Pont aux Dames, a privilege of which she did not attempt to avail herself. The same applied to Nicolas du Barry's wife, who through the countess's influence had obtained a place at court but who now showed an indecent haste in persuading her husband to change his name for a title belonging to her family.

The permission granted to her sister-in-law and her nephew's wife was persistently refused to the countess's mother, Anne Bécu, who after living with her niece in the aristocratic convent of St Elisabeth had returned to her husband only to find that the rent of their apartment had fallen into arrears and that the proprietor was threatening to sue. A police interrogation brought up unpleasant details of the past, of furniture bought in her daughter's name and paid for by du Barry. Jeanne was so upset by this news that one of her first acts on regaining her freedom and on completing the sale of her house in Versailles was to buy a large and comfortable manor house for her mother and stepfather and her beloved little niece. But nearly a year was to elapse before Louis XVI consented to her leaving the abbey. A letter written in August 1774, claiming that convent life was endangering her health, remained unanswered. Even a personal request from the abbess praising her exemplary conduct and asking for a remission of her sentence, when shown to him by Maurepas, elicited no more than an uncompromising 'No'. The Prince de Ligne, who had known Jeanne in the early days at the rue Jussienne and had remained a devoted and loyal admirer, took advantage of his friendship with the young Queen to intervene on her behalf. But Louis had not yet forgiven the favourite's unfortunate slights on his manhood, and with a somewhat heavy sarcasm reproved the prince, 'That is a fine mission you have undertaken,' to which the irrepressible prince replied, 'Sire, no one else would have dared to make it.'

No more was said at the time, and Jeanne remained at Pont aux Dames throughout the long and rigorous winter which, far from being detrimental to her health, considerably improved it. The quiet convent life, the plain food, the cold baths which she found so beneficial that she took them for the rest of her life, cured her of the nerves and agitation she had suffered from during the last months at Versailles.

The woman who came out of Pont aux Dames in the early spring of 1775 was far stronger and more able to cope with life than the pampered favourite who had been admitted a year ago. Though no longer the graceful nymph whom Drouais had loved to paint in the guise of a Flora or a Hebe, she was still a very beautiful woman. The delicate skin might have suffered from exposure, the figure might have grown somewhat fuller, but she was still as fascinating, perhaps even more fascinating than before, with a look of sadness in her lovely eyes, a wistfulness in her smile.

She was given her freedom in May 1775, but even then freedom was conditional, compelling her to keep at a distance of ten leagues from both Paris and Versailles. Unable to return to Louveciennes, she acquired with characteristic impetuosity a large estate thirty miles south of Paris in the neighbourhood of Corbeil. St Vraiň, a moated castle with a lake surrounded by a large park, had been familiar to her from her earliest youth, when it belonged to one of the daughters-in-law of her first employer, Madame de la Garde. Since then it had passed into the hands of one of the King's secretaries, who had put it up for sale at the price of two hundred thousand *livres* – an exorbitant sum for a woman still with many debts. But d'Aiguillon, who on his dismissal from office had received a payment of half a million *livres*, was prepared to advance her the sum plus a further fifteen thousand *livres* for the furniture.

When Madame du Barry left Pont aux Dames, the good nuns wept at her departure and even the abbess was sad to see her go. But the woman who in the past year had wept so many tears and said so many prayers was now eager at the age of thirty-two to get back to the world, her youthful optimism unimpaired, full of hope for the future, for a new life and new loves.

15

Only someone as extravagant as Madame du Barry would have acquired a château as large as St Vrain and kept on the same number of servants she had employed as royal favourite at Versailles and Louveciennes. She spent the first weeks of freedom in a euphoric mood, regardless of the fact that she was still uncertain of the future, not knowing whether she would be allowed to return to Louveciennes or to retain the revenues granted her by the late King. In the next few years some of the loveliest pictures of her collection, including Greuze's *La Cruche cassée*, would go to pay her outstanding debts. For the moment she settled down quite happily to the delights of country life made fashionable in Rousseau, which had become the favourite reading of the young court. Her favourite role was that of Lady Bountiful. In the years to come, her neighbours would speak of her generosity towards the poor, of the lavish fêtes she held for the village people, with dancing in the park; fêtes she appeared to enjoy as much as a masked ball at Versailles. She loved young people, especially newly married couples, to whom she was always ready to give a helping hand in supplying a trousseau and acting as godmother to the first child.

She had no longer the affected airs of a capricious favourite or spoke with the childish lisp that had enchanted the old King. The neighbours found her delightfully natural, ready to give and to accept hospitality, to consult them on the planting of trees and the making of preserves, and to join them in a game of cards, playing for the low stakes adapted to their incomes.

There was a joyful reunion when Chon du Barry arrived from Toulouse, for the sisters-in-law were genuinely devoted to each other. And Jeanne found Chon's trenchant wit a welcome change from the prayers and sermons of Pont aux Dames. Chon, who was unable to live without a man, had imported a middle-aged lover from Toulouse, a certain

Monsieur de Faugas, who in turn had produced a friend, a Vicomte de Langle, both of whom were prepared to settle down for the winter at St Vrain and justify their keep in paying court to the two ladies. The modest games of *vingt-et-un* and *trou-madame* played with the country neighbours gave way to wild gambling, when in a moment of boredom the countess made stakes it would have been impossible for her to pay, had not the viscount, who was more than a little in love with her, been sufficiently gallant to let her go on playing till she had retrieved her losses.

The most welcome of all the visitors to St Vrain was Adolphe du Barry, as charming and as adoring as ever, though it was sad to see the brilliant young officer reduced to the role of a hen-pecked husband with a shrewish, complaining wife who had come to St Vrain for no other reason than to ask for an advance on her marriage settlement. The du Barrys brought news of Paris, of the latest plays and the latest fashions; of the brilliance of the Opéra balls patronized by the young Queen, and the horse-racing on the plain of Sablons, made fashionable by the young Duc de Chartres and the Comte d'Artois. Forgetting the vows she had made at Pont aux Dames, the thirty-two-year-old Jeanne began to be bored in her role as a country chatelaine and to have an ever growing nostalgia for the past. There were occasional visits from old friends who, braving the anger of Marie Antoinette, made pilgrimages to St Vrain: the elegant Duc de Cossé and the faithful Duc d'Aiguillon, who though dismissed from office was still Colonel of the Light Horse with turns of duty at Versailles. But these two accomplished courtiers only made her elderly house guests appear more petty and provincial.

Though Maurepas would have been more than willing to give the countess a free pardon, and even Madame Adelaide had been heard to say that if asked she 'would be in favour of giving her a complete freedom', the young Queen had not yet forgiven 'the creature who had dared to call her "the red-haired child"'. When d'Aiguillon came to take his orders at Versailles, she snapped at him, telling him 'he had better go and pay his court at St Vrain', and Jeanne du Barry's friendship with the former minister did little to help her at Versailles.

Jeanne stayed on at St Vrain throughout the long winter of 1775–6, the coldest in living memory, in which she opened her kitchens to the poor and needy of the neighbourhood, while her spoilt, undisciplined servants quarrelled among themselves. The most troublesome of all was the Indian Zamor, who had grown from an amusing little blackamoor whose playful antics had amused the old King, into an ugly, misshapen sixteen-year-old, hated by the other servants, insolent towards the steward, whom he was for ever reminding that he was still in possession of the document signed both by the late King and the lord chancellor which appointed him governor of Louveciennes. Both her steward and her lawyers were for ever telling the countess that it would be wiser to dismiss Zamor, even if it meant adding to the pension he already received, but she had not the heart to throw the poor, friendless boy out into the world. Zamor stayed on, lonely, embittered and as much out of place in the frozen countryside as Madame's pet parrot who, whenever his mistress came into the room, had been taught to screech. 'There goes the lovely lady!' But at least the parrot, with its gleaming black feathers, was exotically beautiful, whereas Zamor had become so repulsively ugly that the countess could not bear to have him in the room.

In the autumn of 1776 the Comte de Maurepas profited by the absence of the court at Fontainebleau to give Madame du Barry permission to visit Louveciennes and complete her negotiations for the sale of her villa at Versailles. The buyer was none other than the Comte de Provence, who had always been on good terms with his grandfather's mistress and now profited by his friendship to drive a hard bargain with a woman who, for all her peasant blood, was not a match for a Bourbon prince known to have one of the best business brains in the country.

The sale enabled Jeanne to pay back her debt to d'Aiguillon and acquire a comfortable manor house for her mother and stepfather. And in October came the long-awaited permission to return to Paris and Louveciennes. After two and a half years of exile she was again a free woman, able to enjoy the revenues which the young King, who had loved his grandfather, was generous in allowing her to retain. Apart from her large income, there was Louveciennes, with its treasures brought from the palace of Versailles and the villa in the avenue de Paris: pictures and furniture which once had been a part of the royal collections and which Louis xv had given in free gift to a woman he had loved more than any of her predecessors. The greatest part of her fortune lay in her jewels valued at millions of *livres*. In comparison with Madame de Pompadour, who had died poor and in debt, Jeanne du Barry's financial situation was sufficiently enviable to arouse the jealousy of those who, like Choiseul, would have liked to see her reduced to poverty and want. On meeting one of her friends, the duke enquired 'as to whether Madame du Barry's income enabled her to keep so many servants and live in such a grand way'. To hear that she could well afford to do so was bitter news for the proud old man who, bankrupt and discredited, was hoping in vain to be returned to power. But in those first months of freedom Jeanne du Barry was too intelligent to indulge in any form of ostentation which could arouse the resentment of Versailles.

Louveciennes, and the pavilion where she had entertained the King, was now to be transformed into a country house where even the humblest of her Bécu relatives could feel at home. She was affectionate with them all, but Betsi, with aquamarine eyes so like her own, was still her favourite, whom Drouais was commissioned to paint and on whom she was already planning to settle a large dowry.

She was in Paris for the first months while works were being carried out at Louveciennes. But her pleasure on returning to the capital was spoilt by the unhappy atmosphere in the du Barry household, the continual bickering between husband and wife, with Adolphe who had been indulged from his earliest youth unable to reconcile himself to the loss of his regiment, and the beautiful Hélène resentful at being forbidden to appear at Versailles. Jeanne, who had loved him as a younger brother, was sad at seeing all her ambitions for him come to nothing. His only interest lay in gambling, and he was talking of leaving Paris where he had no future and of trying his luck on the ridotto at Spa. His father, Jean du Barry, was still in Switzerland making desperate efforts to return to Paris, a return his sister-in-law dreaded, due to his continual demands for money. Fortunately she had Chon to protect her with the loyalty and love she no longer gave her brother: Chon, who was waiting for the work to finish at Louveciennes, to help her to settle for the first time in a house she could really call her own. Together they unpacked the precious objects in which everything down to the King's golden pens with which he wrote his letters and the silver urn with which he liked to brew his coffee held memories of her royal lover: the chair he always sat in, one of a set of eighteen carved by Guichard and gilded by Cagny and known as the King's chair, always remained empty and many months would elapse before another man was allowed to lie on the white-brocaded couch where Louis xv had rested after a day's hunting at Marly. For the present she was faithful to his memory, and during her first year at Louveciennes she slept alone in her golden bed. Old friends might be welcomed to the house, but even the most ardent of her admirers felt it was too early to disturb the past.

Versailles was quick to forget her. Ambitious courtiers now revolved round the Queen's favourites, the brilliant Princess de Guemenée, the ravishing Yolande de Polignac. But in the spring of 1777, only six months after Madame du Barry's return, a distinguished foreigner was seen one day inspecting the hydraulic works at Marly, which supplied the water for Versailles and straddled the Seine below the terraces of Louveciennes. Whether by accident or design, the countess happened to be strolling in her garden, looking her most charming in a simple morning gown of striped taffeta, with a large straw hat held with blue ribbons. Permission was requested for a Comte de Falkenstein to visit her pavilion. This incognito adopted by the Holy Roman Emperor on his visit to France was no longer a secret. It annoyed both his sister, Marie Antoinette, and their mother and irritated his brother-in-law the King, but gave him immense popularity in Paris. His refusal to live in the palace of Versailles, the interest he took in every form of public life made him the idol of a city so ready to welcome whatever was original and new. The *salonières* raved about him, the academicians fawned on him, and large crowds followed him wherever he went. At eight o'clock each morning he was already on his way, visiting museums, hospitals and factories, seeing ministers, bankers and economists, but spending sufficient time at Versailles to instruct his ignorant and innocent little sister and her still more ignorant husband in the performance of their conjugal duties.

A tour of the hydraulic machine at Marly was all part of his programme, but it must have been on a sudden impulse, when seeing the white pavilion on the hill, that Joseph ii had the wish to meet the legendary woman who in the last five years of the old King's reign had been the uncrowned Queen of France.

No visit could have been more flattering to a woman who at thirty-four was beginning to doubt her powers. Modestly and simply she welcomed Comte de Falkenstein to Louveciennes, making no effort to change the dress which became her so well, allowing her golden hair, which had not yet a hint of grey, to fall in natural disarray, and greeting him with the charm no man was able to resist. Joseph II was fascinated, though later he admitted to a friend that he was disappointed in her appearance. After two years of the hard life at Pont aux Dames the countess could no longer be regarded as young. But he was impressed by her taste and refinement, the exquisite décor of the pavilion with the ceiling by Boucher, the picture gallery in the château where she showed, with a certain pride, the Greuzes and Fragonards, the Vernets and Hubert Roberts she had chosen in the artists' studios, and, above all, the great Van Dyck of Charles I of England she had acquired at the Crozat sale by outbidding the Empress of Russia. She spoke easily, in the manner of a woman who had lived long at court, and tears came into her eyes when she referred to the old King. Time passed swiftly in her company. Walking with her in the gardens along the flowering terraces where the fountains played in the sunlight, the Emperor gallantly offered Madame du Barry his arm, whereupon she protested, dropping all pretence of his incognito and saying, 'Sire, I am not worthy of such an honour.' Emperor Joseph, who was not given to paying compliments and whom the ladies of Versailles had wooed in vain, replied, 'There is no need to protest, Madame, for beauty is always queen.'

There is no record of this conversation which caused consternation at court, infuriating the Queen and embarrassing Comte Mercy, who described it to his mistress 'as having lasted no more than a few minutes'. Long enough for Maria Theresa to reply, 'I would have preferred my son to have kept away from that despicable woman.' The old Empress had been prepared to pity the unfortunate prisoner of Pont aux Dames, but to have the Emperor honouring her with a visit, and at the same time ignoring Choiseul who had been the architect of the Austrian alliance, was an affront both to her and her daughter.

The visit of the 'Comte de Falkenstein' filled others with curiosity to see for themselves the chatelaine of Louveciennes. Among these was the Duc de Croy, one of the few who during the late King's reign had made no effort to curry favour with the reigning favourite. The fame of Ledoux's pavilion brought him that summer to Louveciennes: 'And on the excuse that there was no way of visiting the pavilion and the gardens without visiting the lady of the château, I paid a call on Madame du Barry, to whom I had never spoken and whom I only knew by sight. I found her still beautiful with a greater air of distinction than I had expected. She took me to visit her pavilion, one of the most delightful places imaginable, with a wonderful view over the river, where the hydraulic machine forms a kind of windmill with the water tumbling in cascades. All that taste and money can provide has gone into this charming little pavilion. As we stood on the terrace, admiring the view, I spoke at some lengths to her about the late King and was very much astonished to find that she spoke extremely well, so that it was difficult to be aware of her former condition in life.'

This is one of the last times in which anyone refers to Madame du Barry's humble origins. From now on she was accepted as the chatelaine of Louveciennes; *grisette* and courtesan were buried in the past, together with the scurrilous pamphlets and libellous verses which no one now troubled to read.

16

Barely a year after she had returned to Louveciennes, Madame du Barry acquired a new neighbour, a fifty-year-old Englishman who, with a young French wife, a baby son and a grown-up daughter by a previous marriage, had come to live in the adjoining château of Prunay.

Henry Seymour, a nephew of the powerful eighth Duke of Somerset and half brother to the wealthy Earl of Sandwich, was a man who for all his grand connections had never realized his talents. His many years in the English parliament representing safe constituencies had brought him little political advancement, for, though handsome and intelligent, his insufferable arrogance and uncontrollable temper rendered him unfit for public life. And after quarrelling with every member of his family and running into debt, he decided after the death of his first wife to settle in France. Here he married for the second time a charming French countess, twelve years his junior, and two years after the birth of a son settled in a small château only a few miles distant from Louveciennes.

It was a time when England was very much in the countess's thoughts. The young du Barrys were living in Bath, having hired one of the largest houses in the Royal Crescent, and keeping open house for the smartest society in town. With them was an Irish adventurer, a certain Count Rice whom they had met at the gambling tables of Spa, and who had become the inseparable companion of both husband and wife. A soldier of fortune who had fought in the imperial armies and been given a title by the Emperor, Rice, like du Barry, was an inveterate gambler. Ugly rumours reached Louveciennes of illicit games of faro being played in the elegant drawing rooms of the Royal Crescent, rumours all too reminiscent of the 'roué''s card parties in the rue Jussienne when the beautiful Mademoiselle de Vaubernier had served as decoy to attract young men ready to lose their

money at the faro table. As a habitual visitor to Bath, Henry Seymour
was able to enlighten his charming neighbour on the society which
revolved round the pump room of England's most fashionable spa.
He may even have heard of the du Barrys, for the beautiful Hélène
and her pretty fifteen-year-old sister were to be seen at every ball
in town. But whatever stories he may have heard of the Vicomte
du Barry and his Irish friend and of their unnatural luck at cards,
he would certainly not have repeated them to the lovely aunt who
spoke of her favourite nephew with tears in her eyes.

It was at the end of November 1778, in the first weeks of their
acquaintanceship, that Madame du Barry heard of the tragedy which
brought her close to Henry Seymour, the one person who could give
her details of a duel fought in the early morning on Claverton Downs,
a duel in which the hatred of the opponents was such that the two
seconds were unable to impose the customary regulations. Adolphe
du Barry, mortally wounded, asked his opponent Rice, the Irishman,
for his life, but the request was granted when it was already too late
to save him. There were stories of Hélène du Barry leaving her house
in the middle of the night in pursuit of two desperate young men
fleeing through the streets of Bath, and of being found by a servant
half fainting in a gutter; of her husband being left for two days
untended on the duelling ground, while his opponent was driven back
to hospital. Scandal was rife, though popular sympathy was largely
on the side of the unfortunate widow. Generous Englishmen came
forward to pay her debts, friends offered to accompany her back to
France. She did not even stay in England long enough to attend her
husband's funeral.

Henry Seymour must have been familiar with the little church of
Bathampton where Adolphe du Barry lay buried far from his relatives
and friends. And he was probably one of the few who knew how bitterly
Madame du Barry resented the behaviour of her niece who, posing
as a mourning wife, kept plaguing her for money. Only a few weeks
after her return to Paris, Hélène du Barry put in a request to return
to her maiden name. The request was granted, and in the spring
of 1780 the Comtesse de Tournon was back at Versailles to the fury
of her father-in-law who, having returned from exile, was so outraged
by her behaviour that he presented a memorandum contesting her
right to continue claiming financial benefit from a family she had

disowned. The '*roué*', who had been a proud and loving father, wrote for the first time a document which was completely sincere. But he lost his case, for in the hypocritical world of Versailles it was considered natural that a beautiful young woman like Hélène de Tournon should disown the shameful name of du Barry while continuing to enjoy the legacy of her former aunt. After marrying one of her kinsmen, the Marquis de Claverynon, she still went on claiming her share of the du Barry estate, and many years later, when both she and Jeanne were dead, her husband's name was to be found among the heirs to the du Barry inheritance.

Even someone who knew Madame du Barry as well as d'Aiguillon still played the game according to the rules of Versailles; and in his letter of condolence on her nephew's death he writes: 'The Vicomtesse du Barry is much to be pitied at this time. But I know your affection for her only too well not to be persuaded you will do all in your power to soften her misfortune.' Jeanne Bécu had lived long enough in the hothouse atmosphere of Versailles to accept his false and hollow sympathy.

Henry Seymour was probably the only man who did not try to buy her favours, who offered her his friendship before he attempted to become her lover and was too supremely sure of himself to woo her with expensive gifts. He was moody and temperamental, cold and passionate in turn. She who could be all things to all men, who knew how to pander to every taste thanks to the lessons of a Richelieu, and the training of a du Barry, now at the age of thirty-five suddenly found herself in love, stirred by an emotion she had not felt since the days of her first romance with the young hairdresser from the rue St Etienne. Even then she had been acquisitive, accepting the gifts he could not afford to give. But now it was she who was anxious to please and ready to give – a little dog for a daughter who had been ill, a rare coin for Seymour's collection, gifts exchanged between country neighbours, driving over to visit each other's estates or to chat over a cup of tea. Neither appears to have given a thought to Seymour's young wife and baby son: wives had never played a part in Jeanne's life and he was probably already bored by domesticity. To have the most notorious woman in France as a neighbour was a challenge for a man who, at fifty, still prided himself on his sexual virility, and Jeanne du Barry found in this Englishman, outwardly so proud and cold, an ardent and passionate lover able to give her a happiness such as she had never known. The sensual lusts of the old King, the nights of debauchery which left her in the morning as tired as if she had never slept, belonged to another world. Seymour was strong and healthy and for the first time physically obsessed with the most beautiful woman he had ever met. A handful of letters written by the countess are all that remain of an affair which from necessity called for discretion and led to jealousy on the one hand and bitter heartache on the other. Thirteen of these letters have been published, others have been lost or were stolen from Seymour's home at Prunay when, like most of his compatriots, he escaped from France after 10 August 1792 and the sacking of the Tuileries. Seals were then put on his property, which was later sequestered, and it was only many years later at a Paris auction sale in 1837 that these letters came to light and were bought by a certain Monsieur Barere who distributed them piecemeal to Madame du Barry's earliest biographers.

The letters are simple and direct, for Jeanne was no gifted letter writer and most of her official correspondence from Versailles was dictated by her clever sister-in-law. She makes no pretence of being anything other than a woman in love, giving herself heart and soul to a man whom she hardly knew, but by whom she was entirely subjugated. The first letter is no more than a friendly note enquiring after a daughter who has been ill. In the second there is already the hint of a growing intimacy. In sending him a Louis xiv coin he had admired she writes, 'Monsieur must be aware of the solicitude felt at Louveciennes in regard to what might please or satisfy him.' She goes even further; identifying herself with her sister-in-law she adds, 'Sometime the ladies of Louveciennes will find more serious ways of demonstrating their friendship for him.' In the third letter there is no more mention of Chon du Barry, for by now she and Henry Seymour had become lovers. 'I have a thousand things to tell you, a thousand things to communicate. Never have I felt so much as at this moment, how necessary you have become to me, what happiness if I could be with you always.' She waits for their assignations with all the eagerness of a young girl. 'What an age there is between now and Saturday. My heart finds these two days very long. I await you with the impatience of a soul that belongs entirely to you and wants only the joy of proving to you how dear you are.'

The letters of Henry Seymour have apparently been destroyed, either by Madame du Barry when she was trying to forget his disturbing and unhappy memory, or when her papers were sequestered at the time of the Revolution. It is doubtful whether they would have had much to contribute to an affair of which so little is known, but which on his part never appears to have been more than a violent physical attraction inspired by the vanity of a man who considered himself to be irresistible to women and refused to accept the slightest compromise. The cloudless summer days of a short-lived idyll were soon shadowed by quarrels and recriminations. Both were jealous: Jeanne du Barry resented the presence of pretty Mrs Seymour presiding over the garden fêtes at Prunay, with an apparently devoted husband at her side. 'I wish it were possible for you to live only for me, just as I would live only for you. But your ties cannot be broken. Every moment of my life, even those I pass with you, are embittered by this cruel fact.' But Seymour saw no reason why his beautiful mistress, a former courtesan, should be jealous of his family ties. He, on the other hand, expected complete fidelity from a woman who did not know the meaning of the word, who, while assuring him that her heart was entirely his, was already confessing to a 'mysterious visitor' from Paris, 'a visit I found embarrassing, because I believe you were the object of it'. And she who was used to the coquetry and dalliance of Versailles could not understand the furious rage these apparently harmless lines aroused in a man who would sometimes spend days without sending her a word. She was at pains to assure him that the visit gave her no pleasure, that she was far too absorbed in him to be interested in anyone else. 'How cruel and unjust you are. Why must you torment a heart that cannot and shall not belong to anyone but you?' Tears and protests appear to have had no effect on a man too proud to tolerate a rival. He refused to admit that his mistress had any right to a life of her own and made no allowances for a woman who, having lived all her life in society, wrote, 'Since we cannot spend our lives together in a *tête-à-tête*, I am in need of a few diversions.'

Poor Jeanne, who had been so spoilt and adulated, was now pathetically in love with an Englishman who showed neither tenderness nor kindness in his eagerness to put an end to an affair that was beginning to pall. 'Your letter has torn my soul apart. Only your sweet friendship can heal my wounded heart – come back to me, my beloved one, for I cannot live without you.' And again she writes, 'I am so ill that I believe it would be impossible to live without you.' She will not believe that all her sensibility and pathos leave him unmoved. She, who had always been pursued, becomes the pursuer. In letter after letter she tries to rekindle a passion that has burnt itself out in bitterness and recriminations.

Were these letters entirely sincere, or was the *grande amoureuse* using all her wiles to reconquer? Was there someone else with stronger claims to a heart as volatile as hers; someone who long ago, living as a neighbour under the eaves of Versailles, had coveted what he did not dare to claim?

At the end of 1780, the death of the Duc de Brissac, Maréchal de France, had made his only surviving son, the Duc de Cossé, into one of the wealthiest men in the country. Louis-Hercule-Timoléon de Cossé, Duc de Brissac, colonel of the Cent Suisses, captain of the King's Guard and governor of Paris, was forty-six when he came into his vast inheritance. Married to a lady of the Queen's household, by whom he had a daughter and a son who had died in early childhood and with whom he now lived on amiable but distant terms, he had remained devoted to Madame du Barry throughout her imprisonment at Pont aux Dames, and had even dared to incur the Queen's anger by visiting her at St Vrain. But for a loyal courtier like the Duc de Cossé, the old King's mistress had always appeared to be inviolate, and it was only when he learnt of her affair with her English neighbour, at a time when her relationship with Henry Seymour was already becoming strained, that he appeared as a 'mysterious visitor' to Louveciennes.

Jeanne du Barry may still have been in love with Seymour whose varying moods, changing from that of a romantic lover to a brutal egotist, kept her in a continual state of agitation. But there was too much of the realistic, peasant woman in her character not to appreciate all that the Duc de Cossé, now Duc de Brissac, had to offer, and to let her head dictate rather than her heart. Till now no lover had exacted fidelity of her other than the King, and long after becoming Brissac's mistress she was still hoping for the return of Henry Seymour. Her colossal vanity, fed on continual admiration, made it impossible for her to understand that Seymour was ready to go on living at Prunay for the next ten years without making any attempt to see her. In the last of the pathetic bundle of love letters, which is all that survives of that stormy and passionate affair, we read: 'I will not tell you of my tenderness and feeling for you. You know them. But what you do not know is what I have suffered. You have not condescended to reassure me about what disturbs my peace of mind. Therefore I believe my peace of mind and happiness touch you very little. I speak of this with regret and for the last time. My mind is clear, but my heart suffers. With courage and resolution I may cure it. Farewell.'

There may well have been other letters, all of which remained un-answered. But the cruellest of all was when Seymour returned the double-backed miniature which the artist Lemoine had executed at his orders. Copied from a larger picture, it shows Madame du Barry wearing a straw hat with ostrich feathers. The picture is still to be seen but the miniature has disappeared. Lemoine may have bought it himself in one of the sales at Louveciennes, for in 1796 he copied Seymour's portrait from the miniature, even to including the lines written in English at the bottom, which read: 'Leave me alone.'

17

On a July day in 1782 the Condé Dragoons, newly returned from the War of American Independence, held a review in the neighbourhood of Bayeux. In command of the regiment was the self-styled Marquis d'Hargicourt, formerly known as Nicolas du Barry, who had been so anxious to change his name after his sister-in-law's disgrace. But times had changed. At the brilliant spectacle, which culminated in a sham battle and was followed in the evening by a great ball attended by all the leading families of Normandy, the guest of honour was none other than the Comtesse du Barry. It was her first public appearance since the death of the old King and the first time she was seen in the role as official mistress to the Duc de Brissac.

Now in her fortieth year, recovering from a humiliating love affair, she still retained her seemingly indestructible beauty. There were those who found her looks more perfect and remarkable than ever. Captain Belleval, who had seen her eight years before at Versailles where he had gone to plead for the life of a young deserter from his regiment, visited her in 1782 at Louveciennes and was amazed at finding her so unchanged. 'I had only to mention my name and she exclaimed as she used to do in the old days, "Oh, it's my redcoat." But instead of the happy peal of laughter, tears now sprang to her eyes. She talked to me of the past, in which I saw with pity that she took as much refuge as possible. I must have reminded her of what had gone and all that she had lost. When I left, she gave me her hand and said "Adieu" in a voice full of feeling.'

Were those tears for her lost youth or for the glittering splendours of the times when young men like Belleval came begging for favours, or did he remind her of his friend, young Adolphe du Barry, the beloved nephew so full of promise, now buried in a foreign graveyard? With a nature as volatile and emotional as Jeanne's, tears and laughter were always very close. But there was little reason for tears in the early 1780s, for on the threshold of middle age she began what were to be the happiest years of her life. In the Duc de Brissac she found a lover ready to protect and cherish her in the luxury which had become necessary to her wellbeing. While Henry Seymour had compelled her to discretion, denying her the right to rival his wife, Hercule de Brissac was proud to proclaim himself her lover. His wife had long since resigned herself to his infidelities and, since the death of their son, played little part in his life. All she demanded was to live in a part of the house, in which she would not have to share a staircase with Madame du Barry, who on her visits to Paris stayed openly in the Hôtel de Brissac, occupying an apartment adjacent to her lover's. The society of those days accepted the situation: as the mistress of the Duc de Brissac, the notorious Madame du Barry became respectable. Women who at Versailles had turned their backs on the royal favourite now visited Louveciennes and were surprised to see her so charming and simple in her ways, so essentially *Honnête*, a word much used at the time which can best be translated as 'genuine'. One finds the Marquis de Breteuil, minister of the King's household and a friend of Marie Antoinette, inviting himself to dine, and the Prince and Princesse de Beauvau, who were cousins to the Duc de Choiseul, and who had formerly forfeited their court appointments rather than curry favour with Madame du Barry, now sending her affectionate letters inviting her to stay at their château in the Île de France. On one of these occasions Jeanne is supposed to have questioned her hosts as to why she had been so hated at Versailles, whereupon the princess replied, 'There was no hatred but we all wanted to have your place.' The people who now avoided her were the ones she had once called her friends: the raddled old women whom the Duc de Richelieu had collected in order to give her the semblance of a court, the *soupeuses* who night after night had sat at her card table and attended her supper parties and had their debts paid for by the King. Ignored by the young Queen, they now rarely ventured out of Paris and had no longer any interest in the sylvan delights of Louveciennes.

Madame du Barry now lived in another world. Brissac was in every way the opposite of the brilliant, cynical men she had known in her youth, and the du Barrys and Richelieus would probably have dismissed him as a bore. He was the prototype of the *grand seigneur*, brave, honourable and true, loyal to a King he did not admire and to a system he did not believe in. Both simple and arrogant, he was one of those idealists who dreamt of a better world in which all men were equal, who read the works of Rousseau and sat at the feet of d'Alembert, but was not yet prepared to sacrifice the smallest of his feudal privileges. A man of immense wealth, he could afford to indulge his mistress in every extravagant whim. A patron of the arts who owned one of the finest collections in Paris, he would accompany Madame du Barry to exhibitions at the Louvre and enrich the gallery at Louveciennes with landscapes by Vernet and paintings of classical ruins by Hubert Robert. Hubert Robert's famous portrait of one of the last *messes* celebrated at the Tuileries was bought by the Duc de Brissac as a gift for Madame du Barry. There were those who said that Madame du Barry would ruin the duke in the same way as she had ruined so many men in the past. But she was now a very wealthy woman in her own right. Calonne's appointment as controller-general to the treasury, which was disastrous for a country which the American war had brought to the verge of bankruptcy, was highly advantageous to his friends. Among these was the Comtesse du Barry, who had known him since her early days at Versailles when he had supported d'Aiguillon in his struggle with the Breton *parlements*. In an operation in which the treasury was the loser, the countess's comparatively modest pension of fifty thousand *livres*, which at the end of 1769 had been granted her by the late King, was converted into a capital sum of one million, two hundred thousand *livres*. This transaction passed almost unnoticed at a time when Calonne was lending millions to the royal princes and paying the debts of the bankrupt Duc de Choiseul.

Thanks to Calonne and the generosity of the Duc de Brissac, Madame du Barry lived in a manner more like that of a reigning royal favourite than a retired courtesan in her fortieth year. She always drove out in a coach and six and had her own box at the opera, to which she went incognito and heavily veiled. But at carnival balls and receptions at the Hôtel de Brissac she appeared in her former splendour, wearing her magnificent jewels. In the autumn of 1782, in the first months of her liaison with Brissac, we hear of her ordering from Rose Bertin, the Queen's dressmaker, an elaborate ballgown embroidered with golden sheaves of corn, blue stones and seed pearls costing no less than two thousand *livres*. But for all her extravagance and the enormous sums spent on the upkeep of Louveciennes with its many servants, most of whom robbed her, the greater part of her income went on charity, in gifts to her family and donations to the poor. She even endowed two scholarships at the Royal School for drawing classes for artisans who required a knowledge of drawing for the practice of their trade.

Contemporary diaries give many accounts of her generosity in various fields. Madame Vigée-Lebrun, who in 1786 was commissioned by the Duc de Brissac to paint the first of three pictures of Madame du Barry, wrote in her memoirs: 'During my stay at Louveciennes we often visited some unfortunate person together, and I still remember the countess's righteous indignation on seeing some poor woman in childbirth who lacked every necessity and to whom the servants had omitted to send the linen and provisions she had ordered. I cannot describe the passion with which she reprimanded the housekeeper while putting together a bundle of the necessary linen, which together with soup and claret was to be taken at once to the poor woman's cottage.'

All those who visited Madame du Barry in these peaceful, uneventful years have nothing but good to relate of their charming hostess with her winning ways and lovely smile. Contented and at peace with a lover who adored her, recovered from an unhappy love affair, she had begun to put on weight and the plain white dresses she affected in her youth were now cut loosely like *peignoirs* and made out of the finest linen and batiste. She never felt the cold, and summer and winter alike kept to the habit she had acquired at Pont aux Dames of taking a cold bath every morning. The pampered royal favourite, who spent days resting on her gilded bed, had matured into a strong and healthy woman who took long walks in her park and allowed her delicate, transparent skin to become reddened by sun and wind. But she was still infinitely desirable, a beautiful matron who carried herself superbly and moved with grace. The Comte d'Espinchal, who devoted many pages of his memoirs to her, described the last time he saw Madame du Barry on the eve of the Revolution. 'She had grown somewhat stout and her face was a little pitted. But she was still most attractive. She owed much of her charm to the most scrupulous attention to cleanliness.' Twenty-five years had passed since he had seen her for the first time, seated in du Barry's box at the Paris

Opera House. She was twenty-one at the time, making her début as the *'roué'*'s official mistress, and d'Espinchal wrote: 'In all my life I have never seen anything more charming than this divine creature. She was Hebe. She was one of the Graces, perfect in every way.'

But all who saw her in her middle age, whether out of friendship or curiosity, were fascinated by the ease of her manners and the flow of her conversation. She liked to talk and she sometimes talked too much. But her stories of the past were always interesting and she never said anything unkind, not even of Choiseul, whose friend she regretted never having become, a fact which she considered to have been the fault of the Duchesse de Gramont.

The Comte Dufort de Cheverny, a former protégé of Madame de Pompadour, met her at the house of a Spanish nobleman who had escaped from the prisons of the Inquisition. He wrote: 'We had a thoroughly delightful dinner in the company of Madame du Barry, who carried all before her. She left us with the impression that with unexampled good sense she had been able to return quite happily to a less pretentious position in life. We were not surprised at the part she had played in the life of a man of sixty-four who was weary of every pleasure, for she must have been a most delightful mistress.'

Brissac, who in the past had been renowned for his amatory exploits, was becoming every year more devoted to her. She combined the talents of a courtesan with the cosiness of *une bonne bourgeoise*, caring for his comforts, sharing his tastes for the arts and for reading, which d'Espinchal tells us 'was next to her toilette her greatest interest in life'. In imitation of Brissac she had fallen under the influence of the *encyclopédistes*, and had become an admirer of Necker, the King's director of finance and a friend of Choderlos de Laclos. This brilliant cavalry officer, whose lack of quarterings had barred his promotion in the army, had taken his revenge on society in a novel depicting the corruption and decadence of a world which had refused to accept him. But the author of *Les Liaisons Dangereuses*, the creator of Madame de Merteuil, was kinder and more tolerant in the picture he gave of Madame du Barry. 'When Elmire', as he called her, 'had to leave the Palace of Kings she retired to a peaceful and sylvan retreat, where she lived far removed from the cabals and intrigues of the capital. It was wise of her not to remind the public of those moments of error which encourage the malicious to recall a splendour which breeds the serpents of envy. Elmire need not fear the judgment of posterity, for one can forgive the frailties of a woman who never made her lover either cruel or unjust and who never tried to alienate him from his people or from his duties as a king.'

So wrote Choderlos de Laclos at a time when no invective was too vile to besmirch the favourite of Versailles. Nor was he the only revolutionary to uphold a woman whose 'only fault lay in her birth and in those who had debauched and debased her'. At a time when the cafés of the Palais Royal were crowded with lawyers, journalists and politicians in the pay of the Duc d'Orléans who were working to undermine the structure of the *ancien régime,* three men, Mirabeau, Laclos and Brissot, sat together in the Café Aurore, discussing among themselves the deplorable role played by the royal favourites in the past two reigns. The one they blamed the most was the Marquise de Pompadour, who in her inordinate ambition had made and unmade ministers and generals and been largely responsible for the most unpopular of wars. But all three were inclined to be indulgent towards her successor, in particular Brissot, who recalled meeting Madame du Barry in the spring of 1778. He was then a young and unknown lawyer waiting outside the door of Monsieur Voltaire, who had returned to France after a voluntary exile of twenty-eight years. The whole of Paris was on the great man's doorstep, but few were admitted. Clutching a manuscript he was anxious to show him, but too timid to force his way in, Brissot was about to depart when he saw coming down the stairs a beautiful woman who gave him such a kindly smile that he had the courage to address her and to ask her whether there was any hope of his meeting the great man. 'He is seeing very few people,' she repied, 'But as I have obtained such a favour, I am sure that also you will be received.' And, noting his embarrassment, she retraced her steps and led him up the stairs to introduce him to Voltaire. Remembering the sweetness of her smile, Brissot agreed with Mirabeau that 'La du Barry's only fault lay with the gods who had made her so fair'.

It was her kindness and amiability which people remembered even more than her extraordinary beauty and which made her so loved even in middle age. No one who asked of her a favour was ever refused, and with a lover as powerful as Brissac she had many favours to bestow. There came a time when even the Queen's ministers solicited her help in persuading the old Duc d'Orléans to sell his property of St Cloud to the Crown. The people, who were already exasperated by the Queen's extravagance, the millions of *livres* spent on Trianon, resented the acquisition of another royal home, and the price of ten million *livres* demanded by the old duke was so exorbitant that even the King hesitated. But Marie Antoinette, who had just given birth to a second son, had set her heart on having St Cloud. The health of the little Dauphin was already causing concern, and St Cloud was known to have better air than either Versailles or Trianon. Breteuil, who was always anxious to please the Queen, knew that Brissac was on friendly terms with the old duke's morganatic wife, the Marquise de Montesson, and hoped with the help of the Comtesse du Barry to obtain St Cloud at a lower price.

His efforts were successful; the King bought St Cloud, but committed the irretrievable blunder of buying it in the Queen's name. A notice posted on the gates declaring it to be her private property aroused a storm of indignation, with angry deputies standing up in the *parlements* to protest that it was both immoral and illegal for royal palaces to belong to the queens of France. It appears that the acquisition of St Cloud, which added to the Queen's growing unpopularity, reconciled Marie Antoinette to 'the infamous' du Barry, even if we are inclined to discount an incident related by d'Espinchal. He wrote that during the Opéra ball of the 1785 carnival season, profiting from the anonymity of their masks, the Queen, the Duc de Choiseul and the Comtesse du Barry spent several hours together, and that the Queen was so pleased with the countess's behaviour that she promised her the protection of the court should she ever have the need. D'Espinchal is usually a truthful chronicler but this whole story is unlikely. In the early months of 1785, Marie Antoinette was in the last stages of pregnancy and Choiseul was already a dying man. Nevertheless, the part played by Madame du Barry in the acquisition of St Cloud earned her the gratitude of the King's ministers. When Jean du Barry returned from exile, seedy, impoverished, more ready than ever to batten on the sister-in-law whom he still regarded as his property, he found that as the mistress of the Duc de Brissac she was more independent than when she had been the mistress of the King.

18

The Duc de Brissac was a proud and possessive lover, more prepared to accept his mistress's connection with the humble Bécus than with the dissolute du Barrys. Having little sense of humour, he failed to appreciate the witty sallies of Mademoiselle du Barry, his mistress's sister-in-law. The imitations and light-hearted mockery which had entertained the old King left him singularly unamused. Little is heard of Chon after the coming of Brissac: the loyal and devoted sister-in-law, on whom Jeanne had relied for companionship and advice, and who had guided her steps during her first perilous years at court, now gradually drifted out of her life. We hear of her visiting her old lover, d'Aiguillon, whom the Queen's enmity had driven into exile, and finally retiring to her family home at Levignac, which the du Barrys had entirely rebuilt at their sister-in-law's expense. Jeanne missed her 'little Chon' and time hung heavy on her hands when Brissac's duties as governor of Paris and captain of the 'Cent Suisses' kept him away from Louveciennes. It must have been tantalizing to have Henry Seymour still living in the neighbourhood, to hear of him from mutual acquaintances who were only too ready to tell her of his infatuation for the fascinating Madame de Canillac who earlier in life had provoked a scandal at Versailles by bringing about a duel between two Princes of the Blood.

In the absence of Brissac one suspects that the countess made several attempts to renew her relationship with Seymour, and the portrait by Lemoine on which the one-time lover had written the chilling words 'Leave me alone' probably dates from those years.

The country reverberated with the scandal of the diamond necklace in which a scheming adventuress succeeded in destroying the reputation of the Cardinal de Rohan, grand almoner of France. But few people at the time remembered that the legendary necklace, said to be the most expensive in the world, had originally been intended as a present for Madame du Barry. Her name came up at the trial of the infamous Jeanne de la Motte as one of those whom the adventuress had petitioned for help in her claim to be descended from the Valois kings. But the countess had been so put off by the woman's insolence and pride that she had ended in throwing the petition into the fire. She had little to say in evidence at the trial, but the very name of du Barry was sufficient to attract the attention of every gossip writer in Paris, reviving all the salacious stories of her past.

No one was spared in a trial which shook the foundations of the throne, heaping calumny on the innocent Queen. To protect his wife the King committed the greatest blunder of his reign in bringing the grand almoner of France to trial before the *parlement* of Paris. The cardinal was acquitted, Jeanne de la Motte was branded as a thief and sent to Salpetrière. But the one who suffered most was the Queen, whose unpopularity rose to unprecedented heights.

Neither Madame du Barry nor the Duc de Brissac played any part in the stormy arguments which divided the society of the day, he on account of his loyalty to the King, she because she secretly sympathized with the handsome cardinal whom in her romantic fashion she imagined to be madly in love with the Queen.

This was the year when Madame Vigée-Lebrun paid a visit to Louveciennes to paint the first of the three portraits commissioned by Brissac. It shows us the countess wearing a morning gown with a plumed straw hat, practically the same costume in which she was painted twenty years earlier by Drouais. The charming features, the little nose and exquisite mouth with the pearly teeth were still the same; the blue half-closed eyes, '*les yeux en coulisses*', were still the eyes of a coquette; only the skin, pitted and somewhat *couperosé* or blotched, was beginning to spoil. At forty-five Madame du Barry was still a beautiful woman. But the artist, who was then at the height of her fame, was more inclined to criticize than the admirers who came to Louveciennes only to praise. Ten years younger than Jeanne du Barry, Vigée-Lebrun, who was a friend and confidante of the Queen, the intimate of the Comte de Vaudreuil and the mistress of Calonne, the King's controller-general, two of the most fascinating men of the day, found life at Louveciennes too restricted for her taste. The situation was delightful, but her rooms overlooking the hydraulic machine of Marly were so noisy that she was unable to sleep at night, while the gallery in the castle, 'so full of treasures that it might have belonged to the mistresses of several kings', was overcrowded and badly arranged. But the pavilion, where they always took coffee after dinner, was perfection. They would sit in the beautiful drawing room looking out over the Seine and the distant spires of Paris, a room in which almost every piece of furniture came from one of the royal collections and every door handle was a masterpiece of the goldsmith's art. Madame du Barry would entertain her in reminiscing on her past. But the painter was disappointed by the discretion with which she spoke of the late King. 'His Majesty would do me the honour of coming to dine here,' she would say before passing on to another subject. Or she would stroke a brocaded sofa, saying gently, 'His Majesty would come and rest here after a day's hunting.' Now it was the Duc de Brissac who, when staying at Louveciennes, would accompany the ladies to take coffee in the pavilion before retiring to rest on that same brocaded sofa.

Madame Vigée-Lebrun wrote little of Brissac. As he was her patron she was hardly in a position to criticize. Nor would these two middle-aged lovers, so exquisite in their manners that in public there was never anything to suggest they were anything more than friends, be particularly interesting to a woman used to the wit and sparkle of Marie Antoinette's *société* at Trianon. As for her hostess, she found her charming, genuinely kind and generous, but not particularly intelligent, while the childish lisp she still affected when in the company of men, and which delighted her lover, seemed slightly out of place in a woman of her age.

There was one occasion at Louveciennes which Madame Vigée-Lebrun was never to forget. It was at the time of her second visit in 1788 when Madame du Barry received the emissaries of Typoo Sahib, sultan of Mysore, come to solicit help from France in his struggle against the English. News travelled slowly in the East and the envoys appear to have been under the impression that the countess still had influence at Versailles. They came laden with gifts of exquisite muslins embroidered in gold, and with characteristic generosity Jeanne du Barry presented her guest with the loveliest of them all. When Vigée-Lebrun returned to France after many years of exile, she still had the Indian muslin in her baggage and, finding herself invited to a big reception in the Paris of the Consulate and having nothing to wear, she created a sari wonderfully adapted to a year when Bonaparte's Egyptian campaign had made fashionable everything Eastern.

But there were not many exotic evenings at Louveciennes, and when Brissac was busy with his manifold duties in Paris and Versailles, or visiting his estates in Anjou and Normandy, Jeanne filled the house with her relatives. Now, in place of the du Barrys, there were the Bécus, a family which had prospered since the days when poor Madame de Cantigny had committed the error of marrying her handsome '*rôtisseur*'. Fabien Bécu's superb physique had been inherited by his descendants. This family of handsome major-domos and footmen in princely households had bettered themselves; one of them, Charles Bécu, in the service of the exiled King of Poland in his palace at Lunéville, had found eligible husbands for his two pretty daughters: one of them an officer in the guards of the Comte d'Artois called Graillet, the other a government official by the name of Neuville. Both of them in turn had daughters and the two families spent many weeks at Louveciennes, which must have been a fairyland for children with its menagerie full of exotic animals, the white deer in the park, and the rooms full of exotic toys. But jealousy arose when Betsi arrived at the château. Throughout the reign of the late King the so-called daughter of Nicolas Bécu had lived with her aunt in the aristocratic convent of St Elisabeth, where the nuns had given her an excellent education. Her pretty face and taking ways gave Madame du Barry high hopes for Betsi's future. But she was only fifteen when King Louis's death put an end to these ambitions and, in 1781, she was quietly married in the chapel at Louveciennes to a cavalry officer considerably older than herself. It was a good match for a Bécu, and the bridegroom, who was heir apparent to the Marquis de Boisseson, was a man of considerable ability who helped sort out the countess's chaotic finances. The generous dowry of one hundred and sixty thousand *livres* given to Betsi on her marriage, of which five per cent was paid quarterly to her husband, and the suite of rooms given to the Boissesons at Louveciennes, aroused considerable resentment among the cousins. Further resentment was caused by the Duc de Brissac's predeliction for pretty little Betsi, his agreeing to stand as godfather to her two children, both of whom were given Brissac family names, the boy being christened Hercule Timoléon after the duke.

But the chief bitterness arose when Jeanne's mother died in 1788, making Betsi her exclusive heir. Some of Madame du Barry's biographers have written that Madame Rançon de Montrabé was an ungrateful parent in cutting her daughter out of her will and in leaving everything to her niece, but in all probability it was Jeanne herself who dictated the will to provide for Betsi's future. Horrified by the family quarrel which ensued, she hastened to make amends by giving the Graillets a house in the grounds of Louveciennes and persuading them to provide a home for poor Monsieur Rançon, who had been cut out of his wife's will. Her stepfather's wounded feelings were placated with an annuity of two thousand *livres*. The charming letter which accompanied this gift 'extolling his perfect probity and expressing her gratitude for the kindness he had always shown her' is excessively grateful, when one remembers it was written to a man who had not hesitated to sell her to du Barry and who later sent her whining letters of complaint, claiming furniture he and his wife had acquired as the price of their complaisance. Neither of the Boissesons appear to have shown much tact on this occasion, and Jeanne, who was always so prodigal with her money, was distressed at the rapaciousness with which her relatives disputed her gifts. But it was not only the humbly born Bécus who battened on her: the aristocratic Marquis de Claveyron, whom Hélène du Barry had married shortly after her husband Adolphe's death, continued to claim the legacy Madame du Barry had given to her favourite nephew long after both his wife and her first husband's aunt had died.

Jeanne was still in mourning for her mother when in 1788 she lost one of her oldest friends, the ninety-four-year-old Duc de Richelieu. A survivor from three reigns, he had remained an unrepenting reprobate to the end, marrying his last wife, a fifteen-year-old girl, shortly before his death, which came at a time when the Versailles of which he had been the most brilliant ornament was threatened with disruption. The young men who had volunteered to fight in the American wars had returned to their country no longer content to be frivolous in the make-believe world of Trianon, and the spoilt beauties of Parisian drawing rooms were now studying political philosophy and speaking of the 'rights of man'. Even Jeanne de Vaubernier, a former *grisette* from the Maison Labille, produced for Richelieu's pleasure by du Barry, now read Rousseau and d'Alembert. But the former *grisette* was one of the few to remain loyal to a man who in the past had given her the first lessons in the complicated etiquette of Versailles. The tears she shed at his funeral were sincere. The family vault of the Richelieus was barely closed before it was reopened for another of her old friends, the Duc d'Aiguillon, who had returned from exile to die lonely and forgotten in a Paris which barely remembered his name.

The halcyon days of Calonne's ministry were drawing to a close. The most popular man in France had dared to raise the spectre of a giant deficit, breaking to the King the news that the country was in debt for over one hundred million *livres*, that it was impossible to raise any further loans, and that drastic economies were necessary to save both France and the monarchy from complete collapse. Too late he realized, as Turgot and Necker had realized before him, that no country could survive in which certain provinces were more privileged than others and in which the ruling classes, both the nobility and the upper clergy, were practically exempt from taxation, for which the whole burden fell on the working man. It was no longer the polished, urbane courtier but a man hollow-eyed from lack of sleep, haunted by the fear of bankruptcy, who now presented King Louis xvi with a detailed programme in which taxes such as the *taille* and the *corvée*, both of which were borne by the poorer section of the people, were either lightened or abolished and a land tax was to be imposed on the upper classes and above all on the clergy, who owned one-tenth of the country's land. Knowing how bitterly these measures would be opposed by those who till now had been his strongest supporters, Calonne suggested that the land tax should be presented for approval to an assembly of notables made up of one hundred and forty-seven of the leading citizens. Once these measures were approved, the *parlements*, always ready to uphold the nobility against the Crown, would have no other choice than to submit.

Assemblies of notables had been summoned in the past, both by King Henry iv and by Cardinal Richelieu, then sufficiently strong to cow the nobles into submission. But neither King Louis nor Calonne were dominating personalities. His minister's proposals came as a bombshell to the King: the man who till now had been his favourite minister was behaving like Necker, whom he abhorred. He did not make any serious attempt to cut expenditure. The autumn journey to Fontainebleau, the most costly of all the royal journeys, for which

138

no fewer than two thousand horses were commandeered, continued as before. The winter season at Versailles, with the extravagant round of balls and entertainments, went on as usual. But the atmosphere of disintegration was apparent to every intelligent observer. Madame du Barry's old friend the Prince de Ligne, who returned to France in the summer of 1786 after an absence of several years, was shocked at the growing spirit of discontent, the change for the worse both in manners and customs. Wherever he went in Versailles people were either boring or bored. What he saw as a sure sign of revolution was that the very classes whose interest lay in supporting the government did nothing but criticize.

Sedition was rife, and not even the one hundred and forty-seven notables, ostensibly chosen for their loyalty to the Crown, could be relied on, for the majority, and in particular the richer members of the clergy, thought of themselves rather than of their country. An idealist like Brissac, who dreamt of a better world, found himself distrusted both by the court party and his fellow nobles in Anjou. Excluded from the assembly of notables, he was pained at finding one of his younger relatives appointed in his place as president of his province. Writing to Madame du Barry, he confessed to being somewhat provoked at not having been nominated as president of the assembly. 'Of course I had not asked for it, but whose fault it is that I have been forgotten and passed over is beyond me to say.' Jeanne grieved over her lover's wounded pride. In the past she had only been interested in politics in so far as they served her ambition, but now she was involved heart and soul in the destiny of a man whose illusion of liberty and justice, combined with a staunch loyalty to the Crown, would make them both into the victims of a revolution neither could understand.

19

Ministers came and went, unable to stem the rising tide of inflation. Two assemblies of notables failed to agree on the necessary measures of reform. The Paris *parlement* restored by the King had become an unruly, undisciplined body which, since the acquittal of the Cardinal of Rohan, was only out to humiliate the Crown, declaring that no one had the right to introduce the land tax without the consent of the Estates General, a consultative body made up of the clergy, nobles and commoners which had not met since the beginning of the previous century. Challenged on what he believed to be an infringement of his royal prerogatives, the King exiled the rebellious *parlement* to Troyes, but the riots and demonstrations were such that within a month it was back in Paris, its members more fractious and arrogant than ever.

By the spring of 1788 the situation had become so alarming that the government had no other choice than to show its strength and, in a solemn *lit de justice* held in the palace of Versailles, the King invoked his right to carry through the land tax without the consent of *parlement*. Troops were sent to clear the Palais de Justice, and both the *parlement* of Paris and those of the provinces were deprived of their powers. The leaders of the opposition, one of them the King's cousin Philippe d'Orléans, were placed under arrest. It was an unexpected role for the duke, a weak, dissipated young man who had but lately come into his father's vast inheritance and who, dominated by the ambition of Choderlos de Laclos and his hatred of the Queen, had adopted the role of the people's champion. But the people themselves played little part in this first year of revolution. The revolts which broke out in the various provinces, and in particular in the Dauphiné, were led by the local nobility and the rising bourgeoisie, members of the rural *parlements*.

In Paris the disturbances were round the Palais Royal, the centre of the seditious printing presses and cafés, where out-of-work deputies aired their grievances to hysterical audiences. As governor of Paris, the Duc de Brissac did little to control a situation that was rapidly getting out of hand. Both Philippe d'Orléans and Choderlos de Laclos were his friends, and he had nothing but praise for the young prince who had put some of his finest pictures up for sale and given the proceeds of eight million francs to be distributed among the poor of Paris. In his intrinsic goodness, Brissac failed to understand the bitterness of Laclos, the brilliant and disappointed artillery officer who, by way of the masonic lodges, had become the *éminence grise* of a prince whose vanity and wealth were his only claims to greatness.

In the rue de Grenelle and at Louveciennes, Brissac and his mistress entertained the progressive elements in the government. When the King was forced to accept Necker as his minister of finance, Brissac was the first to hold a large reception in honour of the Swiss banker, who was generally regarded as the 'financial wizard' who would bring back prosperity to France; while Madame du Barry cultivated the friendship of the pedantic Madame Necker, inviting her to theatrical performances at Louveciennes. Such was Necker's reputation that he was no sooner in office than government funds rose by thirty per cent. Bankers who had had no faith in his predecessors were ready to subscribe to his emergency loans. A certain optimism prevailed in those few months before the opening of the Estates General, which Necker had persuaded the King to convoke in the spring of 1789. 'The word "revolution" was never uttered. If anyone had dared to use it, he would have been considered mad.' So wrote the Marquise de la Tour de Pin in memoirs dictated at the end of a long life spent in exile. 'We laughed and danced over a yawning abyss, thinking people would be content just to talk of abolishing all the abuses. We thought that France was about to be reborn.'

But even the elements conspired with revolution: the terrible drought, which decimated the countryside, ending in a hailstorm of such magnitude that it destroyed the greater part of the crops, was followed by one of the coldest winters on record, brought bread to famine prices and aggravated the misery of the poor. Both the Duc de Brissac and Madame du Barry gave enormous sums in charity, and no one gave more than the King who, on his private account, brought one and a half million hundredweight of wheat from abroad.

But there was no brilliant press officer at Versailles, no Choderlos de Laclos to sing the praises of 'the best of kings', and in Paris the Duc d'Orléans was hailed as the 'hero of the day'. But the duke was not only opening soup kitchens for the poor: he was also subsidizing the beggars, evil, sinister-looking men ready to join in any riot for the sake of a few *sous*. The Opéra ball had never been more brilliant nor the theatres more crowded, but noblemen's carriages were being stoned in the streets and well-dressed women insulted. Paris was not a pleasant place to be in after dark. But Necker still saw himself as the saviour of his country, and true to his democratic principles had persuaded the King to recall the rebellious *parlements*, while the idealistic Brissac wrote to his mistress: 'There may be a few unpleasantnesses, a few disturbances. But the way for reform is always hard.'

Jeanne, with her gay and carefree nature, was ready to believe him on that sunny day in May, when there was still laughter in the air and the whole of Paris had converged on Versailles in a good-humoured holiday mood to witness, in the opening of the Estates General, what was to be the last of the glittering pageants of the *ancien régime*. As mistress of one of the most important officers at court, Madame de Barry would have occupied one of the best windows on the route, from where she could see the great procession wending its way through streets hung with tapestries and banners, with pages and halberdiers still flaunting the fleur-de-lys on their gold-embroidered uniforms. The King and Queen walked behind the Holy Sacraments, carried by the four royal princes; the King a stolid, uninspiring figure in a suit of cloth of gold, but for all his lack of charisma still loved by his people, who were all monarchists at heart, while the Queen, so proud and beautiful in her gown of silver cloth, did not get as much as a single cheer. Jeanne may have been sufficiently compassionate to spare a tear for '*la petite rousse*' who had once banished her to Pont aux Dames and whose dying son was now lying, propped up on cushions, on a nearby balcony, a witness to his mother's humiliation. There were no cheers for Marie Antoinette, no cheers for the Comte d'Artois, at whose wedding the reigning favourite had played the part of the uncrowned Queen of France. Then he had been the most popular of all the royal princes, a popularity he had forfeited through his frivolity and pride.

Walking among his fellow peers, the Duc de Brissac looked splendid and serene. Not even the frenzied applause for the Duc d'Orléans could disturb his olympian calm. The prince had ostentatiously identified himself with the Third Estate, the six hundred deputies who had doubled their representation and were now marching in serried ranks at the end of the long procession, their sombre suits and unadorned *tricornes* in strong contrast to the red and purple robes of the clergy and to the plumed hats and jewelled sword hilts of the *noblesse d'épée*. They were men of the new order, idealists and opportunists, theorists and rationalists, many of whom had never visited Versailles, but to whom within the space of a few months the proud nobility of France would have surrendered the whole of its feudal privileges.

A weak, unhappy King, favouring conciliation rather than force, a minister upholding his democratic principles, a clergy of whom the lower orders had within the first few days gone over to the First Estate, and a nobility divided among themselves had within a month transformed the Estates General into the National Assembly representing ninety-six per cent of the nation. A brief show of strength on the part of the King to assert his prerogatives by a *séance royale* ended in a series of humiliating capitulations which placed the throne at the mercy of the Third Estate.

In a situation rapidly turning into anarchy, Brissac was still writing to Madame du Barry, 'The destruction of our feudal privileges will not prevent what is right and good from being respected. One has to be calm and philosophical and be patient in the hope that the Estates General, which is working so slowly at present, will end in achieving tranquillity for our country.' With Paris in a state of ferment it was hardly the moment to philosophize. Troops called in at the eleventh hour could no longer be relied on. Even the Gardes Français were in a state of mutiny. As governor of Paris, Brissac himself came under attack, and in a long and licentious poem called *Organt* an anonymous author of little talent exposed the duke's relations with a former prostitute. It was only later that the author was revealed to be the twenty-year-old Louis de Saint-Just, the beautiful and implacable 'angel of terror', the sanguinary accomplice of Robespierre.

Jeanne du Barry had suffered from too many libels in the past to take much notice of an obscure pamphleteer from the Palais Royal, and life at Louveciennes continued untroubled by what were still dismissed as 'disturbances'.

On the morning of 14 July 1789, a beautiful summer's day, Jeanne was sitting under an oak tree in her garden, where Vigée-Lebrun had installed her easel and paintbrushes for the second sitting of what was to be the third portrait commissioned by Brissac. This time the artist was making no attempt to evoke a beauty which was long since past its prime. The woman sitting under an oak tree with a book in her lap is definitely middle-aged and the new fashions in dress, with high waist and low-cut neckline, are unbecoming to her full figure. The complexion of milk and roses, once eulogized by poets, is now marked and pitted. The eyes are smaller, the expression sadder, and the smile is more constrained. This is the face of a woman still making an effort to retain her beauty, but the effort is becoming a strain.

The head was already taking shape and the artist was making an appointment for a second sitting when the cloudless sky was rent by the sound of gunfire and spirals of smoke were seen rising over the distant spires of Paris. A messenger arrived with the news that Necker had been dismissed and that all hell was let loose in the capital, with hysterical crowds screaming for his recall. Vigée-Lebrun packed her easel, promising to return, but by the time she got back to Paris the Bastille had been stormed, the governor de Launay and his staff assassinated, and their heads, mounted on pikes, were being paraded through the streets. The artist, who had been a favourite of the Queen and mistress of Calonne, never went back to Louveciennes; she was in one of the first of the hundreds of carriages which headed for the frontier within the next few weeks. It was an exile which was to last for nearly fifteen years, and on her return she revisited Louveciennes to find Madame du Barry's enchanting pavilion desecrated. It was only then that she finished the portrait of a woman who, as one of the last victims of the guillotine, lay buried in an unnamed grave.

'If King Louis xv had been alive, nothing of this kind would have happened.' Jeanne spoke with sadness of her proud old lover who had lived and died as a Bourbon despot and would never have taken the road to Canossa to accept a tricolour from a revolutionary mayor. In his day the assassination of faithful servants like de Launay and Flesselles would never have gone unpunished, and she wept for the two charming old gallants who in the past weeks had visited her at Louveciennes. But in Paris, given over to an explosion of joy, people talked of the glorious revolution 'which had been achieved with very little loss of life', and the latest craze among fashionable women was to wear jewels *à la constitution*, carved and polished stones taken from the Bastille and elaborately set in gold.

Jeanne du Barry remained at Louveciennes throughout the summer of 1789, during which revolution spread all over the country, and at the end of July occurred what historically became known as the 'Great Fear' when, on a given day and hour, mysterious horsemen appeared in various towns and villages, terrorizing the population by announcing that armies of bandits were on the march and that foreign mercenaries were planning to invade the country and restore the King's lost power. In every province a systematic campaign of hate incited the people against the 'aristos', the peasants against their masters. Brissac was among the first to leave for Anjou, where a handful of agitators had brought terror to a hitherto peaceful province. Châteaux were being pillaged and destroyed, the owners pulled out of their beds and murdered in front of their children. There was no longer any central authority, for the King's administrators had abandoned their offices and the archives had been burnt.

Brissac had barely reached the town of Le Mans when he was arrested by a band of revolutionaries. They were found to be mistaken in his identity and he was allowed to proceed in peace. But it was already dangerous to have a great name like his, and Jeanne trembled for her lover, who still persisted in taking an optimistic view of the future. 'There are three or four people', he wrote, 'who disturb the peace that otherwise reigns in the neighbourhood. The calamitous fact of their existence has to be borne with patience, for liberty is too precious a thing to be sacrificed for a little ease. Whether we shall be any the better for it is perhaps doubtful. But at least we should be happier.'

This man, who had but lately escaped death, wrote of the celebrations held at Brissac in honour of his birthday: 'I felt my fellow citizens put their hearts into their demonstrations of affection.' He was anxious to help his country, but he appears to have been overlooked both by the ministers at Versailles and the deputies of the National Assembly, leaders such as the Abbé Siéyès and the Comte de Mirabeau, who had little use for the metaphysical meanderings of an elderly courtier.

By September even Brissac's enthusiasm for the new order was beginning to wane and one finds him writing, 'The future is as disheartening as the present. How many are the men with sufficient loyalty to agree to arrangements that are to the benefit of all? There are very few or else they are not heard or do not speak or do not even exist. What melancholy feelings do these reflections arouse. My only happiness lies in hearing of you and in thinking of you and of my sincere and eternal devotion to you.'

Jeanne was very lonely without her lover. A great number of her friends had already fled the country, many of whom still believed they would be back within a few weeks. Betsi, who had become her favourite companion, had gone with her children to join her husband at the military headquarters in Metz. Chon, from whom she had been inseparable at Versailles and who had run her household so efficiently, superintended her accounts and prevented her from being robbed by spoilt, lazy servants, was now living in Toulouse. Occasionally there was a letter from a du Barry, usually asking her for money. But she turned a deaf ear to their pleadings, for the chaotic state of the country was such that no taxes had been paid nor revenues collected and, like most of her class, Madame du Barry was suffering from a shortage of funds. This, however, did not prevent her from visiting the *Salon* and acquiring for her garden another group of statues by Caffièri or Lemoine. And while there was burning and pillaging all over the country, Jeanne and her lover were discussing the merits of a new painting by Vien – an old-fashioned allegory called *Love Fleeing from Slavery*, representing Cupid escaping from a cage opened by a woman.

It was one of the strange anomalies of those first months that a picture so insipid and typical of the *ancien régime* should have been shown at the *Salon* at a time when Paris was seething with new ideas, and in the National Assembly the Declaration of the Rights of Man, 'giving civil equality' to all, brought the King into direct opposition with his government and his people. Men like Brissac were still totally unaware of the spirit of hatred growing in the country, of which the liberal-minded Marquis de Ferrières wrote, 'The revolt against the nobility is widespread. Among the deputies are people who hate us without knowing why. Their hate is all the stronger and more active for having no definite cause. They do not stop to think that they will end in being the victims of the troubles they have provoked.'

It was said that the faces of many of those who were murdered showed surprise at the hatred they had inspired in peasants they had thought to be devoted.

It must have come as an unpleasant shock to Madame du Barry when, in September, an obscene pamphlet from the Palais Royal published the news that 'that infamous Messalina, widow of King Louis xv, wishes to sell half a dozen old horses for the sake of getting a new colt which the Prince de Beauvau has procured for her'. It had taken a revolution to make Jeanne Bécu of Vaucouleurs into one of the hated 'aristos'.

20

It was a misty October morning when Jeanne du Barry woke to the sound of a tremendous banging on the doors and the cries of her frightened servants. A maid came bursting into her room to tell her that there were two wounded men, officers of the Royal Guard, begging for admittance, that Versailles had been stormed by a mob of fishwives and the Queen had barely escaped assassination. Regardless of the risk of giving them asylum and the fear that Louveciennes might at any moment share the fate of Versailles, Jeanne immediately gave orders for the officers to be taken in and nursed. Without waiting to get dressed, she personally reassured them that they were to remain at Louveciennes as her honoured guests until they were completely cured'. This spontaneous generosity, which was later to earn her the grateful thanks of Marie Antoinette, was later to be judged at the revolutionary tribunals as the first of the many acts of treason which in the end would lead her to the guillotine.

Though Versailles was only a short distance from Louveciennes, Jeanne knew nothing of the events which in the last twenty-four hours had culminated in a banquet given in honour of the Flanders regiment brought in to reinforce the local garrisons. The banquet, which began in a friendly atmosphere with the various regiments, including the newly formed National Guard, joining in a loyal tribute to the royal family, had rapidly turned into an ovation, which the revolutionary press in Paris lost no time in transforming into an orgy in which the Queen was said to have distributed white cockades to the men and the tricolour to have been trampled underfoot. How much was truth, how much was propaganda? So little was needed to light the flames and to incite the crowds which in the past weeks had been rioting outside the bakeries for bread. There was no real shortage: enormous stores had been released by the government, sufficient to feed the population. But mysterious agents, many of them paid by

Orléanist gold, had sabotaged the supplies. In her well-stocked larders at Louveciennes even Madame du Barry was finding it difficult to find food for the local poor, and Brissac wrote to her from Anjou of his regret in not being able to send her some of the fine fruit which 'the Angevin Ceres' had given him that year. He added: 'It would be both difficult and imprudent of me to try to send them. The municipalities fear people who are dissatisfied with the necessities and want to share the superfluities of life.' That summer in France not even one of the richest men in the country dared to send as much as a hamper of fruit to his beloved mistress.

The duke was still at Brissac when the events of 6 October, the attack on Versailles, changed the whole course of their lives. The blood of the wounded guardsmen staining the marble floors of Louveciennes had turned Jeanne du Barry into a passionate royalist, bitterly opposed to the men of the new order and in particular the Orléanists. Many were said to have been implicated in the storming of the palace, and there were those who maintained that the Duc d'Orléans, the King's cousin, had even been seen directing the mob to the Queen's apartment. Others suspected Choderlos de Laclos of having been the master-mind who had organized the march on Versailles.

Loyal courtiers rallied round the King when he was forced to leave Versailles for Paris and the Tuileries, the vast dilapidated palace where no French king had resided since Louis xv had lived there as a boy. The Duc de Brissac was among those who, taking up his hereditary post as royal pantler, came to be with the King and Queen.

It was an unhappy autumn, when all efforts to maintain the illusion of a court could not prevent the royal family from feeling as if virtually in prison, subject to the continual intrusion of the Parisian populace camping in the gardens, singing and shouting obscenities. Brissac suffered from his enforced stay at the Tuileries as much as his royal masters. Confined to his bed with a bad cold, he wrote to Jeanne: 'Tomorrow I may be better company for you ... My cold is largely due to the stagnation of too long a stay in Paris to which I am far from accustomed. If I cannot move soon it will end in driving me to despair and killing me. Farewell, dear heart. I love and kiss you a thousand times with the deepest affection of our hearts – my heart, I should say – but I shall not scratch out what my pen has written, for I love to think that our hearts are forever one. Farewell till tomorrow.

I shall try to sweat and spit – what a pleasant prospect. The occupation is less disagreeable as things are at present, than if the weather were calm and consequently fine. All that happens is confusion and folly, and the wisest thing we can do is to be together. Farewell, sweet friend. Farewell, dear heart. I love you and embrace you.'

The King and Queen disapproved of Brissac's liaison and it was not through him that Marie Antoinette conveyed her thanks to the Comtesse du Barry for helping the two wounded officers of the Royal Guard. One of the countess's earliest biographers, Lafont d'Aussonne, published what purports to be her reply to the Queen but the style is too elegant for Jeanne, who in her reign at Versailles had all her correspondence dictated by Chon du Barry. She would neither have been capable nor would she have dared to write the following lines: 'The two wounded youths I helped only regret that they did not die with their comrades for a princess as perfect and as worthy of being honoured as Your Majesty. Louveciennes is yours Madame, for do I not owe my renewed possession solely to your good will and kindness? Influenced by some sort of presentiment, the late King compelled me to accept thousands of precious things before sending me away from him. Allow me, I implore, to render unto Caesar that which is Caesar's.' The wording of this letter may be largely apocryphal, but the sentiments are sincere. For barely a month later, in November 1789, Madame du Barry transacted the sale of her diamonds through her Paris bankers, Vandenyvers, which according to the receipts realized one hundred and thirty-three thousand *livres* – a sum reserved as part of a secret fund which was to help the royalist cause.

Letters from her brother-in-law du Barry importuning her for money remained unanswered; the dressmaking bills of Rose Bertin remained unpaid. But in Paris she rented three separate *pieds-à-terre*, where royalist meetings took place unknown to the police. Unfortunately no one was less suited to the part of a political conspirator. Letters were left open and drawers unlocked in a house full of untrustworthy servants, none more untrustworthy than Zamor who was now approaching thirty and had little to do except to stir up trouble, taking endless trips to Paris where he frequented the cafés of the Palais Royal picking up sinister acquaintances, foreign spies and agents, some of them English, paid by a government who had not forgiven France for the loss of her American colonies. Zamor boasted to his new friends of the days when the late King had created him governor of Louveciennes and custodian of its treasures. He spoke with bitterness of his ungrateful mistress who had forgotten these promises and treated him as the lowest of her servants. Some of these men may even have come to the village of Louveciennes, spreading their subversive doctrines among people who felt nothing but gratitude for their noble benefactress, but who now began to read seditious papers such as *L'Ami du Peuple* in which the venomous pen of Marat wrote that 'the National Assembly had spent for a whole year barely a quarter of what that old sinner Louis xv spent on the last and most expensive of his whores.'

It may have been at this time that a middle-aged Englishman by the name of George Grieve, claiming to be the friend of Marat and of Franklin, took lodgings at Louveciennes and began to take an interest in what was happening at the château. Grieve appears to have been one of those curious psychopaths who, eaten up by envy, flourish in revolutions. Of a respectable family from Newcastle, he had been educated at Eton and had literary tastes. He prided himself on being an iconoclast, bent on destroying what he regarded as the vicious depravity of the *ancien régime* – a depravity represented by the beautiful woman he saw driving out of the gates of her park, distributing her smiles on those whom she still believed to be her friends.

Jeanne du Barry refused to believe that her world was coming apart. Louis's return to his capital had brought a revival of his popularity. The average Parisian was glad to have his King living in his midst, and even the Queen was cheered when she appeared in the Tuileries gardens holding the little Dauphin by the hand. Many who, a year ago, had applauded the glorious revolution, now felt it had gone on for too long. The Orléanist bid for power had failed: Choderlos de Laclos had been unable to turn his weak and vacillating prince into a leader. Incriminated in the excesses committed at Versailles, accused of treachery by Lafayette, the King's cousin had been only too ready to save his face and accept a spurious mission for England where Laclos made a last attempt to intrigue with the opposition. But Philippe d'Orléans preferred to tour the English racecourses with his pretty young mistress rather than listen to the dangerous counsels of a man he had begun to fear. When he finally returned to France he was no more than another hated Bourbon prince with no future left to him other than the guillotine.

1790 saw the apotheosis of Lafayette and Mirabeau's eleventh-hour attempt to save the throne. Neither of them trusted the well-meaning idealism of a man like the Duc de Brissac any more than did the King and Queen, whom he continued to serve with a devotion which, as the months went by, became ever more disillusioned. Louveciennes was his only escape, the only place in which he found some measure of happiness. Food supplies were back to normal and there was still a great deal of entertaining among a nobility who preferred to risk their lives in Paris rather than embark on the discomforts of exile. Jeanne du Barry's cook still produced the best dinners in Paris, even if Marie Boisseson kept warning her that he was stealing some of her most precious porcelain, and courtiers who had turned their backs on her at Versailles were only too pleased to accept her invitations.

In the first months of 1791, when people were being murdered all over the country and hundreds of châteaux burnt down, the Duc de Brissac celebrated the feast of the Epiphany by holding a banquet in his town house in honour of Madame du Barry. It was on the day of 10 January, four days after the actual feast day, and the weather was so cold and wet that Brissac had persuaded Madame du Barry to spend the night with him in town. Though already approaching fifty, Jeanne was still as gay and frivolous as in her youth, ready to enjoy a party of which she would be the undisputed queen. Sparkling with diamonds, wearing a dress as extravagant as any she had ever worn at Versailles, she set out in her coach-and-four accompanied by two maids and a footman, leaving behind her faithful factotum Denis Morin and a handful of servants. There had been rumours of rowdy characters in the neighbourhood having threatened to kill the rare animals in her park, in particular a white deer she kept as a pet, and Madame du Barry had taken the precaution of asking the commandant of the Swiss Guards, stationed at Reuil, to allow one of his men to patrol her grounds. At the same time she had collected her silver and hidden it in one of the outhouses inhabited by a gardener. But no special precautions appear to have been taken in guarding her house, especially her bedroom, where later events were to prove that more than one person living there at the time was aware of an enormous amount of valuable jewellery she kept locked in an elaborate commode with bronze fittings, decorated with Sèvres medallions.

These included some magnificent diamonds she had recently been trying to sell abroad.

For the first time in many years, the Comtesse du Barry was hard up. Rents were not being paid and not even the generosity of the Duc de Brissac could prevent her from accumulating debts. She had even gone to the municipal authorities at Versailles to ask for a reduction of her taxes, which was hardly likely to gain a hearing when the applicant was known to be one of the richest women in the country. Later it was to be one of the accusations brought against her at the revolutionary tribunals.

On the morning of 11 January, Jeanne woke from a night of love to hear that thieves had broken into her house and got away with the greater part of her jewellery. Drowsy with sleep, she did not grasp the extent of the disaster till she returned to Louveciennes and found in her ransacked bedroom the broken commode, the empty drawers, with the smashed Sèvres medallions scattered on the floor. Overcome with grief she broke down and wept like a child.

Throughout her life her jewels had been the leitmotif of her existence, since the time when as a child of six Francesca had given her a little pearl bracelet to console her for being sent to a convent; since the time when her first lover, the infatuated young hairdresser, had ruined himself in buying golden ornaments for her hair. One after another her lovers had won her favours with diamonds. Every necklace held a memory, every pair of earrings recorded a triumph. On quiet evenings spent with her relatives at home she would amuse herself in dressing up her pretty little cousins in pearls and diamonds given her by the King. To see their velvet boxes now lying on the floor, the exquisite settings torn apart, was as if she herself had been violated by clumsy, brutal hands. The open window with the ladder left against the wall; the servant who had failed to carry out her orders to sleep in a room adjoining her bedroom; above all the defection of the Swiss Guard, who had been persuaded to leave his post and go and drink in the village – all added up to a combination of events which enabled a gang of thieves to carry out an audacious robbery without arousing the slightest suspicion in a house full of sleeping servants. Morin, who had his own house in the grounds, knew nothing till the following morning at seven o'clock, when a farmhand saw a ladder stolen from a field propped up against the wall of the countess's bedroom.

After inspecting the bedroom and ascertaining the extent of the robbery, Morin immediately sent a message to the Hôtel de Brissac and got in touch with the local authorities both at Versailles and Louveciennes. In spite of a growing antagonism against the nobility, Madame du Barry was still a sufficiently important person in the neighbourhood to command the services of the head of the gendarmerie and the leading officers of the municipality, while the Duc de Brissac, who shared in her distress and regarded himself as responsible in having persuaded her to come to Paris for the night, was prepared to pay for all the expenses. The celebrated court jeweller Jean Joseph Rouen, of whom Madame du Barry was the most profitable client and who was familiar with the weight and value of every stone he had set for her over the years, was called upon to make a detailed account of the stolen jewellery which was to be published in all the leading towns of France, offering a reward of two thousand *louis* for the return of the whole amount and a reasonable percentage for whatever was recovered.

The notice, which ran to several pages and dwelt in detail on the rarity and beauty of the gems – the *parures* of diamonds, the ropes of pearls, the jewel cases containing twenty-five rings of emeralds, sapphires and rubies, the numberless objects in crystal, gold and lapis lazuli – was hardly a document to appear at a time when sensible people were doing their best to remain as inconspicuous as possible. Rouen, who was a master craftsman with an intense love for his art, had no idea of the effect this list would have on the inflammatory passions of the day. Neither Jeanne nor her lover, who was as honest as he was stupid, realized the bitterness and envy such an advertisement would produce in revealing the details of the fantastic wealth amassed by a royal mistress. Jeanne du Barry was once more attacked in venomous articles describing her as 'the infamous prostitute of a lecherous old monarch'. The revolutionary journals took up the cause of Badoux, the young Swiss guardsman 'guilty of no other crime than a certain negligence, who on Madame du Barry's orders had been put in chains and thrown into prison'. There were those who maintained that the whole story of the robbery was fictitious, deliberately invented by the countess to solicit sympathy from the authorities and receive some reduction in her taxes. This was later repeated at the revolutionary tribunal both by George Grieve and his associate, the despicable Zamor, who may well have played a part in a robbery so audacious that it can only have been carried out with inside help.

Gangs of thieves flourished in those first years of revolution, when the constant riots and pillaging of shops enabled them to scavenge among the ruins. Many of these men were foreign Jews, operating as itinerant tradesmen in the populous district of St Martin. But someone with a special knowledge of Louveciennes, its treasures and the habits of its owner must have brought robbers to break into Madame du Barry's château on that cold and windy night in early January, when she was known to be in Paris.

It was only a month later, on 15 February, when Jeanne was beginning to despair of ever retrieving her jewels, that she received a letter from London telling her that three foreigners and a Frenchman, all of them Jewish, had been found in possession of what appeared to be her stolen jewellery, and that her presence in London was necessary for purposes of identification. The letter was signed by Nathaniel Parker Forth, a mysterious Irishman who in the past years had travelled often across the Channel dealing in horses, politics and pictures, trusted and distrusted in turn by ministers, princes and ambassadors, and probably known to Madame du Barry when he was buying horses for Henry Seymour.

21

Nathaniel Parker Forth was one of the many Irishmen who, in the time of the penal laws against Roman Catholics, migrated to the Continent. Born of a landowning family in County Longford, with little money but good connections, he started his career in studying law at the Irish Bar, for which he was temperamentally unsuited. At the age of twenty he was already wandering round Europe, where like so many of his countrymen he ended up settling in Paris, dealing in carriages and horses. This and his brilliant horsemanship brought him into contact with the wealthy young nobility who were passionately interested in hunting and racing, of whom the leaders were the King's youngest brother, the Comte d'Artois, and his cousin, the immensely rich Duc de Chartres. The duke's anglomania was such that his estate at Raincy was described as being practically an English colony, with English servants, gamekeepers, coachmen and grooms as well as an English huntsman with a pack of hounds. When in 1776 the first horse race on English lines was run in the Bois de Boulogne, Lord Forbes and Nathaniel Forth, both of them from County Longford, won the first two races.

From now on the young Irishman lived in a world beyond his early aspirations. Brilliant, impudent and witty, he became the general factotum and intimate of the Duc de Chartres, who found Forth invaluable in supplying him with English dogs, horses and mezzotints. This relationship with a Prince of the Blood first brought Forth to the notice of the British ambassador, Lord Stormont, at a time when the British government was anxious to know to what extent the French were secretly helping the American colonists. Meanwhile the French minister Comte de Maurepas was finding this gregarious young Irishman with his excellent French to be a very useful go-between in unofficial talks with the British ambassador, where suggestions could be made on both sides without previously consulting their respective governments. It was at Maurepas's request that Forth was appointed as a special envoy to the court of Versailles, with a commission signed by Lord North and two secretaries of state, giving him a thousand pounds a year for his expenses.

Right up to the declaration of war and even after, Forth continued to act as agent for his government, though never entirely trusted either by King George III or his minister Lord North. In France, where his reputation was far higher than in England, people would have been surprised to know how little he was paid. Fortunately he had a generous and wealthy patron in the Duc de Chartres, who in the middle of the war asked him to carry out the strangest of commissions, to find him a little English girl, preferably a foundling, to be educated with his children. The idea had originated with their governess, the Comtesse de Genlis, a former mistress of the duke, who had stipulated that the child had to be pretty, speak no French and have no relations to claim her back. This may not have been as difficult as it first appeared for, according to rumour, the 'charming little creature' whose arrival sent the duke into 'transports of joy' was none other than his bastard by Madame de Genlis. Chartres's gratitude was such that from now onwards Forth gained not only a patron but a friend. In 1785, when Chartres succeeded his father as Duc d'Orléans and became one of the wealthiest men in Europe, Forth was living rent free in his London mansion in Portland Place and was his inseparable companion on English racecourses. The portrait the duke had painted by Reynolds as a gift for the Prince of Wales was presented to the prince by Forth, who as an *habitué* of the Carlton House set did a brisk trade in commissions on the nine hundred bottles of champagne given him to sell by his friend the Marquis de Sillery.

By the beginning of 1790 Forth had prospered to such an extent that, when Madame du Barry's stolen jewels were discovered in London, he was living with a wife and family in an elegant house in the fashionable quarter of Manchester Square, and had become a justice of the peace for the county of Westminster with sufficient capital to figure on the board of the newly-formed insurance company known as the Westminster Society. But for all his outward respectability he was still very much the Irish adventurer at heart, ready to become involved in any business which might be both lucrative and exciting.

Nathaniel Forth had come into Madame du Barry's life at the

beginning of 1780, before her finances had been settled by the generosity of Calonne or she had acquired a wealthy lover in Brissac, and
had returned to Louveciennes to find a mountain of debts and a two
hundred thousand-*livre* loan from d'Aiguillon still unpaid. Forth must
have been a friend of Henry Seymour, frequenting the same horse
racing world and recommended to Madame du Barry as someone
who, through his connections with the Duc de Chartres and the Carlton
House set, could be helpful in negotiating the sale of some of her
jewels in England, without attracting too much publicity in France.
At that time Forth had been supplied with the exact list of the jewels
for sale, giving the weight and size of every stone. But the London
jewellers found that Madame du Barry demanded too high a price,
and her diamonds remained unsold.

As Brissac's mistress, the countess could afford to keep her jewels.
But ten years later, when the five men who had carried out the robbery
at Louveciennes arrived in London with the booty they had not dared
to sell in France, they made the fatal mistake of approaching one
of the few honest jewellers in the city, Baron Lyon de Symons, the
great diamond merchant, who by chance had seen in a coffee house
a notice circulated by the French embassy concerning the robbery
at Louveciennes. Ten years before, a certain Mr Forth, acting as agent
for the Comtesse du Barry, had offered to sell him some of her
diamonds, and no sooner was de Symons shown the stolen jewellery
by Levet, the leader of the gang, who posed as a French marquis
emigrating abroad, than he suspected that he and his companions
were thieves and that the diamonds were part of the collection he
had been shown by Forth. Being a timid man who did not want to
commit himself before he was sure of his facts, de Symons got in
touch with his lawyer and, acting on his advice, paid Levet £1,500
in part payment for the gems, which was one-sixth of their value,
on condition he was shown the others in Levet's possession. He then
wrote to Mr Forth addressing him as an agent of the said Comtesse
du Barry, telling him he believed he had discovered her jewels and
asking to be indemnified for the money he had paid out. Forth, who
knew nothing of the robbery, refused to pay the money but nevertheless
produced the catalogue made in 1780, in which the weights and value
of every stone tallied with those in de Symon's possession. Seeing
that neither the jeweller nor his lawyer would ever have the courage

to denounce the thieves, he himself wrote to a friend at the French embassy asking for any detail they might have on a recent robbery committed at the Comtesse du Barry's château of Louveciennes.

But in 1791 the French ambassador, the Marquis de la Luzerne, had sufficient difficulties without involving himself in the matter of the Comtesse du Barry's jewellery. Nor had he a very high opinion of that 'firebrand' Forth, whose patron the Duc d'Orléans was by now discredited both in England and in France. A secretary was sent to Manchester Square to tell Forth in person that the ambassador had no further information to give on a matter which was none of his concern. Forth, however, had sufficient self-confidence to act on his own. Taking advantage of his position as justice of the peace, he had Levet and his companions arrested and thrown into Newgate, an ill-considered action which was later to complicate the case by giving the thieves the opportunity of suing for unjust imprisonment.

In a letter to Madame du Barry, recalling their former friendship, Forth now offered to act on her behalf in an affair which he regarded as practically settled. The thieves were under lock and key; her jewels were safe, and all that was needed was for her to come to England to identify her property. His eagerness to act as her agent makes one suspect that there may have been some other reason in wishing to cooperate in a case which would entail several journeys across the Channel. It lends an element of truth to the accusations brought against Madame du Barry at the revolutionary tribunals when she was denounced as having acted as a royalist conspirator with 'the Machiavellian' Nathaniel Forth, the notorious English spy.

The countess was overcome with joy to hear of the recovery of her jewels, and she never hesitated at the prospect of a journey which, given the unsettled state of the country, would have filled most women of her age with nervous apprehension. Brissac, who was unable to leave the Tuileries, feared for her safety and insisted on her being accompanied by his aide-de-camp, a chivalrous but not very sensible idea as the Chevalier d'Escourre was elderly, had never travelled abroad and did not speak a word of English. With characteristic generosity, Brissac insisted on paying the expenses of the journey and, at a time when the expropriation of Church property had brought a fresh exodus of priests and 'aristos', Jeanne du Barry, with no other thought than the recovery of her jewels, set out in her luxurious coach escorted by four servants, Brissac's aide-de-camp and her jeweller to identify the jewels.

Nathaniel Forth was waiting for her at Boulogne, exuding a self-confidence and charm which filled her with optimism. After crossing the Channel on the night of 19 February, they arrived in London and went to Greniers Hotel in Jermyn Street, kept by a former chef of the Duc d'Orléans and renowned for its cuisine. Greniers was the first port of call for all French refugees, but most could not afford the prices and left after a few days.

In comparison to the riots and discomforts of Paris, Jeanne found London wonderfully peaceful and prosperous, and the blue-eyed Irishman with his gaiety and exuberance was the perfect companion with whom to go sightseeing and shopping in between the sessions with bankers and lawyers. To begin with everything went smoothly. Madame du Barry, Forth, the English and French jewellers, together with their respective lawyers, met at the Pall Mall offices of Ransom, Morland & Hammersley, the highly respected bankers where the jewels had been deposited. Rouen had no difficulty in identifying the diamonds as being the property of the Comtesse du Barry, and Jeanne expressed her thanks to the English jeweller who told Forth he would not accept any compensation or reward and only hoped the countess would be his client at some future date.

A few days later, on 24 February, a further meeting took place in the presence of Sir John Boydell, lord mayor of London and a famous printer and engraver who, at a time when English mezzotints were the fashion, had amassed a large fortune exporting them abroad. Here again Rouen was asked to identify the jewels, and after swearing on oath that the diamonds were her property Madame du Barry was confronted with the five thieves, brought in from Newgate to be cross-examined. The Englishman Joseph Harris, alias Abraham, was the only one who made a full confession, naming his accomplices in France. Levet, however, continued to maintain he had bought the jewels in all good faith in plying his trade as an honest broker. The meeting ended with all five men being committed to trial for felony, and Madame du Barry was bound over to prosecute.

There was nothing more to be done than to await the opening of the spring sessions, and after a banquet given for her and her party by the lord mayor, and a few mornings devoted to shopping where

Jeanne, with characteristic extravagance, acquired two carriage horses for her stable, she left for France still without her jewels. In March she was back at Louveciennes, delighted to be in her lovely home, where the spring flowers were just coming into bloom and Brissac, who had been miserable without her, welcomed her with the ardour of a young man in love for the first time.

In gratitude to Forth, the duke invited the Irishman to stay at his house in the rue de Grenelle. This was immediately noted by a revolutionary spy called Blache, who unknown to Madame du Barry had been shadowing her in London for the past month, and had reported to Paris that the Englishman Nathaniel Forth never left her side and accompanied her on her visits to Madame de Calonne, 'the wife of a former minister of Louis XVI', who acted as the unofficial representative of the French government in exile.

There can be little doubt that Forth was an agent spying in France on behalf of the British government and assisting French royalists in escaping from the country. Madame du Barry and her jewels were a useful cover for underground activities, and from now on her subsequent visits to London involved her ever more in the lives of the émigrés.

The political situation in France was rapidly deteriorating. The decree which forced priests and bishops to become salaried officials of the state had resulted in serious disturbances. The departure of the King's old aunts, who set out for exile in the middle of winter rather than submit to the new laws, would have resulted in their arrest had it not been for a brilliant defence by Mirabeau, who ridiculed his colleagues in the Assembly for trying to arrest two useless old women. A few days later a mob attacked the Tuileries after a rumour had gone round that the King and Queen were contemplating flight, and every day their position was becoming more untenable. Even beautiful and peaceful Louveciennes was changing. The place seemed sad and empty with Boisseson having gone to fight in Condé's army, taking with him his wife and children. Such friends who still came were full of fears for the future. But Jeanne still kept up her old way of life, and a week after her return visited a warehouse in the rue St Honoré, where she already owed a lot of money, and bought a large bronze equestrian statue of King Henry IV which cost her over a thousand *livres* and which, like so many of her other bills, was never paid. She had always had her whims and fantasies satisfied by her lovers and as yet could not envisage a holocaust which would destroy the greatest fortunes in France.

In the following month she was back in England, so confident that her affairs would soon be settled that she only applied for a passport for three weeks. In these circumstances it is strange that Nathaniel Forth should have rented her a house for what was supposed to be a short visit and that she should have applied for an unlimited amount of money to be placed in her account in a London bank.

Everything on this journey conspired against her. A stormy passage kept her over twelve hours at sea. She arrived in London early in the morning of 8 April, feeling so ill that she was confined to her bed for several days. On attending the first session at the Old Bailey, she heard the unpleasant news that a criminal could not be tried in England for a felony committed in France, a fact which Forth, who had been trained at the Irish Bar, should have already known. All of the thieves, with the exception of the Englishman Harris (alias Abraham), who had made a full confession, were released. And the leader, the Frenchman Levet, who had always persisted in his role as an honest broker, now had the temerity to bring an action against de Symons and Forth, claiming the money the English diamond merchant had promised for the jewels and suing the latter for unjust imprisonment.

From now on the story of Madame du Barry's jewellery becomes ever more involved. How was it that an apparently penniless thief, with no connections in England other than Harris and his brother, a second-hand iron dealer in Petticoat Lane, could find the money to embark on an expensive course of litigation? Was there some connection between the thieves and the sinister Grieve, with his passion for Louveciennes and his insane hatred of Madame du Barry? We know Grieve to have been in correspondence with Blache, the Frenchman who spied on Jeanne while she was in London, and later gave him the information which was to send her to the guillotine. Either of these men may well have supplied Levet with sufficient funds for a long and expensive litigation. But by the summer of 1791 her jewels were no longer Madame du Barry's principal preoccupation. When she returned to Louveciennes on 21 May the diamonds were still deposited in a London bank. But the courier who forty-eight hours later woke her in the middle of the night to tell her that her presence was urgently needed in London brought letters which had nothing to do with her jewels. The royal family was planning to escape and was desperately short of funds. England, the former enemy who had never forgiven King Louis the loss of her American colonies, was the only country which could help.

22

Jeanne du Barry was no conspirator by nature. If she allowed herself to be carried away in a vortex of royalist intrigue it was probably out of the compassion and pity she felt for those pathetic exiles she had known in the days of their glory at Versailles. Though all her sympathies were for the King and Queen, she took no side in the quarrels between the various factions, some of which supported the Queen and the others the Comte d'Artois, whose bellicose declarations from the safety of his father-in-law's court at Turin were as dangerous to the 'prisoners of the Tuileries' as the threats of the Jacobins. Her friendship with Madame de Calonne, encouraged by Forth for his own purposes, was probably for no other reason than that her husband had befriended her in the past. And she never stopped to think that this friendship was as suspect to the court of the Tuileries, who detested Calonne, as to the French embassy in London.

Never did Jeanne du Barry show herself as shallow and as intrinsically frivolous as on this third visit to London. Nathaniel Forth still directed her movements but made little headway in settling her case, and she was beginning to find the processes of English law to be both cumbersome and expensive. In the courts she had to face an action brought by Baron Lyon de Symons who, in fear of being sued by Levet, now claimed the two thousand *louis* she had offered as recompense on recovering the jewels, which were still under seal in a bank. It was a difficult situation to understand for a woman who had lived in a world where everything could be arranged providing one had the right connections. Acting on Forth's advice she sought help in England by resurrecting old friends from the past, one of whom was the powerful Duke of Queensberry whom she had known as the 'wild Lord March' when he was an *habitué* of the '*roué*''s card parties in the rue Jussienne. Through him she was introduced to the Prince of Wales, who was curious to meet the notorious Madame du Barry.

At Queensberry House she also met Sir Horace Walpole who remembered her from the days when she appeared for the first time in the royal chapel at Versailles. Before long the countess had become one of the attractions of the London season. She was painted by Cosgrave; of which only an engraving still exists. Looking at it one finds it hard to believe that this is the face of a woman who is nearing fifty. She appears so young, so free of care. The blonde curls are powdered to hide the streaks of grey, the full white throat with its rope of pink pearls is still unlined; the half-closed eyes, the famous *'yeux en coulisses'*, are still provoking, teasing, encouraging love; the charming mouth is still ready to be kissed. It is the portrait of a woman who has always been adored and has never been refused. She could not understand that those delightful Englishmen so full of flattering attentions would not raise a hand to help her in her difficulties. Lord Hawkesbury, a rising politician and future prime minister, gallantly offered to be of assistance, but warned her 'that the laws of his country forbade any judge, even the Lord Chancellor himself, to interfere in the actual course of a trial'.

Her case was finally to come up at the Old Bailey towards the end of July, to be tried by the Lord Chancellor and a jury of City men. Meanwhile, she consoled herself by indulging in social life, giving card parties and dinners at her house in Margaret Street, where many a courtier who had snubbed her at Versailles was only too glad to partake of her exquisite food, and malicious and witty Frenchwomen delighted in making fun of their English hosts. She made friends with the beautiful Mrs Hobart, who had known Adolphe du Barry in the gambling rooms of Bath, and was a frequent guest at her villa on Ham Common. The news from France, which became ever more alarming, did not prevent her from dining and dancing at Ranelagh and Vauxhall. And while many of her compatriots were selling their last jewels, she herself was never short of funds, thanks to the liberality of her Dutch bankers, Vandenyvers, who advanced her money on the rents she still received in France. The more depressing the news, the more she sought consolation in shopping, acquiring rare plants for the gardens and hothouses of Louveciennes, a fine set of Shakespeare printed by Sir John Boydell and a portrait of the Prince of Wales. And though the laws against the *émigrés* were already in force, she seems to have had no difficulty in getting the goods shipped back to France. What she bought for herself was only a fraction of what she gave away in charity to people who in the old days had never been her friends, but to whom she now gave generously and unquestioningly. No account was made of these sums, but it may be one of the reasons why in 1795, two years after her death, the sale of her legendary diamonds at Christie's realized barely a third of the amount recorded in the catalogue made in 1780 by Nathaniel Forth.

The delays in the London courts were becoming ever more tedious and expensive and she was homesick for Louveciennes and her lover who, after the disaster of the flight of the royal family to Varennes, had lost the last of his illusions and all hope in the future. With unconscious egotism she still counted on Brissac, who was living in unhappy conditions at the Tuileries, to carry out the smallest of her wishes. Writing to her steward at the beginning of July, she tells him to ask the duke's advice 'about putting her valuables in safety', but to do it carefully so that no one will suspect it. In another letter she informs him that 'Monsieur de Brissac is sending the money to pay off my outstanding debts', and that he will procure a passport for a maid who is to join me in London. Though she herself is only staying there till August, she gives a long list of what the maid is to bring, which includes 'several bottles of essence of orange flower and cherry blossom, and some of the pots of preserves made last year if any is left' – all of which were no doubt intended as gifts for English friends.

Her world might be falling apart, but she still clung to her old way of life. Her interests still centred round her garden, her *potager*, the products of her still room, her presents for her friends. She was still the simple, warm-hearted peasant woman, the granddaughter of a handsome *rôtisseur*, and it was this combination of simplicity and sophistication, of total immorality and unquestioning generosity, which rendered her so irresistible to a man like Brissac, whose passionate attachment to this woman of the people made him distrusted both by the King and his entourage. In planning their ill-starred flight to the frontier, neither Louis nor Marie Antoinette had taken the duke into their confidence, 'as it was impossible to confide in a man who told everything to La du Barry'. But after the humiliating return from Varennes when they were mocked and insulted by the Parisian crowds, Brissac was one of the few waiting on the steps of the Tuileries to pay homage to his King who, fat and sweaty, covered in dust and disguised as a steward, had lost the charisma which might have saved him his throne.

Two months later Madame du Barry, escorted as always by the ubiquitous Nathaniel Forth, returned from England still without her jewels. In August the London courts had finally come to the decision that 'since the theft had not taken place on British soil, it would be necessary to obtain the condemnations of the thieves from the French courts together with an official declaration that the property belonged to the Countess du Barry'. During her absence the Tribunal Criminel, one of the new courts established since the Revolution, had been making every effort to bring the thieves to justice. But the ringleaders had fled the country, leaving only their wives and accomplices to be placed under arrest, and they had ultimately to be released for lack of evidence. The Swiss Guard who had neglected to carry out his duties had been handed over to be disciplined by his regiment and finally acquitted, and in the end the Englishman Harris (alias Abraham), who had been committed for perjury, was the only one of the thieves to be left in jail. It was not a very satisfactory outcome for Madame du Barry but, by the summer of 1791, the state of France was such that she may have preferred to know that her jewels were safely deposited in a London bank.

Forth's presence in France was required so that he could appear at the Tribunal to furnish documents of the various proceedings in the English courts. But it was unwise of Madame du Barry and of the Duc de Brissac to be seen so much in the company of a notorious English spy. Paris was no longer a place where the privileged were immune. Republican feeling was growing day by day. Lafayette, who had been the idol of the masses, lost his popularity overnight when his cavalry broke up a demonstration in the Champs de Mars which called for the abolition of royalty. But for the moment he was still in power, one of the so-called 'triumvirate', of whom the other three, Adrien Duport, Antoine Barnave and Alexandre Lameth, were all men who had hitherto detested one another, but had come together in an uneasy alliance to support a constitution which they believed to be the remedy for all evils. As the constitution required a King, Louis was to be pardoned for the part he had played in the flight to Varennes where, as the victim of a royalist plot, he had been abducted against his will. General Bouillé, who had waited for him in vain at the frontier, and was now safely in Brussels, encouraged this story by writing to the Assembly, taking upon himself the full blame for the expedition.

The King was led to understand that his future depended on his acceptance of the constitution, which from the beginning he knew to be unworkable. A civil list of twenty-five million *livres* was allotted to maintain the semblance of a court. But only a few as disinterested as the foreign minister, the Marquis de Montmorin, and as loyal as the Duc de Brissac took up their appointments. Louis, who was too sunk in despondency and too apathetic to make the slightest effort, told Brissac, 'We are resolved to do nothing for the time being and to remain quiet until our people have come to their senses and put us back in our place. And we desire that the nobility should do the same.' To which Brissac replied, 'Sire, it is all very well for you who have twenty-five million *livres* for your civil list. But we nobles, who have nothing any more, who have lost everything and sacrificed everything to serve you, are faced with only two alternatives, either to join your enemies and depose you or go to war and die on the field of honour. And Your Majesty, if he believes in us, knows that is what we will do.' Now at the eleventh hour, the King was made to realize that the man he had distrusted as the friend of Madame du Barry was the most loyal of all his courtiers.

Jeanne returned to France to find her lover sadly changed. His bearing was still as proud and upright as ever, but the kind blue eyes were faded and the face was that of a man who had lost all hope and who carried on with his duties because, to quote his own words, 'he owed it to his ancestors and the ancestors of his King'. The only happiness he knew was at Louveciennes, where Jeanne kept up the even tenor of life as it was led under the old regime, and where friends came from far and wide to have news of the relatives she had seen in London. Madame du Barry's pavilion had become the centre of royalist activities, where Zamor, dressed in his handsome uniforms, still served the coffee, listening and spying on every word. Despite the growing power of the Jacobins in the Assembly, the Republican demonstration in the Champs de Mars, she continued to hold her charming dinner parties where the conversation was as witty as ever and elegant women still wore the latest creations of Rose Bertin, who had opened a branch of her dressmaking establishment in London.

A letter from Brissac, written in the Tuileries, refers to one of these dinners. It is a pathetic, banal little note written by an unhappy man still trying to pretend that life was normal. 'I am without my glasses, so I will write you only one thing, which covers all: I love you and will love you all my life, however much envious old people may criticize. Tomorrow I will come to dine, bringing with me Madame de Bainville and the Abbé Billiardi. Today I rode eight leagues with the King, who shot three pheasants ... I love you and embrace you with all my heart ... I have just made a blot on the paper for which I beg your pardon.'

The King's acceptance of the constitution momentarily relieved the tension. The restrictions were lifted from the Tuileries, the gardens were again opened, and the majority in the Assembly voted for the restoration of royal authority and a general amnesty which included the release of all those who had been implicated in the King's flight. The King and Queen appeared again in public, and for the first time in many months Marie Antoinette heard again the cheers of '*Vive la Reine!*' While she drove out with her children to Meudon and St Cloud, the King roused himself from his apathy to go shooting in the Bois de Boulogne. Royalists, who in the past months had not dared to show their faces, appeared again at court and Sunday mass in the royal chapel was as crowded as before.

In characteristic fashion Madame du Barry celebrated this wave of euphoria by acquiring for her garden a large marble group by the sculptor Allegrain. It was entitled *Beauty Disarming Love*, one of her favourite subjects, but singularly unsuited to the times, for the optimism of those weeks was short-lived. Neither Louis nor Marie Antoinette had any faith in the constitution, and the few aristocrats left in the Assembly did nothing to help their unfortunate sovereign. They were so bitterly opposed to the constitutionalists who had robbed them of their privileges that they were more ready to side with their enemies than with 'renegades of their class' like Narbonne and Lafayette. Abstaining from voting, they left the field free for the triumph of the left-wing Girondins who were in control of the new Assembly. When the King arrived to take the oath he found himself seated in an armchair in a line with that of the president. When he stood up to speak all the deputies remained seated, and neither the applause nor cheers which greeted his words could compensate for what he regarded as a public humiliation – the denial of his divine right to rule by putting him on the same level as the bourgeois president.

The constitution was completed, with many radical changes made in the administrative and judicial institutions. But the royal army was allowed to remain intact, with the exception of the King's military household which was replaced by what was known as a constitutional guard chosen by the King and paid out of his civil list. He chose as commander-in-chief the Duc de Brissac, whose loyalty he had been so slow to recognize and who now accepted the post not as an honour but as the last duty he could perform for the monarchy. It was a fatal choice, for the officers chosen by Brissac were all aristocrats and counter-revolutionaries. He was even foolish enough to allow Madame du Barry to interfere in recommending some of the sons of her old friends, and for a few weeks Jeanne revelled in a position she had not enjoyed since her days at Versailles. But before long there were complaints from Republicans in the infantry regiment that the cavalry was too devoted to the King and 'that La du Barry was given the task of sounding the opinions of those who were admitted in the ranks'. There were futile arguments over the colour of the uniforms, and Brissac's appointment became anathema to the members of the legislative assembly, and in particular to the foreign minister, General Dumouriez, and to the minister of war, the Comte de Narbonne.

The spring of 1792 brought a series of disasters. The French monarchy lost the bravest and most ardent of its allies when Gustavus III of Sweden was assassinated in the middle of a masked ball. In Paris his murderer was acclaimed as another Brutus and publicly cheered outside the windows of the Tuileries. In that same spring the Queen's younger brother Leopold, who had succeeded the Emperor Joseph II, died after a year's illness in which most of his energies had been devoted to stamping out rebellion in his empire. Pacifist by nature, he was the cleverest of all the Habsburgs and might have been able to save his sister and brother-in-law had it not been for the disaster of Varennes. But once Louis was prisoner in the Tuileries Leopold preferred to accept him as constitutional King of France rather than to mobilize his forces in a war he could ill afford. Leopold's son Francis, with none of his father's brilliance and very little interest in an aunt he had never seen, was nevertheless of a far more bellicose disposition and was ready for a conflict which was wanted by all parties in France. King Louis, who had tried to resist to the end, had finally to give in to this growing war fever, and on 29 April 1792, in a sad little speech vociferously cheered by all members of the Assembly, he declared war on the Queen's nephew.

Hatred against the Austrian Queen rose with the news of the first military defeats. The constitutional guard came under attack from left-wing deputies, and barely a month later was disbanded and the commander-in-chief, the Duc de Brissac, accused of treason and summoned to appear before the high court at Orléans.

It was one o'clock in the morning when the young Duc de Choiseul, who was on duty in the palace, brought the news to the King and Queen who were in bed. Prisoners themselves, they were powerless to defend the man they had chosen for his loyalty. All they could do was to send Choiseul to the duke's room, proposing to him the means of flight in the few hours of liberty he had left. 'I gave him their message,' wrote Choiseul, 'and warned him he would be notified of his arrest within a few hours, and begged him to take advantage of the time that was left. His age and confidence in his innocence prevented him from accepting; the only thing he did was to write a long letter to Madame du Barry.'

23

Brissac's last message from the Tuileries was destroyed in a holocaust of papers by a frightened woman in fear of her persecutors. But one senses some of her anguish when she first heard the news of his arrest and wrote a letter which never reached him and was later found at Louveciennes and used against her at the revolutionary tribunal. She must have felt that this note might fall into alien hands, for it is not so much a love letter as a defence of a man who meant everything in the world to her, and who till now had never been in need of defence.

'I was seized with mortal terror, Monsieur le Duc, when Monsieur de Maussabré was announced. He assured me that you were well and were calm with the tranquillity that comes from a good conscience. But that cannot satisfy me ... Why am I not near you? I should endeavour to console you with my faithful, tender love. I know you have nothing to fear if only the Assembly is governed by reason and good faith ... I am certain you have not transgressed in any way in forming the King's guard, so that I fear nothing for you from that side. Your conduct has been so blameless at the Tuileries that you can be accused of nothing. Indeed your patriotic actions have been so many that I cannot see what they can find to attack.'

In writing this letter, she realized that for the first time in her life she was alone, that the kindest and most chivalrous of men would no longer be able to protect her. Even the journey to Orléans was fraught with danger, for one of the most sinister aspects of the Revolution was the murderous gangs, many of them led by foreign criminals, the most notorious of whom was known as Fournier l'Américain, who attacked and robbed convoys of prisoners and whom the National Guard were powerless to protect. But two days later, on 3 June, his aide-de-camp brought a message that the duke had arrived safely in Orléans without encountering the slightest incident. Imprisoned in an old convent with fifty others, including Lessart the former foreign minister, who in the previous year had given Madame du Barry her first passport to England, Brissac was to remain in Orléans for two months before being put on trial. The prisoners' quarters were reasonably comfortable, though the duke had now to content himself with one servant. Calm in the confidence of his innocence, he made no attempt to prepare his defence, and spent his days in studying geography and in organizing recreations for his fellow prisoners, turning a disused refectory into a court for shuttlecock.

For the second time in her life Jeanne du Barry displayed a heroism for which history has never given her credit. At the time of the old King's death she had risked her beauty and her youth in remaining by his sickbed, breathing the pestilential air and stroking his forehead ravaged by smallpox. Now she summoned the courage to identify herself with a lover accused of high treason, undertaking the journey to Orléans, travelling along roads infested by bandits, through hostile villages, where at any time the sight of a private coach might arouse a cry of '*A bas les aristos!*' Like any other visitor, she had to wait at the convent gates for her permit to be examined, while her frightened coachman opened up the parcels she had been allowed to bring, clean linen, jars of preserves, fruits from her orchard, the simple gifts that any prisoner's wife might bring and for which Brissac was pathetically grateful. Some say she took a large sum of money with which to bribe the jailors and enable him to escape, but this is unlikely for she would have known he would only have said that a 'Brissac does not run away'.

Orléans was peaceful in comparison to Paris, where the bad news from the front brought a renewal of mob violence. Back at Louveciennes Madame du Barry trembled for her lover, who remained in prison through the months of June and July, when the growing power of the Commune and the emergence of the sansculottes inaugurated the blood bath of the reign of terror. On 20 June an attack on the Tuileries was repulsed thanks to the bravery of the royal family, the courage of the defenders and a spirited speech made in the Assembly by Lafayette in support of the monarchy he had been among the first to attack. But, left in their vandalized palace, both the King and Queen must have realized that 20 June was only a dress rehearsal for what was still to come. The disastrous effect of the Duke of Brunswick's ill-fated manifesto, in which the commander-in-chief of the Prussian and Austrian armies fighting on behalf of the royalist cause called on all Frenchmen to lay down their arms in support of their rightful King or have their homes razed to the ground, united the whole country in a blaze of patriotism and an outburst of fury against the foreign Queen. The tenth of August saw the destruction of the Tuileries, the massacre of the Swiss Guards and the royal family forced to put themselves under the protection of the legislative assembly.

No sooner had he heard the news than Brissac knew that he was doomed. That same night he dictated his last will and testament, appointing his daughter, the Duchesse de Mortemart, to be his residuary legatee and adding a codicil in which he recommended to her 'a person very dear to him, who might be placed in a situation of the greatest distress by the upheaval of the times'. To Madame du Barry of Louveciennes he left a yearly income of twenty-four thousand *livres* or, should she prefer it, the full sum of three hundred thousand *livres* in cash. What is particularly touching about this legacy is that he begs a woman who had never been known to refuse a gift of money to accept 'this small token of his gratitude', while his daughter is requested 'to prevail upon her to accept it'. And he adds that it is his express wish that 'no other legacy should be paid out until this one is discharged in full'.

Having completed his will, Brissac wrote one of his last letters to Madame du Barry. It is a simple, heartfelt letter in which, in spite of his limited vocabulary, he manages to convey his overwhelming love for the woman who had filled his life from the day when he first saw her, ravishing and unattainable, as the royal mistress at Versailles.

'I have received this morning the dearest of letters and one which made me happier than I have felt for a long time. I kiss you a thousand times, and you will be my last thought. Oh, my dearest heart, why can't I be alone with you in a desert? But I am only in Orléans, where it is most unpleasant to be. I embrace you a thousand, thousand times. Farewell, dear heart. So far the town is quiet.'

But neither Paris nor Louveciennes was quiet. Bands of assassins were roaming the countryside in search of those who had escaped the massacre of the Tuileries. '*Têtes à prix*' ('a price on their heads') was their slogan as they tramped along the roads chanting the revolutionary song, '*Ça ira*'. No manor house was immune, no aristocrat

174

was safe. Two days after the 20 June attack on the Tuileries, young Maussabré, de Brissac's eighteen-year-old aide-de-camp, who had taken part in the defence of the palace, arrived wounded and exhausted at Louveciennes, begging for asylum. Jeanne du Barry never hesitated: Maussabré was hidden in the furthest corner of the château and nursed with the same loving care she would have given the duke. A few days later the strident strains of the 'Ça ira', echoing across the park, told her the assassins had reached the village, but when the leaders came clamouring at her gates she proudly denied that there were any refugees hidden in the château. As Brissac's mistress she had no claim to courtesy. Armed with pikes and knives, the murderous mob burst into her lovely rooms, ripping down the curtains, sticking their weapons into the brocaded chairs, disfiguring the Gouthière bronzes till they came to where poor young Maussabré lay hidden behind a screen. Like a pack of wolves they fell on their prey, dragging him out of the house, ignoring Madame du Barry's tears and pleas, leaving behind a trail of devastation, the marks of their filthy boots on the parquet, the smell of sweat and of cheap tobacco. The unfortunate Maussabré was dragged off to the Abbaye prison to die a terrible death during the September massacres. Alone at Louveciennes, Jeanne waited for news she was afraid to hear.

Verdun was in the hands of the Prussians and Austrians and Paris was in a state of panic, with the Jacobins whipping up the blood lust in a people crazed by fear. The September massacres, which began as an organized attack on the prisons and in which over a thousand people were brutally murdered, could only have been possible in an atmosphere of fear. Girondins and Jacobins were accusing each other of treachery and the insurrectionary Commune had become far more effective than the government. Georges Danton stood out as the one strong man in France, inspiring the people with the famous words: 'De l'audace et encore de l'audace, toujours de l'audace.' But to his everlasting shame he was among those who condoned the September massacres.

It was a time when even decent and honest workmen believed that in killing 'the aristos' they were protecting their families from the fury of the counter-revolution, and when a paralyzed government was powerless to protect their prisoners from the savagery of the mob.

On 2 September the Assembly decreed that Brissac and his companions should be transferred from Orléans to the castle of Saumur.

Eighteen hundred national guardsmen were to escort the fifty-three prisoners, but by a fatal error they were placed under the command of 'Fournier l'Américain', the vilest and most brutal of revolutionaries, who deliberately disobeyed his orders and set out for Paris. By now the panic in the capital had spread to Orléans, and the prisoners, travelling in open hay carts, left the town to the cries of 'Down with the traitors!' and 'Death to the conspirators!' The nearer they got to Paris, the more threatening became the crowds, and the tall, elegant figure of Brissac in his blue coat with gold buttons was singled out for the greatest abuse.

The faithful d'Escourre followed every stage of the journey, trying to send a few words of comfort to the unhappy woman waiting at Louveciennes. 'On the sixth of September', he wrote, 'the Orléans prisoners will reach Versailles. Two men have been sent by the Commune to meet them and to tell the national guard bringing them that it has already broken the law and must be responsible for what may happen to the prisoners, who ought to be judged legally. We must hope that they will arrive safe and sound, and that by gaining time their lives will be spared. Moreover, the Assembly is weary of bloodshed and is suggesting an amnesty ... I have received ten letters from Orléans for the deputies, begging them to prevent the dangers that threaten the prisoners. I am in despair and shall have no peace till I know that the duke is at Versailles. If one can get there I shall go. Otherwise I will send there. You should send too. But above all be careful to avoid any action that may become public and prejudice people against you.'

Jeanne du Barry was already a marked woman. On 2 September there appeared a false account of her arrest: *L'Ami du Peuple* wrote that she had been taken to Paris. 'It is known that this old heroine of the last government was constantly sending emissaries to Orléans; Monsieur de Brissac's young aide-de-camp was arrested in her house. It is thought that her frequent messages to Orléans had some other purpose than love, which Madame du Barry must now forget. As the mistress of the Duc de Brissac she shared his wealth and pleasures. Who can say that she did not share his anti-revolutionary sentiments at the same time?'

But fears for her own safety were forgotten on hearing of the horror of the massacres in Paris, where in an orgy of blood lust a rabble completely out of control were murdering indiscriminately priests, women and children. In an attempt to save the Orléans prisoners, the Assembly ordered the convoy to proceed to Versailles. But the place was already full of army reservists, most of them out for trouble. There was no suitable prison in the town, and in order to ensure their safety the officials of the Versailles commune decided to shut them up in the disused cages of the palace menagerie. Seeing the proud Duc de Brissac caged like a wild beast would give satisfaction to the sansculottes and hopefully turn the feeling of hatred to one of contempt. Richaud, the mayor of Versailles, risked his life in trying to protect the prisoners. But hostile crowds had gathered all along the route before they had reached the town, and his efforts to reason with the people were defeated by Fournier and his men, who kept shouting, 'Death to the traitors!' The convoy was brought to a halt at the corner of the rue de l'Orangerie, opposite the house which the Comte de Provence had bought from Madame du Barry, where in the days of her splendour she had given the most fabulous of balls. Did Brissac remember them now as he sat quiet and calm on the straw of his wagon, apparently indifferent to the crowds screaming, 'Give us Brissac and Lessart and we will let the rest go free'? Then suddenly there was a mad rush – the horses were unharnessed and the mob fell on the prisoners attacking them with sabres, scythes and knives. The guards made no attempt to defend them and Richaud, who tried to reach them, was overpowered and thrust into a nearby house. Seizing a stick from one of his assailants, Brissac put up a heroic defence till, blinded and mutilated, he was thrown to the ground. Three young boys fought with one another over his mangled remains, cutting off his head in triumph and transfixing it on a pike. Yelling with a fearful joy, they paraded it through the streets of Versailles, forcing an unfortunate woman who later died of the shock to kiss the bleeding mouth.

The massacre lasted for over an hour, in which forty-four of the fifty-three prisoners were either killed or mutilated. A rabble who had degenerated into wild beasts now dragged the remains to the Maison Commune of Versailles, flinging them on the table in front of the horrified councillors, who were forced to make an inventory of the possessions found on their bodies, for with a bitter irony the murderers prided themselves on their honesty.

It was already getting dark at Louveciennes, and Jeanne du Barry was still waiting for the news d'Escourre had promised to bring her. It was a warm evening and the scent of roses drifted through the open windows. There was an ominous stillness in the air, as if no one in the château dared to speak. The only sound was the hydraulic machine of Marly bringing the water from the Seine. Then suddenly the village woke to life. The dreaded echoes of the 'Ça ira', the bursts of drunken laughter came nearer to the gates. Morin, the faithful servant, ran forward to shut the windows and prevent his unfortunate mistress from seeing the wild, ragged procession advancing across the lawns with the swaying lanterns illuminating their grisly trophy. But fear and presentiment had spared her the worst. The countess was lying unconscious on the floor.

24

'In the midst of the horrors and outrages that surround me my health remains good, for one does not die of grief.' So wrote Madame du Barry at the end of a nightmare week in which she struggled to survive. It would have been easier to die than face life without the Duc de Brissac. But she had still a part to play in those mysterious journeys to London for which her jewels, sitting safely in a London bank, provided an ostensible excuse.

It has never been fully explained why she embarked on a hazardous journey to England within a month of her lover's death. The September massacres had brought a fresh influx of refugees to England. Passports were hard to procure and the boats were both crowded and expensive. The Channel ports and woods near the coast were full of priests and 'aristos' in hiding, waiting for a passage. But Jeanne still found friends from the past ready to assist her in getting a passport. She was still on sufficiently good terms with the municipality of Louveciennes to persuade them that she had legal business of an urgent nature to attend to and that there was no question of her becoming an *émigrée*. Le Brun, the new foreign minister, whom she may have known and helped when he was one of Maurepas's secretaries, went out of his way to assist her, writing to her with an old-fashioned courtesy which was later to be quoted against him at the Revolutionary Tribunal. One is astonished that the matter of recovering her jewels should still have been accepted as a valid reason for travel, but the country was in such an appalling financial condition that anyone who could prove they had money or jewels to bring back to France was issued with a passport, usually for no more than a few weeks.

The strength and courage displayed by Jeanne at a time when her heart was breaking gives us another aspect of a woman, who since the age of eighteen, had lived the life of a pampered beauty. Now she spent hours in writing to the local authorities, in safeguarding her interests and in assisting Brissac's daughter, the Duchesse de Mortemart, who was returning from exile to claim her father's inheritance. The duke's last wish was that the two women he loved most in the world should live together like sisters. When she was still prostrate from the shock of her lover's death, one finds Madame du Barry writing to the duchess: 'Your father's wish that I should cherish you like a sister is so much in accordance with my own that I shall never dispute it.' And in her reply Madame de Mortemart assures her father's mistress 'that the last wish of him whom I shall respect and love forever is also my own heart's desire. I shall love you like a sister and my devotion will be lifelong. His wish is to me a sacred command and I hope to be able to carry out all that he expressed or would have expressed in his last moments.'

Jeanne Bécu never received a greater tribute than in this offer of friendship from her lover's daughter, and she appears to have responded with typical generosity, for according to the memoirs both of the Comte d'Espinchal and of the Marquis de Bouillé, 'It was her fatal devotion to the Duchesse de Mortemart which led to her last journey to England and finally brought her to the guillotine.' The impending law suit in London brought by Baron Lyon de Symons, claiming compensation for having retrieved the jewels, was a matter which could have been easily settled by her lawyers and by Nathaniel Forth, and in no way required her presence. It was a dangerous time to travel, particularly for a woman already watched by spies not only in London but also at Louveciennes, which was no longer the peaceful village where she was beloved as 'Lady Bountiful'. Grieve, the sinister foreigner, who for the last two years had been making trouble in the neighbourhood, had taken up residence in one of the local inns and become the leading spirit in the newly established Republican Club, frequented by various troublemakers in the village, among them the Indian, Zamor, who was still living in the château.

The friendless young man suddenly found himself treated as a person of consequence by this cultured Englishman who referred to him as 'an unsullied child of nature' and encouraged him in his reading of Rousseau. Flattered by his attentions, Zamor was only too ready to repeat everything he knew of his mistress and her friends, the names of all the *ci-devants*, former aristocrats, who called at the château, partly to condone in her grief, but also to bring her letters and messages for their friends and relatives in exile. He was aware of those occasions in the gardens when, wrapped in voluminous cloaks, Madame and her steward would be seen going out at night, walking as far as the water machine at Marly, or to the outhouses at the bottom of the orchard. The fact that he was never asked to accompany them was felt as another grievance by a man who had been so spoilt and petted in his youth. He suspected that the countess was burying some of her treasures in the same way as she had hidden away her silver before her first journey to England.

Not only treasures were buried at Louveciennes, for there is a legend that, many years later, a skull was found in the rose gardens where Madame du Barry was said to have buried her lover's head. But there is no mention of this incident in the statement made by the Duc de Brissac's lawyers when they came to Louveciennes to ascertain his death.

Madame du Barry's enchanted pavilion had become a place of sorrow, and even the discomforts of travel by ordinary stagecoach were preferable to remaining in a house haunted by ghosts.

On 19 October Madame du Barry, accompanied by two manservants and a devoted lady's maid, set out for Calais. With her went two friends, one of whom, the Duchesse de Brancas, had a passport in order; the other, the widowed Duchesse d'Aiguillon, having none, had to go disguised as a maid, an imprudent act on the part of the countess, who was already watched by the police. All of them travelled in the same crowded diligence, subjected to endless interrogations on the part of insolent officials to whom Jeanne bravely maintained that she was only forty-two years old, characteristic of a woman who even in sorrow remained eternally feminine.

In London Forth had rented her a large house at the corner of Bruton Street and Berkeley Square, originally belonging to the Abbé de St Phar, a half brother to the Duc d'Orléans. But the time was approaching when Forth would no longer flaunt his Orléanist connections: as Philippe-Egalité, the champion of the people, the duke's name had become anathema to London society. By order of the Prince of Wales his name had been struck off the membership of his London clubs and the Reynolds portrait which Forth had had the honour of presenting to the prince was removed from the walls of Carlton House.

One of the many curious aspects of Madame du Barry's last visit to London which has never been fully explained is the enormous sum of money she was able to dispose of when, only a year later, in prison in St Pélagie, she admitted to being in debt for two million, seven hundred thousand *livres*. Her Paris bankers, the Vandenyvers, had in the last years been involved in the dangerous business of transferring capital out of France, and had been advancing cash to Madame du Barry 'on the security of diamonds deposited in a London bank.' But towards the end of 1792 and in the first months of 1793 two large sums, each amounting to two hundred thousand *livres*, were paid out on her order, the money apparently coming out of the sale of shares she still possessed in France. The first of these sums was a free gift given to the Cardinal de la Rochefoucauld, Archbishop of Rouen, to help in feeding the thousands of starving priests who had fled to England rather than take the oath to uphold the constitution. The second sum was more secret in origin and was in the form of a loan paid by her Paris banker to the Duc Louis Antoine Auguste de Rohan-Chabot, who was in England at the time, and given in exchange for a mortgage on certain Rohan properties in Brittany. The enormous amount of this loan, the fact that it was given at a time when the Rohans were involved in the Royalists' risings in the Vendée, implicated both the countess and her bankers in the plots of the counter-revolutionaries.

There was a certain recklessness in Madame du Barry's behaviour on this last journey to England. An unhappiness bordering on despair, tears which were ready to flow on the slightest occasion led to many an imprudent action she would have been wiser to avoid. By the end of 1792, most of the refugees in England were in a pathetic condition. In the early summer they had believed that the Duke of Brunswick and the Prussian army would be in Paris by August and the King back on his throne. But the extraordinary victory of Valmy, in which Dumouriez and the untrained young armies of the republic defeated the seasoned veterans of the Prussian army, changed the whole course of history, and the *émigrés* who welcomed Madame du Barry on her arrival in London were resigned to a long and dreary exile, both those of 1789 who had followed in the wake of the royal princes, or those of the eleventh-hour constitutionalists like Narbonne and Talleyrand, who in the last Assembly had been sufficiently courageous to defend their King. All were equally unhappy and discouraged, and Madame du Barry gave them generous and indiscriminate hospitality. Courtiers she had known at Versailles and now eking out a precarious living as wine merchants and dancing masters; *les dames aux tabourets* who had become milliners and were spoiling their pretty, dimpled hands in stitching straw and feathers; generals like Bouillé or young officers like Choiseul, who had failed in their efforts to rescue the King at Varennes, or the Comte de Narbonne who had served as Louis's last minister of war: all were made welcome at the dinners and the card parties with which the countess tried to distract those who were as unhappy as herself. A pathetic figure in her mourning robes, she still retained the power to fascinate, and those who met her on her last visit to London were as charmed as the gallants who long ago had bought their sword-knots from the blue-eyed *grisette* who served them at '*le trait galant*'.

For all her unhappiness she still went out in society. In his memoirs General Bouillé's son, the young marquis, gives us one of the last descriptions of the 'notorious' Comtesse du Barry. He recalls that he often met her supping with Mrs Fitzherbert, the mistress of the Prince of Wales. 'As she was about forty-seven at the time it was rather late to make the acquaintance of a woman whose beauty had been her merit, her fortune and her renown. But though the freshness and first splendour of her charms had long since vanished, the traces that remained were sufficient to give some idea of the effect they must have had. Her eyes were still large and blue with the sweetest expression possible. There was still the beautiful fair chestnut hair, the lovely mouth, the rounded oval of the face, whose heightened colour did not detract from its charm. Her noble elegant bearing still retained some of its supple grace in spite of a slight tendency to portliness. And finally there were the voluptuous curves of her figure that her attire specially in the morning scarcely concealed. Her manner was in no sense common, much less vulgar. Though without pretensions to brilliance she had more wit than she was given credit for. Besides her goodness of heart no less than her simplicity was sufficient compensation ... I was as much struck as moved by the fact that the woman whom both the King and Queen had treated so harshly on their accession to the throne could not cease thinking of their misfortunes and wept for them tears that were as sincere as they were frequent.'

At the supper table of the Prince of Wales's mistress, a woman who was some ten years her junior, it was the Comtesse du Barry who stole the limelight. Her aristocratic French friends were introduced by her into London society, and one finds her writing to the Duke of Queensberry to ask whether he would include the Duchesse de Brancas in a supper he was giving for the Prince of Wales. The duke, a former *habitué* of the rue Jussienne, was so delighted with his old friend that he went to the lengths of taking her to Windsor Castle and presenting her to King George III, where the exquisite manners she had learnt at Versailles from her old mentor the Duc de Richelieu were much admired at Queen Charlotte's court.

One wonders how a woman who only a few months earlier had seen her lover's head impaled upon a pike could bring herself to go out in public and be entertained by people whose language she barely spoke. But whether they were courtesans or duchesses, the women of the *ancien régime* who appeared to be so frivolous and superficial had all been taught to dissimulate their feelings, even when their hearts were breaking.

The republican victories at Valmy and Jemappes, with the Duke of Brunswick's armies in retreat across the frontier, destroyed the last hopes of the *émigrés* who now faced a long and hungry winter. In Europe the royal princes were in flight from their creditors, and from Paris came the news of the King being put on trial.

Madame du Barry shared in the tribulations of her countrymen and publicly identified herself with the enemies of the Republic. She made no attempt to hide her grief when, on the evening of 21 January, came the news of King Louis's execution. In London the theatres and other places of public entertainment were immediately closed and the audiences came out into the streets singing 'God Save the King'. Frenchmen of all shades of political opinion crowded the services held in the chapels of the various Catholic embassies in memory of the 'martyred King', and Jeanne du Barry was among those whose presence was noted by republican spies. When the English court went into mourning for the King who in 1778 had supported its rebellious colonists, Jeanne, who was still in mourning for Brissac, could not resist ordering some completely new outfits in St James's Street: one elaborate, black silk gown with fringes, and two others in white and grey damask, what were known as breakfast gowns. Was it loneliness, unhappiness or boredom which made her so reckless with her money, when in spite of the appalling news from France, where every day the guillotine was taking its toll of victims, she still continued to order rare plants from English nurseries to be sent to her hothouses at Louveciennes? Or was there a new interest in the life of this woman who was unable to live without love and in the misery of this London winter had met someone for whose sake she was ready to risk going back to a dangerous and uncertain future?

General Bouillé's young son writes in his memoirs that Madame du Barry risked her life for the sake of Brissac's daughter. But Pauline de Mortemart had already returned to France and was living in hiding at Calais, while Madame du Barry stayed on in London, ostensibly kept by a law suit which never seemed to end and for which Nathaniel Forth was still her principal adviser. In those last weeks matters more important than her diamonds had been claiming her attention. In the last days of January she signed the loan for two hundred thousand *livres* made out to the Duc de Rohan in return for a mortgage on lands in Brittany, an act which incriminated both herself and her bankers, the Vandenyvers. Little is known of this last affair with a man whom some of her biographers assert to have been thirty years her junior, but judging by the one letter that survives, Rohan appears to have been a friend and contemporary of the Duc de Brissac; a widower who, after his wife's death in Brussels, had passed through London before returning to look after his properties in Brittany which were threatened by an imminent war with England. The loan advanced by Madame du Barry was said to have been given for this purpose. But the royalist risings in the Vendée in which the Rohans played a leading part make it seem as if Jeanne, in her usual headstrong and imprudent fashion, gave active help to the counter-revolutionaries.

All that survives of what appears to have been a short, tempestuous love affair is one letter written in September 1793, only a few days before Madame du Barry was taken to prison. It is unsigned and the whole affair might never have come to light had it not been for the implacable hatred of George Grieve, who succeeded in tracing the identity of the writer.

We know that Jeanne met Rohan in London where she was frequently seen in his company, and that he returned to France shortly before the outbreak of hostilities, when she gave the order for a loan. She herself stayed on in London for the final settlement of her law suit with de Symons, and as an enemy alien had to procure herself a passport, which she obtained with the help of her old friend the Duke of Queensberry. Time was pressing, the six-week exit visa given her in France was already overdue, and in the last days of February she received a letter from her steward to tell her that she had been listed as an *émigrée* and that the officials of the municipality of Louveciennes had placed seals on the château and the pavilion. It was alarming news for a woman who had always been ready to help her friends, while regarding herself as being above the law. The lavishness with which she had been spending in the past months had made a considerable drain on her finances, and before leaving England she was reduced to borrowing a large sum from Nathaniel Forth, who was still representing her interests in the law courts.

The Irishman was an astute man of business. If he was ready to give her a loan of £24,000 for which she signed a promissory note giving her diamonds in security, it was because he knew that the jewels were already safe in her hands. She admitted in her note that she was borrowing money to enable her to pay the most pressing of her debts in France, without which she could not have returned to Paris. The terms of the loan were unduly generous to Forth, for the countess was willing to be paid in *assignats*, or promissory notes, which were practically worthless outside France and of which Forth had collected a large amount on his various mysterious journeys across the Channel.

Madame du Barry signed the notes on 3 March and that same evening embarked for France. She left against the advice of all her English friends at a time when the Jacobins had triumphed in the Convention and the advent of Robespierre had brought a reign of terror to a country paralyzed by fear. To those who questioned Jeanne as to why she was leaving, she only replied that 'she had a debt of honour to be settled in France'.

Was it in order to help Pauline de Mortemart, or to save her beloved Louveciennes and its treasures, so carefully hidden in corners of her park? Or was it that this woman, approaching fifty but still radiant with life and health, had fallen in love with the friend of her murdered lover and was ready to risk everything just to see him again? Madame du Barry made her appointment with death, and those questions remain unanswered.

25

England and France were already at war, but the Channel boats under English control were still taking passengers across to Calais, and thanks to her English connections Madame du Barry was able to obtain comfortable berths for herself and her companions. Her troubles began on her arrival in France, where she was met by rude and suspicious officials who, seeing that her passport was out of date, prevented her from proceeding on her journey until her permits were renewed. Gone were the days of privilege when as the Duc de Brissac's mistress, she had accompanied him to military reviews in Normandy, greeted by obsequious mayors and cheering regiments. Calais was a dirty, crowded town full of drunken soldiers and insolent police. The inns were full and for a fortnight she had to share a room with her maid, waiting for a new passport. Also in Calais, hiding under an assumed name, was Pauline de Mortemart, who had been in Paris to see her father's lawyers and ascertain the gruesome details of his tragic end. Now she was hoping to return to England, relying on the help of Madame du Barry. But Jeanne was herself an outlaw, queuing in draughty offices, submitting to endless impertinent questions from men who had little respect either for her age or sex, still having to keep up the pretence that she was no more than forty-two years old, a pathetic delusion, for after the worries and discomforts of the past weeks the stout, middle-aged matron waiting her turn in the customs offices of Calais could no longer hide her age.

A fortnight later she was back at Louveciennes to find guards at the gate, her property under seal, with her steward telling her of a sinister foreigner, an anarchist of the most dangerous kind, who was transforming the village into a hive of Jacobin intrigue and stirring up trouble among her own servants. But the woman who at Versailles had brought about the downfall of the omnipotent Choiseul was not likely to be intimidated by an unknown foreign agitator, and in the first few days she had already addressed a letter to the governors of the district protesting against her treatment and reminding them that 'the reasons compelling her to leave England were sufficiently well known for her not to be considered as an *émigrée*'.

The letter was favourably received, for there were still certain officials under the new regime who, while paying lip service to the doctrines of equality, were sufficiently impressed by the glamour of a former royal favourite to support her appeal. One of these was Citizen La vallery, vice-president of the district of Seine-et-Oise and known to one of Jeanne's friends and neighbours, the Princesse de Rohan-Rochefort. In the spring and summer of 1793 the Reign of Terror in Paris does not yet seem to have penetrated to the surrounding countryside. There were still people living in their châteaux, some of whom had never emigrated, others who had gone and returned when the new laws against *émigrés* threatened the loss of their properties. While the men went to fight in Condé's army, many heroic women remained behind to protect their homes and their family's inheritance. The Princesse de Rohan, who had suffered imprisonment at the beginning of the Revolution and been released, was living peacefully at Versailles under the protection of the friendly La vallery, and appears to have been on intimate terms with Madame du Barry during her last months of liberty.

The fact that she was a Rohan and was only a recent friend makes one suspect that she may have acted as intermediary in a new and mysterious love affair in which a lonely, frightened woman found strength and consolation.

From the one letter which survives it appears that the writer was a friend and maybe the executor of Brissac, and that the *hôtel* in the rue de Grenelle, with its vast collection of pictures, had not yet been sequestered, so that Madame du Barry was still able to receive the paintings she had asked for.

The letter, which begins, 'My dear sweet friend', leaves no doubt as to the relationship between them. 'I send you the picture you wished for. It's a sad and gloomy present, but one which I feel is what you would desire. In a position like ours, with so much cause for pain and unhappiness, all that beseems us is to seek food for our melancholy. I sent for the three pictures which he owned which are here now, and I have kept one of the small ones, the original of the one in which you wear a white shift and a plumed hat. The larger one by Madame Lebrun is delightful – a fascinating and speaking likeness of infinite charm. But indeed I would have thought it indiscreet to choose it, and the one I have kept is so charming, so like you and so adorable that I am transported with joy at possessing it and have no other wish than to have one which I can carry on me and which shall never leave me.'

It is as a passionate lover rather than as Brissac's friend that he writes, 'Do come, dear love, and spend two days here. Come and dine with me and bring anyone else you like. Give me a few moments of happiness, which I only enjoy when I am with you. Come for at least a moment to see him who loves you beyond all else and will continue to do so till the very end of his life. A thousand times let me kiss the most charming woman in the world whose noble heart is worthy of eternal devotion.'

How could anyone as frail and vulnerable as Jeanne du Barry fail to respond to such a letter? Brissac himself, so tolerant and noble, would have been the first to forgive and to understand a woman he had loved with all her weaknesses.

She had returned to Louveciennes in the first days of spring when the trees were bursting into blossom and the lawns were carpeted with jonquils and narcissi. Never had it looked more beautiful and never had it seemed so bereft, with every sofa and brocaded chair haunted by some beloved ghost. Those who had made it into a place of laughter had long since gone: gay, witty little Chon, who was now living in hiding in Toulouse, not daring to write her a line; Marie de Boisseson and her charming children, who had followed her husband into exile. She still had Bécu cousins living on the estate, Neuvilles and Graillets, but they brought her little comfort with their continual complaints, their incessant demands for money she was not able to give.

Not daring to envisage the future, she lived entirely in the present. Hours were still spent at her toilette, her scented baths, her daily massage, the long sessions with her coiffeur. The middle-aged woman who had waited in the queues of the customs houses of Calais revived in the luxury of Louveciennes. Her secret love gave her new hope, a new desire to live. At fifty she was still desirable, anxious to please whoever came within her orbit. The neighbours who remained were entertained as lavishly as ever. 'A chain of *ci-devants* of both sexes exists along the banks of the Seine, who all gather at Louveciennes where they are still addressed by their titles', wrote Grieve in one of his reports to the Committee of Public Safety.

The implacable hatred with which the unfortunate woman was pursued by a man she had never met is so inexplicable that one is tempted to believe in the explanation put forward by Lenôtre, one of the best historians of the period who, in his *Vieilles Maisons et Vieux Papiers*, suggests that Grieve may have been the mastermind behind the robbery which took place at Louveciennes in the early days of January 1791 when he and Blache, the Jacobin spy who dogged Madame du Barry's footsteps in London, connived in an act which might have succeeded had it not been for Nathaniel Forth's identification of her diamonds. Hence his hatred of 'the Machiavellian Mr Forth, the notorious English spy and agent of Mr Pitt', and his calculated determination to destroy a woman whom he both coveted and hated.

His second attempt to ruin her came in July when the Convention introduced a new law by which the local authorities were able to place under arrest anyone suspected of 'uncivic behaviour such as lack of patriotism or aristocratic tendencies'. Profiting by this law, Grieve demanded the arrest of a woman who, despite her wealth and immorality, continued to live in luxury thanks to the protection of 'the traitor La vallery' whom she had seduced with her wiles. Thirty-six inhabitants of the village of Louveciennes were terrorized into signing his inflammatory petition. But due to the friendship of La vallery, Madame du Barry was able to thwart his plans, and he arrived at Louveciennes to be met by several superior members of the department of Seine-et-Oise and severely rebuked for abusing a law which was only intended for use in notorious cases, to be applied solely in times of emergency.

But by now the Reign of Terror was spreading across the country. The Girondins had fallen, the more moderate elements in the Convention had been eliminated, and the dreaded Committee of Public Safety was in the hands of bloodthirsty Jacobins. La vallery compromised himself in going to Louveciennes, exhorting the countess to move to Versailles where friendly authorities could protect her. But she was nervous of leaving her possessions in the hands of servants, some of whom she could no longer trust. Too late she realized the mistake she had made in keeping her Indian page, for the virulent attack addressed by Grieve to the Convention was largely compiled from details supplied by Zamor. No sooner had she read it than he was instantly dismissed and became Grieve's principal ally in his campaign of defamation, repeating every conversation overheard at the dinner table of Louveciennes where the guests still used their titles and drank toasts to the martyred King.

In Grieve's address to the Convention, Zamor is described as 'a pure child of nature, a reader of Rousseau whom the low-born Messalina, the former concubine of the tyrant Louis xv, had been unable to corrupt', and cold-blooded puritans like Robespierre were willing to allow an unknown foreigner and a former slave to bring about the ruin of the unfortunate Madame du Barry. The Convention replied to Grieve's attack by endorsing the arrest of the woman named 'La Dubarry' residing at Louveciennes, ordering her to be taken to the prison of St Pélagie and detained as a person suspected of aristocratic leanings. The Englishman's connections with the Committee of Public Safety appear to have been so powerful as to overcome the opposition of the local authorities and to requisition such armed forces as were necessary to carry out the arrest, giving him supreme control over Louveciennes and its treasures.

Jeanne du Barry knew she had an enemy in Grieve. But she saw him as a leader of the sansculottes rather than as someone animated by a vitriolic hatred. She was totally unprepared for his sudden eruption at Louveciennes and had barely the time to destroy some incriminating papers before he had followed her into her bedroom where, accompanied by the loyal mayor and a squadron of police who unwillingly carried out his orders, he broke into cupboards, opened drawers and, finally, in a struggle to seize her papers, pinned her down on her bed.

In a letter written later from prison, in which she complained of her treatment, the countess wrote: 'My pen refuses to transcribe the horrors and outrages which he perpetrated.' But those people she addressed were no longer in a position to protect her. The day she wrote that letter, the body of the unfortunate La vallery was found drowned in the Seine. Denounced by Grieve in his attack on Madame du Barry, the vice-president of the department of Seine-et-Oise had preferred to take his own life rather than face the guillotine.

Morin and her other loyal servants were in the hands of the police, and Jeanne was left alone to struggle on her gilded bed with a man of almost superhuman strength who, while assaulting her physically, abused her in the filthiest language of the Paris gutter, revelling in her humiliation by treating her as if she were the lowest of prostitutes. Fear and repulsion gave her an added strength. But at the end of an unequal battle he carried her forcibly into the carriage which was waiting to take her to prison. They had barely reached the entrance to the park when they saw the Chevalier d'Escourre driving towards them in a small cabriolet. No sooner did he see them than he turned in the other direction. But Grieve was quick to sight another victim. The police were sent to pursue him, and he was made to relinquish his vehicle and taken off to prison under an armed guard while Grieve mounted the cabriolet and drove Madame du Barry alone to Paris.

What happened on the journey has never been revealed. It is not known whether the 'horrors' Jeanne referred to occurred at Louveciennes or on the way to Paris. It is believed that Grieve offered her her life as the price of her favours, that lust rather than hatred dictated his actions, and that the disgust with which she repelled his advances explained the fury with which he hounded her to her death.

Even the sordid, overcrowded prison must have come as a relief after the terrifying nightmare drive with a stranger she regarded as a madman. There were friendly, familiar faces in that strange conglomeration of women whom the Revolution had brought together in the dank corridors and dirty common room of St Pélagie, where duchesses mingled with prostitutes and among the inmates at the time was the famous Madame Roland, heroine of the Girondins, and Mademoiselle Raucourt, the lovely actress who once had taken Paris by storm in her role as the Queen of Carthage, and whom Madame du Barry, the reigning divinity of the day, had presented with a dress costing over six thousand *livres*. Now they were all reduced to the same miserable conditions in what was little more than an ante-chamber to the guillotine. Only a fraction were ever acquitted, though some were still buoyant with hope, pathetically believing in a justice which no longer existed. Among these was Madame du Barry, who was so convinced of her innocence, so sure of finding champions ready to defend her against the malignancy of Grieve, that twenty-four hours after her arrival in prison, when she was still unaware of the suicide of the unfortunate La vallery, she was already writing to the local authorities of Versailles, vigorously protesting against the behaviour of Citizen Grieve, 'a foreigner of no fixed abode' who had 'violated every form of decency' and, contrary to the spirit of the law, had refused her the right of taking with her either money, linen or produce from her garden.

Nameless friends, many of them in hiding, provided her with the material comforts which could be procured for payment. A devoted maid, who pleading sickness had remained at Louveciennes, still had access to her linen cupboard. And within a few days Jeanne had recovered her natural spirits and, with an optimism one cannot fail to admire, was writing to 'her dear Henriette' asking for supplies of linen, 'a lawn cap and also shifts with little coloured stripes, as well as white ones; handkerchiefs and fichus, as many as can be sent, including a dozen table napkins, some towels and sheets'. Superficial, frivolous, feminine to the last, she was still sufficiently interested in life to make it as endurable as possible. She writes, 'I am well and have everything I need here; also an agreeable companion who shares my cell. Send me news of what happens in the house, if they have confiscated my things and if it is well watched. Speak to the villagers who are still interested in me and find out whether they have petitioned in my favour.'

At a time when the Jacobins were exercising a stranglehold on all the local authorities, fifty-seven inhabitants of Louveciennes had the courage to react against the threats and blackmail of Grieve and his companions by signing a petition in favour of their benefactress, stating that their previous denunciation had been made under duress. A month before, this declaration would have saved her, but in the past few days Grieve had installed himself at Louveciennes, searching in every pigeonhole and blotter for papers she had forgotten to destroy, piecing together incriminating letters and noting in his small, precise handwriting any reference which might help to condemn her, with the result that all the letters in which Jeanne du Barry protested her innocence remained unopened on the desks of the members of the Committee of Public Safety.

26

Madame du Barry spent over two months in prison, the latter part of the time in solitary confinement which, for a woman who had never been alone, was worse than any discomfort. Used to a healthy, outdoor life, she suffered in a cold, damp cell deprived of fresh air and exercise.

Even the most optimistic inmates of St Pélagie lost all hope when, on 16 October 1793, Marie Antoinette was sent to the guillotine, dying with a heroism many hoped to emulate. But for someone like Jeanne du Barry the sound of the tumbrels rattling along the cobbled streets was a reminder of a future too fearful to contemplate. Every day someone was taken away, to be immediately replaced by others who brought news of the outside world, of the royalist risings in the Vendée and in Calvados, and of the British attack on Toulon, news which resulted in fearful reprisals, with the Parisian mob screaming for more heads for the guillotine.

But what the members of the Convention required more than 'heads' were the confiscated fortunes of their victims to fill the empty treasury for a war which never seemed to end. Three thousand *livres* had been advanced to George Grieve to execute the warrant for the arrest of 'the woman named Dubarry' and to enter into possession of what was now known as the 'Maison Nationale de Louveciennes' which, counting the pictures, furniture and gold and silver plate, promised to be one of the richest collections in the country. Most important of all were the valuables which, according to Zamor and Salanave, had been hidden in the park, and none of the villagers, even those who had petitioned for her release, could resist joining in the hunt for the treasures belonging to their former benefactress. The local authorities resented the intrusion of a foreigner who, thanks to his connections with the members of the Committee of Public Safety, 'made fear the order of the day' in which everyone suspected his neighbour of concealment, and anyone who dared to stand up to

Grieve and his assistants was instantly dismissed or thrown into jail.

Later Grieve prided himself on having sent no less than seventeen people to the guillotine, beginning with Denis Morin, the faithful steward who had defended his mistress's interests to the end. The Bécu cousins, Graillets and Neuvilles, still living on the property, were immediately sent to prison, and would have shared their cousin's fate had not the fall of Robespierre put an end to the Reign of Terror.

The members of the Convention were anxious to move in the surveyors and executors who were to make an exact list of the contents. But Grieve and his assistants refused to be hurried. In his morbid passion for Louveciennes, which he described as an 'enchanted palace', he spent hours shut up in the deserted rooms where smiling portraits of the woman he was deliberately condemning to death looked down from the walls, the famous *'yeux en coulisse'*, immortalized by all the leading artists of the day, taunting a man who had never known the delights of life under the *ancien régime*. The first pictures he had removed were those of her lovers, as if he could not bear to work under the disdainful look of the proud old King or face the urbane elegance of Brissac reminding him of a world in which, humble and obscure, he had struggled in vain for recognition. As Citizen Grieve he was at last sufficiently important to be feared, and he spent happy hours seated at the beautiful rosewood desk, decorated with medallions of Sèvres porcelain, sorting the bundles of letters his unfortunate victim had not had time to destroy. In his skilful hands the most harmless of notes became the most compromising of statements. By the time he had finished, a case which was fundamentally insubstantial had become dynamite when passed to the public prosecutor. Jeanne Vaubernier, 'the woman named Dubarry', was accused of fifteen different crimes against the state. Denounced at the same time were her bankers the Vandenyvers, the Chevalier d'Escourre and his nephew, the Chevalier de la Bondie, guilty of no other crime than of having accompanied her on her journeys to England. At the same time Grieve went out of his way to prove that the theft of the jewels necessitating these journeys was a complete fake and that it had taken place at the instigation of that 'well-known English spy' Nathaniel Forth, who had used it as an excuse in maintaining contact between the Court of St James's and the Tuileries. To prove his theory Grieve was able to show that, although the jewels were safely deposited in a

London bank, not one of the thieves had as yet been brought to justice.

Assisted by the treachery of Zamor and of Salanave, he became familiar with every detail of her life, the names of every *ci-devant* aristocrat who had visited her at Louveciennes during the past months, the identity of every *émigré* who had posted her letters from abroad. Every one of his accusations was supported by evidence, some of it puerile in itself but sufficiently important to serve as grist for the public prosecutor. Added to the information supplied by Blache, who had noted her various visits to London, her friendship with leading British politicians and royalist *émigrés*, this was sufficient to sign her death warrant.

Jeanne du Barry began to lose hope when she heard of the suicide of La vallery and the arrest of the Vandenyvers. Such friends as she had left were powerless to help. But alone in her cell she still had the courage to defend herself against those who were trying to destroy her. News of what was happening at Louveciennes had got through to her prison, and the thought of her beautiful possessions being pillaged and violated by unclean hands gave her the strength to hate. With hitherto unsuspected eloquence she appealed to the Committee of Public Safety 'trusting they would be so kind as to examine her conduct as soon as possible and see that justice was done and that she was protected against the malignity of her enemies'.

She did not yet know that her enemies were their friends, and the only answer to her appeal was a visit on 30 October from two members of the Committee come to make the first examination of 'the woman called La Dubarry'; an examination in which she showed remarkable skill in evading any information which could incriminate her friends. After six weeks in prison she still made an attempt to attract, giving her age as forty-two, answering the questions in the soft and gentle voice which till now had never failed to charm. She made no attempt to deny the past, calmly admitting her guilt, the money she had squandered in her years as a royal mistress. 'It was not her fault. What could she have done?' The questioning smile found no response in the eyes of those stern-faced moralists who saw her a depraved and lowborn Messalina.

While admitting the faults she had committed at Versailles, she hotly denied every accusation of having conspired against the Revolution. The robbery of her jewels was too well known to have ever been in doubt. The journeys to England had been made with passports legally issued by the foreign minister of the day. How could one say she was unpatriotic when the municipality and inhabitants of Louveciennes could testify to her patriotism, her voluntary contributions to the state, her gifts to soldiers leaving for the front? The fact that she had returned to France without waiting for her jewels to be released in England proved that she had never been and never wanted to be an *émigrée*.

For two hours she stood up to the questioning of men who had already condemned her and were only interested in making her commit some indiscretion which would implicate others in her fate. At the end of this visit the prisoner known as 'the woman Dubarry' was committed to the state prison of La Force. But it was already overcrowded and she was still at St Pélagie when, on 8 November, Madame Roland, the most famous of the Girondins, went to the guillotine, maintaining to the end the attitude of Roman stoicism which won her a place in history but which frail, human creatures like Madame du Barry had neither the wish nor the will to emulate.

On 22 November, the second day of *Frimaire* of the new revolutionary calendar, she was brought to a private room in the Palais de Justice to submit to a second interrogation by the vice-president of the revolutionary tribunal, the cold-blooded Dumas, who had never been known to let one of his victims escape from his clutches. Hidden in the shadows, making notes, was the public prosecutor, Fouquier-Tinville, one of the most sinister of all the perverted psychopaths spewed up by the Revolution. A stern moralist and exemplary father, he took a sadistic pleasure in sending men to their death, and would hurry from the courtrooms to assist at the execution of his victims. Jeanne du Barry can never have seen him, for one look at that cruel face with the thin mouth and hooded eyes would have told her there was no pity to be expected in that quarter, and she would have saved herself from writing a letter which casts a perpetual slur on her memory when, in a desperate attempt to save herself, she denied a love of which she now proved herself unworthy.

On her return to St Pélagie she addressed to Fouquier-Tinville a grovelling, piteous note appealing for mercy against the evil machinations of Grieve and his associates who were bent on her destruction.

She insists, 'I never emigrated; I never even intended doing so. I never provided the *émigrés* with money, and if I was compelled by circumstances both in London and in France to see persons of the court, and others who were perhaps not in complete agreement with the ideals of the Revolution, yet I sincerely hope that in the justice and equity of your heart you will take into consideration the circumstances in which I found myself, and my relations with Citizen Brissac, which are well known, *and were forced on me by the circumstances of the time*, whose correspondence is in your hands.'

Fouquier-Tinville may never have read this letter, for his only reply was to draw up the warrant ordering the accused and her accomplices to be transferred to the prison of the Conciergerie, known as the antechamber to the guillotine.

At nine o'clock in the morning of 6 December, the sixteenth day of *Frimaire*, Jeanne du Barry, the banker Vandenyver and his two sons appeared on trial in the Great Hall of Liberty which had formerly been the seat of the Paris *parlement*. Jeanne must have remembered it from the day when, with all the pomp and panoply of Bourbon power, King Louis came from Versailles to dismiss the rebellious *parlement*. The golden lilies on the wall were now erased by revolutionary slogans; a tricolour covered the royal throne, and the whole place stank of sweat and cheap tobacco. Every seat was taken by a public eager to gloat over the downfall of a woman who had already become a legend. But most of them were very disappointed, for the stout, middle-aged woman with the pale cheeks and eyes reddened by tears had left little of 'a Lais* so celebrated for her dissolute morals, whose wantonness alone empowered her to share the life of a despot who sacrificed the wealth and blood of his people to the satisfaction of his shameful pleasures'. The purple rhetoric of the public prosecutor hardly applied to the sad-faced woman with the gentle voice who, after two months of prison, was still scrupulously clean with a fresh fichu and well-brushed hair.

After a succession of sleepless nights, she still summoned the courage to maintain her composure through the trial. The only emotion she showed was when Grieve gave his evidence on the papers he had found at Louveciennes, and the spite and venom of his tone brought

* Lais was a Greek courtesan famous for her beauty.

colour to her cheeks and a flash of anger to her eyes. After Grieve came Blache, giving his testimony on her London visits; her assignations with Nathaniel Forth and other royalist spies; her friendship with English politicians and her presence, dressed in mourning, at the memorial service held for the late King, Louis Capet. There were a hundred petty details gathered from frightened servants blackmailed into denouncing a mistress they adored. Blache's evidence was followed by that of the servants themselves; young maids, blushing with embarrassment, were forced to admit having seen her burn a whole pile of papers on the night of Brissac's arrest, and of having sheltered a wounded guardsman who had escaped on 10 August. Then it was Zamor's turn to denounce her, revelling in the role of Grieve's principal witness; daring to assert that since the beginning of the Revolution the house of the accused had been 'continuously frequented by aristocrats who openly rejoiced in the defeats of the republican armies', that time after time he had rebuked the accused on the folly and wickedness of her behaviour but she had never even troubled to reply. Both he and Grieve were convinced there had never been a robbery and that the whole story had been invented in collusion with 'the English spy Nathaniel Forth.' Looking at that dark face distorted with hate, Jeanne du Barry must have wondered what she could have done to deserve so much ingratitude.

Witness after witness appeared in court to testify against her. But those who inadvertently did the greatest harm were the ones who spoke in her favour; the devoted Chevalier d'Escourre, who had been brought from La Force and was so weakened and confused after the long weeks in prison that he faltered and contradicted himself in his replies. Even more damaging were the Dutch bankers who, scrupulously honest in their evidence, supplied the prosecution with the exact dates and details of every letter of credit and promissory note she had signed during her visits to London.

Chauveau La Garde, the brave and honourable advocate who had appeared for the defence both for the Queen and Charlotte Corday, did his best to convince the jury of her innocence. But they had already judged her guilty before the public prosecutor had embarked on a long and verbose peroration 'on the infamous conspiracy of a vile courtesan of a crapulous tyrant'. The vice-president then summed up the case and the jury went out, to return an hour later, at eleven o'clock in the evening, when 'Jeanne Vaubernier du Barry', and the three Vandenyvers were pronounced guilty and condemned to be executed at eleven o'clock on the following morning.

The verdict was heard in silence broken only by a cry which was little more than a whimper. Jeanne du Barry had fainted in the dock and had to be carried back to her cell. But the strange thing was that when she recovered consciousness she was still so active and alive that she was ravenously hungry and ate every morsel of the supper provided by Madame Richard, the kindly wife of the prison warder. On the table there was also a tallow candle, some paper and a prayer book for those who were sufficiently resigned to pray. But Jeanne was not a woman to resign herself to death. Now, at the eleventh hour, her life had never seemed more precious. In the grip of fear, she still believed she could buy her way to freedom. For, hidden in the grounds of Louveciennes, in places which Grieve and his sleuth hounds had never found, were the treasures she and Morin had buried at night: bags of gold coins, piles of *assignats*, diamond, ruby and emerald rings, miniatures framed in diamonds, golden pencil boxes, enamelled clocks; the pink pearls she had worn when Cosway painted her in London; the last diamonds given her by Brissac; a king's ransom waiting to be collected from the lily ponds and the deer park as far as the hydraulic machine of Marly.

Throughout a sleepless night she lay on her cold, hard bed, remembering with incredible lucidity every object and the exact place where it was hidden. If these were not enough, there were still the impounded jewels in London, to be released when she had paid the cost of the court action. This would take weeks and even months, and by then the Reign of Terror might have ended. Hope had returned by the coming of dawn, and the executioner who arrived at eight o'clock to prepare her for the guillotine found her calm and composed, asking for a delay as she had important information to impart to the Committee of Public Safety. The Committee was ready to listen to her proposals, and the poor woman was allowed to delude herself in the belief that she might save her life in divulging her secrets.

Three men, one of them a clerk, were sent to take down her statement, and for over three hours she sat in her cold and draughty cell, enumerating her hidden treasures with a faultless accuracy. It was past midday when they left her in a state of anguish and suspense, but still with a ray of hope. But they had barely gone when the executioner returned to cut her hair and tie her hands behind her back. There was to be no reprieve. The tumbrel was already waiting outside. When she felt the cold touch of the steel on her neck, giving her a foretaste of the horror to come, and she saw her lovely golden curls, barely streaked with grey, lying on the dusty floor, the woman who had once been the beautiful du Barry finally collapsed into a pathetic, whimpering creature dead to all sense of dignity and shame.

The gendarmes carried her struggling into the tumbrel where the Vandenyvers were already waiting, the father and two sons who, through her folly and imprudence, were to share her fate. They must have felt nothing but contempt for the woman who lay struggling and moaning at the back of the cart, now and then letting out a cry of pain as the tumbrel lurched and the horses stumbled on the cobbled stones of the rue St Honoré.

It was already getting dark, and the people who had waited all morning to see the notorious royal favourite being taken to the scaffold had long since gone home. It was too cold to linger in the streets. But in the Place de la Révolution there was still the usual crowd of those who, day after day, attended the grisly spectacle of the condemned being brought to the guillotine.

Only today there was none of the usual animation, the raucous laughter and coarse jokes, for here was no proud, disdainful beauty to be mocked at and reviled but a pathetic, broken creature more like a trapped animal than a human being. Sensing the reaction of the crowds, the executioner hurried her first up the steps of the guillotine. She was still struggling and had to be carried by force, all the time screaming, 'You are going to hurt me! Please don't hurt me!' When the knife crashed down there was one terrible, piercing cry. Then the executioner shouted, '*Vive la Révolution!*' and the lovely head of the last of the royal favourites fell into the basket.

Bibliography

Arneth, Ritter von, *Correspondance Secrète entre Marie Antoinette, Marie Thérèse et Mercy d'Argenteau,* 3 vols, Paris, 1868

Arneth, Ritter von, *Correspondance de Mercy d'Argenteau avec l'Empereur Joseph et le Prince von Kaunitz,* Paris

Aulneau, Joseph, *Madame Du Barry et la Fin de l'Ancien Régime,* Paris, 1937

Baillio, Joseph, 'Marie Antoinette et Vigée-Lebrun', *L'Oeil* no. 308, 1981

Belleval, *Souvenirs d'un Cheveau-Léger,* Paris

Bernis, Cardinal, *Memoirs of,* trans. London

Besenval, Baron de, *Memoirs of,* trans. London

Bouillé, Louis, Marquis de, *Souvenirs et Fragments,* Paris

Brissot, Jacques Pierre, *Mémoires,* Paris

Campan, Madame, *Mémoires Privées sur la Reine Marie Antoinette,* Paris, 1823

Castelot, André, *Madame Du Barry,* Paris

Castries, Duc de, *Madame Du Barry,* Paris

Cheverney, Dufort de, *Souvenirs et Mémoires,* Paris

Choiseul, Etienne-François, Duc de, *Mémoires,* Paris

Condorcet, Marquis de, *Mémoires sur la Regne de Louis XVI et la Révolution,* 2 vols, Paris, 1862

Dard, Emile, *Le Général Choderlos de Laclos, Auteur des 'Liaisons Dangereuses', 1741–1803,* Paris, 1936

Deffand, Marquise du, *Lettres de la Marquise du Deffand à Horace Walpole, 1766–1789,* 3 vols, trans. London, 1912

Diesbach, Ghislain de, *L'Histoire de l'Emigration,* Paris, 1975

Douglas, R.B., *Life and Times of Madame Du Barry,* London

Duthens, Louis, *Mémoires d'un Voyageur qui se repose,* Paris

d'Espinchal, Comte, *Journal de l'Emigration,* Paris

d'Espinchal, Comte, *Souvenirs,* edited by Hauterive, Paris

Falk, Bernard, *The Naughty Seymours,* London

Fejtö, Joseph, *Joseph II,* Paris, 1953

Ferrières, Marquis de, *Mémoires,* Paris, 1822

Funk-Brentano, F., *L'Affaire du Collier,* Paris, 1901

Gaxotte, Pierre, *Le Siècle de Louis XV,* Paris, 1933

Genlis, Madame de, *Mémoires,* Paris, 1925

Georgel, Abbé de, *Mémoires pour Servir à l'Histoire des Événements de la Fin du Dixhuitième Siècle,* 6 vols, Paris, 1817

Goncourt, Edmond and Jules de, *La Du Barry,* Paris, 1878

Gooch, G.P., *The Monarchy in Decline,* London, 1956

Haslip, Joan, *Marie Antoinette,* London, 1987

Hausset, Madame du, *The Private Memoirs of Louis XV from the Memoirs of Madame Hausset,* London

Hibbert, Christopher, *The French Revolution,* London, 1982

Laclos, Choderlos de, *Portrait d'Elmire,* Paris

Langlade, Eric, *La Marchande de Robes de Marie Antoinette,* Paris, 1911

La Tour du Pin Gouvernet, Marquise de, *Journal d'une Femme de Cinquante Ans,* Paris, 1913

Lenôtre, G., *Vieilles Maisons et Vieux Papiers,* Paris

Leroy, Alfred, *Madame du Barry et son Temps,* Paris, 1942

Lescure, Adolphe, M. A. de, *Correspondance Secrète et Inédite sur Louis XVI, Marie Antoinette, la Cour et la Ville,* 2 vols, Paris, 1866

Levron, Jacques, *Le Destin de Madame du Barry,* Paris, 1961

Ligne, Charles Lamoral, Prince de, *Memoirs and Letters of the Prince de Ligne,* translated by Katherine Prescott Wormsley, London

Loomis, Stanley, *Du Barry,* London, 1962

Maugras, Gaston, *Le Duc et La Duchesse de Choiseul,* Paris

Mayrobert, Pidansat de, *Anecdotes sur Madame Du Barry,* Paris

Mitford, Nancy, *Madame de Pompadour,* London, 1968

Morris, Gouverneur, *A Diary of the French Revolution,* 2 vols, London, 1939

Nolhac, Pierre de, *La Reine Marie Antoinette,* Paris, 1890

Nolhac, Pierre de, *Marie Antoinette, Dauphine,* Paris, 1897

Saint-André, Claude, *A King's Favourite, La Du Barry,* with a preface by Pierre de Nolhac, Paris

Saint-Beuve, Charles Augustin, *Portraits Literaires,* vol 3, Paris, 1937

Saint-Priest, Comte de, *Mémoires,* Paris, 1929

Ségur, Philippe, Comte de, *Mémoires et Anecdotes,* 3 vols, Paris, 1894–5

Vatel, Charles, *Histoire de Madame du Barry,* 3 vols, Versailles, 1883

Vigée Le-Brun, Elisabeth de, *Souvenirs, Notes et Portraits,* trans. London, 1904

Walpole, Horace, *Letters of,* edited by Toynbee, Oxford

Ward, Marion, *The Du Barry Inheritance,* London, 1967

Index